POST MORTEM

The Jews In Germany — Now

POST MORTEM

The Jews In Germany — Now

BY

LEO KATCHER

HAMISH HAMILTON
LONDON

First published in Great Britain, 1968
by Hamish Hamilton Ltd
90 *Great Russell Street London WC*1
Copyright © 1968 *by Leo Katcher*

241.01595.2

105984

Printed in Great Britain
by Willmer Brothers Limited
Birkenhead

*For Dee – for understanding above and
beyond the call of duty*

Contents

Preface and Acknowledgment

I WENT to Germany with a specific assignment: to find out what it is like to be a Jew today in what was Hitler's Germany.

For the answer, I travelled for nine months in West and East Germany, in West and East Berlin, and in Austria.

Wherever I went I was treated courteously. Public officials in West Germany went out of their way to be helpful. Busy men and women, everywhere, gladly gave me of their time. If, as was sometimes the case, they believed my assignment fanciful, they were too courteous to say so.

Language proved only a minor difficulty in my interviews. My German was rusty at first – I had not used it in more than twenty years – but I could read and understand it well. In some early interviews (such as that with Mgr. Klausener) I used an interpreter. As the months passed, this became unnecessary.

Most of the persons with whom I spoke conversed fluently in English, but there were instances where a mélange of languages – English, German, French, Spanish and Yiddish – was necessary.

It is unfair to name only a few of those to whom I am grateful for their help, but I must give special thanks to Rabbi Nathan Peter Levinson, of Heidelberg, to Mrs. Gisele Spangenberg, of Roy Blumenthal Associates in West Berlin, to Steven Steinberg, of Radio Free Europe, in Munich, and to Ernest Landau, also of Munich.

Some whom I interviewed asked me not to use their names. In each instance this has been so noted in the text.

It would be untrue to call this a completely objective report. I am a Jew. I was an adult during the Hitler years. Long before I made this trip to Germany I had seen and talked to victims of Nazism. No, I did not go to Germany with an open mind and a forgiving heart.

A*

But I believe that I have fully and fairly given the varying points of view and attitudes I encountered. I did not stack the cards.

These are the questions for which I sought answers:

Who are the Jews now living in Germany?
What kind of lives do they lead?
How do they feel about Germany?
How do the Germans feel about them?
Is Nazism dead or only hibernating?
Is there a future in Germany for the Jews?

In this book I present the evidence I found and the conclusions which I drew. Others may disagree with the conclusions, as is their right. I claim to speak for no one but myself.

January 1968   *Leo Katcher*

1. Numbers

'HITLER turned us into numbers. So many for the labour camps. So many for the gas chambers. So many for the ovens. So many for Mengele to use as guinea pigs. And then we became so many tons of human fat, so many millions of dollars of gold and silver from the tooth fillings and the wedding rings. So much skin for the book-bindings and the lampshades.'

Ernest Landau riffled a stack of papers. 'Today we are still numbers. Just smaller numbers.'

He spoke sadly but without bitterness. Seated in the living room of his apartment in Munich, he stared at another number, the indelible number seared into his skin in Auschwitz. Across the room, his wife stared down at her own wrist, her own number.

The Landaus were two of the people with whom I talked in Germany. Their story – and it will be told in its proper place – was filled with numbers.

Everywhere I went in Germany I was given figures, statistics, numbers about the Jews. After a time, I feared that flesh had turned to paper and blood to ink, that the Jews existed only as numbers. Even to themselves.

The numbers declare that there are about 26,000 registered Jews in the Federal Republic – West Germany. And an estimated 4000 more Jews who have not registered their religion on the rolls. In East Germany, which also provides numbers, only 1500 admit to being Jewish. If there are more, they have become blanks.

There are 45 synagogues in West Germany, 39 Jewish libraries, 15 rabbis and 106 cemeteries.

Twice as many Jews (all these numbers are for West Germany) are over 50 as are below 30. Ten per cent of the Jews are over 70. The death rate is eight times as high as the birth rate.

(In East Germany, 75 per cent of all Jews are over sixty. There

are only 20 who are younger than fifteen and another 13 who are
less than thirty. There are no seminaries, no libraries, one rabbi,
and no figures for the Jewish cemeteries.)

Jews of German extraction number (that word again) about
8000. Their average age is over 60 and they make up most of the
population of the old people's homes.

About 15,000 of the Jews in Germany come from Eastern
Europe. These include Poles, Czechs, Russians, Galicians, Lithu-
anians, Roumanians and Hungarians. Those over 20 became
residents of Germany by way of the concentration and displaced
persons camps.

There are 1500 dark-skinned, exotic, Iranian Jews, mainly in
Hamburg.

The largest Jewish community in Germany is in West Berlin.
It also has the highest percentage of German Jews and the highest
average age. Of the 6000 there, 3750 are more than fifty and 700
are less than thirty.

Sixty-seven Jews live in the state of Schleswig-Holstein and their
average age is the same as their number – 67. 'Don't say that we
live here,' one of them pleaded. 'Say we are waiting to die here.
This will be our revenge on Hitler.'

There are many cities and towns in Germany where not a
single Jew lives. There are millions of Germans under 21 who
have never knowingly seen or spoken to a Jew.

But there are no ghettos in Germany and anti-Semitism is a
felony, punishable by imprisonment. 'The Jews in (West)
Germany,' said Nathan C. Belth, of the Anti-Defamation League
of B'Nai Brith, 'are the most protected people in the world.'

The Chief Rabbi of Cologne agreed. 'If a visitor from Mars
were to survey earth,' he said, 'he would find no other country
where the Jews are so insulated from injury or discrimination. He
would see that we get the same reverence that the Egyptians show
their mummies.'

The pendulum has swung to the other extreme from Hitlerism.
The Germans remember the admonition from John C. McCloy,
military governor and high commissioner for Germany when the
Federal Republic came into being that 'the world would judge how
much the Germans had changed by the manner in which they
treated the Jews.'

The new government, under Chancellor Adenauer, made it a

Federal crime to preach or practise racism. 'We knew,' said Richard Borchardt of the Foreign Office, 'that we had to regain credibility with the world.'

And the symbol of credibility was the Jew. The dead Jews – the six million ghosts that haunted Germany – and the handful who remained alive. Where only a few days earlier the Jew had been sought out for destruction, now he was to be sought for penitence. Yesterday's scum was today's paragon.

'First they threw stones at us,' Ernest Landau said, 'and then they threw flowers.'

And today, the Jews in Germany remember the stones and are fearful. But they see the flowers and so they are bold. They live in Germany but only a few – a very few – say they are Germans. They flaunt their Jewishness but few practise their religion.

They are the descendants of Abel. They cannot forget this. Nor can the Germans forget they descend from Cain.

Before Hitler, there were about 550,000 Jews in Germany. More than 180,000 of these died in camps and ovens and gas chambers. Of the rest, about 300,000 were able to escape from Germany. They fled between 1933 and 1941, during that period when Hitler was satisfied to rid Germany of Jews and before he put into operation his *endlosung,* his 'final solution'.

When the war ended, there were 15,000 German Jews still alive. Most were survivors of the camps, the few whose turn it had not yet come to die. The rest were alive because they had been saved by anti-Nazi Germans or had, somehow, been able to save themselves.

All but 5000 of these left Germany as soon as they could.

But with the war's end, a torrent of East European Jews – displaced persons – swept into Germany. By 1947, there were more than 200,000 in the different DP camps, most of them in Bavaria because that was part of the American occupation zone. Virtually every D P wanted to place what was left of his life and his hopes in American hands.

Few of the D P's wanted to remain in Germany, but the rest of the world was no more eager to accept them then than it had been before the war. The red tape was thick, the quotas low, the visas few. Israel, to which so many looked, had not yet become a nation and Great Britain was sealing off immigration to that haven.

The DP camps remained in operation for seven years. Those inside them lived off food packages from the (Jewish) Joint Distribution Agency and CARE. They lived on aid given by UNRRA, on gifts from friends, relatives and strangers. Some lived on earnings from the black market.

All lived on hope. With the creation of the nation of Israel, the camps started to empty but it was not until 1955 that the last of these was closed. Some DP's still remained in Germany. They were primarily the old and the sick. But some had created a foothold for themselves in Germany. The had married Germans or found a way to earn a living there.

These DPs who remained were double strangers. They were alien both to the mass of Germans and to the German Jews. There had long been antagonism between the German Jews, who looked down on their Eastern brothers, and those brothers. But rapprochement between the two Jewish groups was easy. They remembered that Hitler had not let geography influence him.

Rapprochement with Germans and Germany, however, has still not come.

To these few survivors and DP's, a third group of Jews was added. These would be Jews who came to Germany during the period of German *Wirtschaftswunder* (economic miracle). And there would also be a trickle of *Rueckwanderer* (returnees), those who had once left Germany and came back.

The new Jewish population of Germany is dominated by East Europeans. Many of them speak Yiddish, not German. Some wear kaftans and wide-brimmed black hats. They have earlocks.

But they have been gladly accepted by the German government and most of the German people. They are a natural resource, a political asset. They provide tangible proof that Hitler's Germany lies interred. They are evidence that democracy is at work.

There are, of course, some sceptics. A skit in a political cabaret defines democracy as 'a form of government imposed on Germany each time it lost a war.' And students of German history recall that there had been no contradiction between democratic government and anti-Semitism under the Weimar Republic.

In 1926, as an example, German university students held a referendum on the question: Shall membership in the German Student Organization be made dependent upon certain German characteristics which can be derived from the concept of German culture or from 'racial' concepts?

A large majority of the students, from one end of Germany to the other, voted in the affirmative. Jewish students were barred from membership. After all, they were not members of 'the German race'. And, as a result, the democratic Weimar Republic of Germany dismissed Jewish professors from its schools and ordered the public burning of books written by Jews.

But this did not satisfy the Student Organization. It demanded that Jewish scholars be forbidden to write and publish in the German language. They should be restricted to 'Hebrew and other foreign languages'. The matter was still being argued in 1933 but then, of course, it became academic.

The Jews of pre-Hitler Germany were not surprised by the action of the students. One of the most prominent of them – Walter Rathenau – had shortly before written :

'During the youth of every German Jew there comes a painful moment which he remembers all his life : the moment when he first consciously realizes that he has been born into the world as a lower ranking citizen and that no merit and proficiency on his part can save him from this position.'

This from an individual who attained wealth and power as an industrialist, fame and respect as a statesman, and, ultimately, death by assassination as much for his religion as for his politics. But, behind his words was knowledge gained from the 2000 year history of the Jews in Germany.

They came to that land originally from ancient Rome. They came as traders and settlers, as Roman officials and Roman exiles. When Rome fell, they came – history has so many ironies – as refugees to escape persecution.

Under Charlemagne and his son, Louis the Pious, they were court favourites, holding a privileged status. But when Louis died, the privileges were withdrawn and a series of suppressions and brutalities was begun that culminated in 1012 with the expulsion of the Jews from Mainz and the expropriation of their property.

Ernest Landau was in error when he said it was Hitler who turned the Jews into numbers. That had happened back in the middle of the Twelfth Century.

At that time, Conrad III seeking both to protect the Jews and increase his own wealth, declared the Jews to be his *servi camerae,* literally 'servants of his chamber'. To make sure that all Jews were covered by his proclamation, he had a special census taken and ordered that, thereafter, a complete record of the number of Jews be kept.

Theoretically, by his act Conrad extended his personal protection to all the Jews. Actually, he had reduced them to chattels, property owned by the ruler, which could be bought and sold and which possessed no civil rights.

Other rulers quickly took advantage of this concept and made their own censuses. Soon every feudal lord had herds of Jews as well as cattle.

Being valuable property, the Jews were coveted. But having no rights, they were also persecuted. The German church was among the persecutors. In the Fifteenth Century the church accused the Jews of giving aid to John Huss and inflicted penalities so severe that almost all of the Jews fled the country, leaving behind their homes and other property which were quickly expropriated by both religious and secular barons.

On the other side of the coin, in the mid-Seventeenth Century, when Bogdan Chmielnicki led his Ukranian Cossacks in a pogrom against the Jews, so cruel and destructive that it would not be equalled until the Hitler era, Germany offered to allow all Jews who could pay their way into the country a place of refuge.

Yet, when the Reformation and the Renaissance resulted in greater tolerance throughout Europe, Germany seized on the change to intensify its persecution of the Jews. Anti-Semitism was an integral part of the German Reformation. Martin Luther made that inevitable.

Four centuries before Hitler, Luther prescribed his own 'final solution' for the Jewish problem. He demanded that 'their assets be sequestered, their homes razed, their synagogues levelled, that they be driven off the roads ... put under a roof or stable, like the gypsies ... assigned to the mines and quarries, compelled to fell trees, skin animals and sweep chimneys ... in misery and captivity as they incessantly lament and complain to God about us.'

Obviously not all Nazis were illiterate or ignorant of history. Some, at least, were acquainted with the writings of Luther.

Yet Luther was doing no more than numbering Jews as chattels rather than people. The heritage of Conrad III had long survived him and his line. This concept of Jews as property was not even questioned by such figures of the Enlightenment as Johann Wolfgang von Goethe or Johann Gotlieb Fichte.

Still, even under these adverse circumstances, the Jews survived in Germany. Survived and sought to become Germans. One such was Moses Mendelssohn, grandfather of the composer, probably the greatest figure in the history of German Judaism. Philosopher and student, Mendelssohn attempted to find a side route to equality by championing cultural assimilation. In this manner, the Jews could be both Jewish and German. Different from other Jews.

For the German Jews – the 'Yahudim' – held that they were not like the 'Ostjuden', the Jews of Russia, Poland, the Baltic and the Balkans. They were, they held, a group apart.

But, even as they asserted this, Jews had to purchase their right to live in Berlin and in Austria each year. Every German government in that fractured country imposed special taxes on Jews for being born, for marrying, even for dying. The government of Berlin decreed that only one Jew in each family could marry so that the total number of Jews could be held to a minimum. (Always numbers.)

Jews had to stay in restricted inns, bearing the legend, 'For Jews Only', when they travelled. When they crossed a toll bridge, they were charged for passage as cattle, not humans.

Only one Jew per family in Austria was permitted to own his own home. The only title by which Jews were addressed was 'Jude', Jew.

Yet, both German and Austrian Jews gladly signed petitions which called on their governments to limit entry of the inferior Ostjuden.

Not until Napoleon was ravaging Europe and scourging Germany did any of the German states relax its anti-Semitism. Then, seeking financial and martial help from the Jews, these governments promised them equal rights. And these were given – until Napoleon was defeated.

Then, once again, the Jews were designated as inferior persons. Various German states ordered changes in Jewish ritual. They imposed harsh controls on religious observances. Prussia enacted a law which forbade Jews to take the same first names as Christians. This was later amended so that only New Testament names were proscribed, an irony that escaped the authorities.

(The Nazis were to impose such a law again and its effects are still felt. I encountered an American, Christian, girl, married to a German, who sought to name her son 'David' after her dead father. Her husband and his family forbade this, saying, 'People will think he's a Jew.' A compromise was finally reached, the child being christened Christian David.)

Not all Germans were anti-Semitic. Liberal voices were raised in behalf of the Jews by many. Karl vom und zum Stein sought to emancipate the Jews in 1808 when he was Premier, but he was forced out of office by German conservatives. His successor, Karl August Hardenberg, went even further, declaring the full emancipation of the Jews, but during the later years of his administration fell under the influence of Prince von Metternich, the German-Austrian whose conservatism dominated European politics until 1848.

As a result, not only did Hardenberg make a dead letter of his own reforms, but he cancelled those of Wilhelm von Humboldt, brother of the famed scientist, who reformed the Prussian school system, founded the University of Berlin, and called for an end to discrimination against Jews in education. In 1819, Hardenberg dismissed Humboldt from office and rescinded his liberal enactments.

It was not until 1871, when Otto von Bismarck united Germany, that a nominal, if not actual, equality was granted to the Jews of Germany. Bismarck needed the support of two Jewish political leaders, Edward Lasker and Ferdinand Lassalle, and when the new constitution was drafted it enfranchised all Jews within the newly united Germany and gave them all rights of citizenship.

But that German constitutional provision was about as effective in Germany as the 14th Amendment to the American Constitution was in the American South for so long. Bismarck turned from his old allies and found new ones, among them Heinrich von Treitschke.

Treitschke, a historian, became the ideologist of the new, unified Germany. He had read 'The Inequality of Human Races', written by Count Joseph Arthur Gobineau and adopted Gobineau's concept of the 'master race' as his own, just as Hitler, et al, were to do later. He preached that the Jews were 'foreign matter' which could not be absorbed into the German bloodstream without poisoning it. He suggested obliterating it.

But Bismarck was not Hindenburg and he refused to turn ideology into policy. After all, there were Jews who were helping to build the greater Germany of which he had dreamed and of which he believed himself the architect.

This was the period when Albert Ballin was helping build Germany's great shipping industry, when the Rathenaus were assembling A. G. E., the first major German power and industrial complex, when other Jews were laying the foundation for I Garben. This was also the period when the great Jewish bankers were financing Germany's expansion. 'Foreign matter' the Jews might be, but they were necessary.

This separate and almost equal era ended for the Jews in the 1920s. Germany and the Germans, defeated in war, burdened by reparations beyond their ability to pay, weakened by deflation, torn by internal dissent, sought a scapegoat for all their ills. A new mystique – the phantasy that the Germans had not lost World War I, but had been betrayed – evolved. And chief among the betrayers were the Jews.

The vote of the university students mirrored the opinion of the mass of Germans. Hitler and the Nazis did not create anti-Semitism. It was ready at hand for them and already had a long history. The Nazis did not even have to promulgate the theory that the Jews were sub-human. Many Germans had long subscribed to that. Under Hitler, they would act on that premise.

After 1933, anti-Semitism was an instrument of German policy. The schools taught it. The churches, both Catholic and Protestant, accepted it. German industry, much of it developed by Jews, battened on Jewish slave labour. German jurisprudence found anti-Semitism both legal and enforceable. German doctors added Jews to their list of laboratory animals.

During that period, the Jews were shorn of humanity. No torture, no degradation, no humiliation, was beyond inflicting upon them.

One stepped on ants, pulled wings off flies, destroyed Jews.

There came a moment in 1942 when Hitler could announce the *endlosung* and most Germans could accept it without horror or revulsion. (The record is written in the Nuremberg and other trials.)

And so bullets and gas and fire and scalpels and clubs and fists were used to kill some six million Jews. When the guns ceased firing on May 7, 1945, the ovens remained hot and the gas seeped for a time into the death chambers.

This was the time of 'liberation' under Allied control. In 1948, the Federal Republic of Germany came into being and, with it, an experiment was launched. Materials for the experiment were those Jews living within the borders of the new country. The object was to determine if the land of Conrad III and Luther, of Trietschke and Hitler, could accept that these Jews were fellow human beings.

Twenty years have elapsed since that experiment was begun. What are the results? Can we give one, two or three cheers for them?

I sought out the answers from the Landaus, from the rabbis, from the laymen. From Jews and non-Jews. From taxi drivers and government officials. From priests and ministers, educators and cafe-owners. From farmers and from librarians. From writers and from textile salesmen.

Above all, I wanted to find out how true was the charge that Gudrun Tempel, once a member of the Hitler youth, made in her recent book, *Deutschland? Aber Wo Liegt Es?* (Germany? Where Does It Lie?) that 'the sin of the Germans was not that they were Nazis in the Hitler years, but that they were not anti-Nazis then and they are not anti-Nazis now.'

2. Relics

THE Jews of Germany are like a sand hill. From a distance, they appear a solid mountain. Close up, it is obvious they are an accumulation of single grains.

And all the grains are different. The only thing they have in common is that they are Jews and each is a different kind of Jew.

From Hamburg to Munich, from Dusseldorf to Passau, I searched them out and talked with them. All these were different from the Jews of West Berlin and these Jews were different from those of East Berlin. The Jews of Leipzig differed from those of Stuttgart. And all of them differed from the Jews of Vienna and Salzburg – except that all were Jews.

There was Erich Warburg in his panelled office in Hamburg, surrounded by pictures of his German banker ancestors, by mementoes of Imperial Germany, by letters from Kaisers and Prime Ministers, by evidence that he is the product of centuries of Jewish background. He is sophisticated, cultured, urbane.

Schmuel Rubinstein was born in Poland, survived Auschwitz, immigrated to Israel and then returned to Germany. Today he drives a taxi in Munich. He is an alien, embittered.

Emil Januscek, Czech-born, is a successful manufacturer in West Berlin. His body still carries bullets fired into it by S S men. His business takes him over much of the world. He is shamed when he tells his customers that he lives in Germany.

Hilde Walter, Berlin-born journalist, is a Jew because the Nazi race laws made her one. She practises no religion, but she is a Jew.

Gisele Bloch was born a Protestant, grew up in Hitler's Germany. She married a fiery, bitter, Zionist and converted to Judaism. She attends a synagogue; her husband does not.

Arthur Brauner, Polish born, lived like an animal for five years in the forests of Poland certain that he would survive. He did and today he is the best known movie producer in Germany. But how does he describe himself? As a German? 'I am a Jew and nothing else.'

Blonde, blue-eyed Birgit Rosenthal, is fifteen. She was born in post-war Berlin to a father who survived because Christian Berliners risked their lives to save his. 'Of course I'm a Jew,' she said. 'That means I am not a Christian.'

The Jews of Germany are all these and more. They include the Iranian rug dealer in Hamburg, the Justice Minister of North Rhine-Westphalia, the bar owner in Munich, the cigar store proprietor in Cologne, the newsboy in Dusseldorf, the television director in Berlin, the Lord Mayor and Federal Senator of Hamburg, the lawyer in Frankfurt, the editor in Cologne and the garage mechanic in Mainz.

But, then, there is the question : What is a Jew?

The definitions vary from individual to individual. Hitler had his and so do the rabbis of Germany. So, too, has Birgit Rosenthal.

If it means being pious, observing creed and ritual, then there are very few Jews in Germany. One rabbi puts the figure at less than a thousand and all the rabbis agree that the least pious of all Jews in Germany are the more than a thousand Israelis who now live in Germany.

Gobineau and his followers called the Jews a race. His disciple and Hitler's mentor, Houston Stewart Chamberlain, devoted the longest chapter in his book, *Foundations of the 19th Century,* to describing the racial characteristics of the Jews, from the shape of their heads to the size of their noses. Yet the Jews of Germany are round-headed and long-headed, Roman-nosed and snub-nosed, tall and short, thin and fat, blonde and dark.

Each man has his own answer to the question: What is a Jew? The Russian-born librarian at the Jewish Community Centre in Berlin said, 'Don't you know? A Jew is a Jew.'

And what is a German Jew – or, more realistically, what are the Jews in Germany?

For this, the cafe-owner in Munich had an answer. 'Here,' he said, 'a Jew is one whose past is in the graveyard and whose future is an old folks' home. A Jew is someone with a double-lock on his door and a ticket to some other country hidden away.'

But Hendrik George van Dam impatiently disagreed. He is

secretary of the *Zentralrat,* the governing body of the Jews in Germany, and its spokesman. It is he who deals with government officials, with foreign diplomats, with newspapermen and T V interviewers, with foreign V I Ps. Van Dam said, 'The Jew in Germany is basically no different from a Jew any place else. His life is what he makes it. And any man who says he is a Jew is a Jew.'

Van Dam is not interested in philosophical discussions. He does not care how many Jews can dance on the head of a pin. What concerns him are the political and economic relations between the Jewish community and the Federal and *Laender* (state) governments. Philosophy can wait.

So, if there is a question of just what a Jew is, there are other matters that could be dealt with rapidly and efficiently without finding that specific definition. One of them was to erect places for the Jews to worship.

And in the past twenty years, new beautiful synagogues have been built and old ones restored: Munich alone, of all large German cities, is without such a synagogue.

In Bonn, capital of West Germany, the handsome, modern synagogue stands across the street from the Foreign Office. Every diplomat and statesman who comes to call on the Foreign Minister sees it. It is a visible reminder of Germany's concern for its Jews. But the visitor is not told that the synagogue is in use only a couple of times each year. The truth is that Bonn has a synagogue – but not the Jews to use it.

The rebuilt Spanish-Byzantine synagogue on Freiherr von Stein strasse in Frankfurt is a magnificent example of its type of architecture. The state of Hesse spent 800,000 marks to erect it. Every guided tour stops outside it while the guide gives the details of its construction and of its cost. But the visitor does not enter it. The doors are locked and the building empty except on the High Holidays.

The synagogue in Dusseldorf has a great glass entry door. A door of a most modern glass, transparent from the inside of the synagogue but opaque from the outside. If only the doors of the synagogue had had that type of glass in the Hitler years, lives might have been saved, destruction prevented.

The remnants of the oldest Jewish building in Germany are included in the rebuilt synagogue of Worms. First completed in 1034, the synagogue has been destroyed seven times by Germans, the last time on that night of horror, the *Kristalnacht* (Crystal Night), November 9th, 1938, when every remaining synagogue in Hitler's Germany was first desecrated and then levelled.

The Federal government, the state of Rhineland-Palatinate and the city of Worms combined to finance the rebuilding. Inside the synagogue are ancient holy writings, sacred documents, accumulated over the centuries, but they are copies, not originals. The originals are in Israel.

That these originals exist at all is due to Dr. George Iller, an 'Aryan', who was Director of the Worms Museum on Crystal Night. When the rioting mob began its depredations, Dr. Iller was able to reach Heinrich Himmler and get him to agree to save the documents because, as Dr. Iller put it, they were 'evidence of Jewish decadence'. Himmler agreed and the treasure was turned over to Dr. Iller.

He kept it safely through all the Nazi era and when that ended, he returned it to the first Jewish authorities to appear in Worms.

But Israeli authorities felt that it would be a mockery for Germany to house such Jewish treasures and a shamed German Government agreed. Besides, at the time there was no sacred place to keep them. When the synagogue was rebuilt, Israel had a set of replicas made and these are the documents now on view in Worms. If the synagogue should be destroyed an eighth time...

But there was another practicality involved in keeping the originals in Israel. When the new synagogue was completed and dedicated, there were not ten male Jews, the minimum needed to hold services, in all Worms. Only fifteen months later, when Ilan Walzer celebrated his *Bar Mitzvah* (Confirmation), did Worms attain its necessary quorum of Jewish men to make up a *minyan* (legal congregation).

There are synagogues enough – and more than enough – in Germany today. Synagogues in Berlin and Hamburg, in Hagen, Duisberg and Cologne, in Muenster and Muelheim and Saarbrucken, in Heidelberg and in Mainz, in Padeborn and Hanover and Wiesbaden. All that is lacking are worshippers to fill them.

The architects who designed some of these synagogues had that in mind. The one who made the plans in Stuttgart provided that the building could be converted into a movie theatre. In

Dusseldorf half the space allotted was used to build a public garage which provides considerable income. (The garage does a capacity business; the synagogue is almost empty.)

Still, the synagogues serve many purposes. The fact that they stand proves the sincerity of the German government. For the Jews, the synagogues are evidence that they can practise their religion freely. And for the old Nazis and the new ones, they are obvious targets for their latent hate.

The buildings have been desecrated and smeared, daubed with swastikas and defiled with excrement. Together with synagogues, graveyards and Jewish community buildings have suffered. During the 1960 Christmas season, an epidemic of outrages occurred. They took place in Wiesbaden and Coblenz, in Ingelheim and Memmingen, in Bamberg and Berlin.

The last attracted the most attention. Forty gravestones were smeared with anti-Semitic inscriptions. Old graves that had only recently been cleared and remarked, were turned into a shambles. Flowers were uprooted and headstones, dedicated with tears and memories, flattened and broken. A still unveiled monument to Jewish victims of Nazism was daubed with brown paint.

Heinz Wasserman now lives in Bamberg. He is over seventy, a thin worn man who survived Dachau and Belsen. All who were his family lie now either in the Bamberg cemetery or in some lime pit. He recalled the events of that night. 'We asked ourselves,' he said, ' "Why? Why?" There are so few of us. (Only seventy Jews in a city of 75,000.) We wondered if we were to hear fists banging on the door again. We were not afraid because we have grown beyond fear. But, if it should be happening again, this time they would not take prisoners. They would find only corpses.'

But it was not happening again. Instead, the people of Bamberg demonstrated that much, much had changed. The flags in the city were flown at half-mast. The city Youth Council cleared the debris from the cemetery. The headstones were raised and cleaned. Those that had been broken were replaced. Fresh flowers were planted and they were blooming when more than 5000 people gathered in a rain storm days later to express their regret and disgust.

Four months afterwards, the cemetery was re-dedicated. Most of those who attended were non-Jews. They heard the rabbi who officiated say, 'We know you shared our shock. We also know that you could not share our memories.'

The series of outbreaks shook all the governing bodies of West Germany. The Federal Ministry of the Interior convened an advisory council of experts to examine German education and determine if it was meeting its responsibilities. Various *laender* governments called for an overhauling of text books and curricula.

(The perpetrators of many of the outrages were discovered. Almost all of them were found to be mentally disturbed youths, filled with a hatred they could not explain. Most were found sane enough to be sent to prison rather than to mental institutions.)

'We were in the position of parents whose children had gone astray,' a government official said. 'We wanted to know what we had done wrong. We suddenly realized that we had been doing only half of the necessary job. We had been thinking in terms of what could be done for the Jews and ignoring what had to be done with the German people themselves.'

Certainly the things that could be done for the Jews had been undertaken. Special care and solicitude had been shown. So much so that a Jewish writer said, 'We are like American Indians on a reservation, wards of the government.'

Financial aid in many forms has been generously provided. In addition to various types of restitution and reparations (including payments and aid to Israel), there is a continuing subsidization of Jewish institutions. The letter of the law has been stretched to provide pensions and security payments to individuals.

If money alone could have dissolved the differences between Jews and Germans, those differences would be well on the way to disappearing.

As of 1967, the West German government had paid out more than six billion dollars, at the most conservative estimate, in restitution, reparations and payments to Israel. Under the terms of agreements now in force, total payment will reach about eight billions.

(The Institute for Jewish Questions has drawn up a balance sheet which reveals that the total amount of Jewish property, valuables, investments and income lost by European Jews was more than twenty-seven billions.)

More than half the payments have been made to individuals and the average payment to individuals, both Jews and non-Jews has been $3750.

(German reparations payments to Norway, Denmark, Greece,

Holland and Luxemburg have totalled about $250 million.)

The government has made these restitution payments despite their being a liability in domestic politics. As early as 1953, the U. S. High Commission in Germany published a study which revealed that at that time two of every three Germans was opposed to restitution. When an added factor – the possibility of Arab retaliation against West Germany – was included in the questionnaire, only 12 per cent of those polled said they favoured restitution.

Every poll taken since reveals a large majority against such payments, but they have been continued.

And so have payments for the development of all aspects of Jewish life in Germany.

Synagogues and cemeteries, old-age homes and community centres, have been built and paid for from treasury funds. Libraries have been established. Institutes for Jewish studies have been staffed and subsidized.

The relationship between church and state is close and entangled in Germany. This has been true ever since Charlemagne ruled as Holy Roman Emperor and symbolized the union of both. Members of all faiths – including of course, the Jews – pay a surtax on their income tax which is collected by the state and then turned over, without strings, to religious authorities.

But, while the churches are financed by the state, they are more free of state control now than at any time in German history. This is part of the reaction against Nazism, when the Nazis wrote the religious textbooks, supervised the clergy, and insisted upon a vow of fealty to Adolf Hitler from all teachers, both religious and secular.

But subsidization of the Jews goes beyond subsidization of religious institutions. It includes the entire structure of the Jewish community. There exists today a fund of about $35 million to finance that community. Administration of this money is in the hands of the elected leaders of all the Jewish communities.

Many Jews are unhappy about this situation. Most ignore it. Certainly it has had one beneficial effect. It has helped weld together all the Jews of Germany.

Before Hitler's time, the cleavage between *Yahudin* and *Ostjuden* had been deep. Walter Rathenau, bright star of the *Yahudim,* had expressed this feeling when he wrote of the

Ostjuden as 'closely linked together, strictly secluded from the outside world, they live in a voluntary ghetto, not as a living branch of the nation, but as a foreign element within its body.'

Hitler, Himmler, Rosenberg and Streicher had seized on these words but had applied them to such Jews as Rathenau as well as those Jews whom he castigated. To them, a Jew was a Jew was a Jew.

The keepers of the flame, the injectors of cyanide and the club-wielders of the camps had not distinguished between one Jewish region or another. And the Jews who suffered had learned that lesson. (Though it was ironic for me to hear some of the old prejudices voiced by Jews who had escaped the Hitler terror.)

After the 'liberation', the Jews who remained quickly formed organizations. The first officials were chosen even as the vanguard of Allied troops tore down the barbed wire.

German officialdom, addicted to bureaucracy, welcomed the creation of official Jewish communities. These were made up of Community Boards of Management, Advisory Councils and Provincial Organizations. Over a period of time, they were all integrated into a national organization, the *Zentralrat*. Headquarters were established in Dusseldorf and Dr. van Dam was chosen to head it.

Local groups, however, were not dissolved, but continue to function. All are autonomous and all operate democratically. The Community Boards and community managers are chosen by direct vote of registered Jews in the locality.

(Only registered Jews, those who pay their religious tax, are eligible to vote in these elections.)

What has evolved is a corporation with more than 26,000 stockholders. Management is in the hands of a board of directors whose chairman, to pursue the analogy, is van Dam. He heads the parent organization, the holding company. It is his function to produce 'profits' for the stockholders.

The operation is decentralized, with each local community autonomous. These are secular-based and handle the distribution of funds, deal with local government officials, hire and fire, and choose the rabbis.

Who are these men, the chairman and the local managers? What manner of men are they? What are their ideas as to the condition of the Jews in Germany and their future in that country?

3. The Chairman

HENDRIK GEORGE VAN DAM fits the part of the modern corporation executive. In his sixties, he is tall, handsome, articulate, well-read, immaculate in dress. He is a lawyer by profession, his mind honed to legal distinctions. His tools are facts. Multi-lingual, he switches languages as easily as a racing driver switches gears.

His office is in an impressive post-war building in one of the better districts of Dusseldorf. There is an air of well-being in the office, of quiet efficiency. Book-lined walls and good pictures give it warmth.

He is not a man of warmth. Of all the Jews with whom I talked in Germany, he was among the least emotional. Or, perhaps better, he displayed the least emotion. He was direct, a stick-to-the-facts pragmatist, who considered each word, each phrase, he used as if he were in a courtroom. He is the unofficial ambassador of the Jews in Germany both to the German government and the world.

'We Jews,' he said, 'go in for too much self-examination and self-criticism. We deal with hypothetical questions rather than facts. There is mysticism instead of realism.'

But, if that is so, then van Dam has separated himself from 'We Jews'. He deals only with the facts. He deals only with what is, not with what was or what might have been. And what is, in this case, is the fact that there are Jews in Germany and it is his task to make their lot as good as possible. To obtain for them the maximum in human rights, in financial goods and in civil equality.

In his large private office, which resembles the library in a gentleman's home, he stated his premise. 'The right of Jews to live in Germany must be assured and protected. I believe this is being done.' Then he ticked off the evidence. This included the constitutional ban on anti-Semitism, the close working relationship between government and the Jewish community, the financial obligations assumed, and met, by the Germans.

He found an article he had written (he writes voluminously for publications in many countries) to give his views of the financial settlements involving Germany and the Jews. This way, he could be directly quoted. What he had written was:

'In all its negotiations and in giving the reasons for its various laws, the Federal Government has always stated that it was impossible to make complete reparations for all the wrongs committed by National Socialism.

'... The amount of injustice done under the National Socialist regime was tremendous and the legislation which the Federal Republic has passed to give redress for it is certainly not perfect ... Nevertheless, the various details and statistics which have been given do indicate that the efforts made to remedy the injustices have been on such a scale as to deserve international recognition.'

This was the lawyer for the plaintiffs summing up. A wrong had been committed and, he acknowledged, a fair effort was being made to compensate for that wrong. However, while like any attorney he was pleased with the verdict in his favour, he believed that the award, though gratifying, did not satisfy him completely.

He is correct in other things as well. Correct and analytical. Van Dam dislikes using the past as a measure of the present because he thinks that the past has been inflated. 'I personally think,' he said, 'that the so-called Jewish influence in Germany before 1933 has been exaggerated. Of course, there were Jews who were important in their fields, but they did not dominate or shape them. (He would modify this soon.) Let me say that I do not think the absence of Jews will do any irremediable harm to Germany.

'Remember, the present Jewish community is far different from the one of before 1933. First, it is much smaller. Second, the majority are non-indigenous who will need at least a generation to become part of Germany. I have no doubt they will be absorbed; other waves of Jewish immigrants were absorbed through the centuries. Third, the Jews have not yet become fixed economically or socially.'

Like a lawyer making an oral brief, he went on, 'While we have only a small number of Jews in the professions, the universities and the laboratories, I do not believe there has been any relative decrease compared to before 1933. I would say the proportion is about the same. However, their importance is less, just as it is in the commercial and financial structure of Germany.'

Here he made his modification. 'Probably our greatest loss is in influence on public opinion. Once there were great Jewish-owned publishing houses. Through their books, magazines and newspapers, they could greatly affect public action and private thinking. Today there are none. Our one means of influencing public opinion today is through the organized Jewish community in Germany. This must continue to speak in one voice.

'History has given the Jews in Germany unique power. It has made them humanity's lobby. For that reason we are able to exert influence far out of proportion to our numbers.'

The phone rang and van Dam spoke a few words into it. One of van Dam's assistants, a very formally dressed, black-suited young man – strange looking in Germany – came in for a word with him. A change had to be made in his calendar. He apologized. When the interruptions ended, he took off on another aspect. This was the relationship of Jews outside Germany to the Jews in Germany.

He objects, most strongly, to the active intrusion of these outsiders. It goes back to the period immediately after the war when most Jews were opposed to any remaining in Germany or returning there. Van Dam's position then was that Jews should live in Germany and it caused him to say, 'Jews living in Germany (after the war) were in the beginning more criticized by some (Jews) than the German Nazis.'

He believes this question is now academic and part of the Jewish self-questioning which he derogates. And he feels the continuing airing of the subject, especially by American Jews, is futile and harmful.

Just as he feels strongly about those Jews who live in Germany but give their first loyalty to Israel. Of these, he said firmly, 'I am of the opinion that a convinced Zionist should stay in Israel.' It has taken courage for van Dam to hold that position and the collateral one that Jews in Germany have an obligation to Germany. 'They must,' he said, 'equate their duties as citizens with their identity as Jews. The fact is they are here and they cannot be emotionalized away.'

Nor does 'assimilation' trouble him. 'All Jews,' he said, 'assimilate, whether in the United States, or England, or France, or Holland, or even in Israel.' For him, this does not mean the disappearance of Jews as Jews, but, rather their blending into the society in which they live. 'I hold it beneficial,' he said, 'that Jews become managers of soccer teams and that they engage in rifle-shooting contests. I am against self-imposed separatism.'

To van Dam, the situation of the Jews is not isolated but falls within the general context of German democracy. 'Even with the best will in the world,' he said, 'one has to admit that Democracy is on trial here. The Germans are still a politically immature people. They did not choose democracy; that was a gift from the Allied powers.

'The Jewish situation relates to this. There would be no new Hitlerism if democracy stumbled because of the small number of Jews and their relative unimportance, but there could well be a rise in anti-Semitism without Jews.'

Van Dam is unhappy about the re-emergence of German nationalism and the growth of the National Democratic Party (N P D) as a political force. But about this van Dam is also coldly objective and stands apart from the majority of the Jews in Germany. 'I believe,' he said, 'that the reaction of many Jews here was hysterical. I have explained this by saying, "Once a persecutee, always a persecutee." Of course all Jews have the memory of the Hitler years in the forefront of their minds. It has to be that way, but we must also have a sense of proportion.'

Here, again, van Dam reverted to outside influences. 'I believe and have stated that the N P D is an internal problem. I do not think that pressures, or fears, or propaganda from outside Germany, have a place in dealing with the N P D.'

As I talked with van Dam, it seemed to me that I was talking to an atavism. His was the attitude of those Jews who had lived in an earlier era, in the time of Rathenau. The years in between had added to van Dam's knowledge but not to his perspective.

I wondered if the reason might not be that the Hitler terror had touched him only lightly. He had left Germany in 1933 and had not returned until after the war. His sister, however, had been a Nazi victim. But he himself had never been inside a camp, never been subjected to beatings and starvation.

He knew all the figures. Intellectually, he was aware of the meaning of Nazism and aware of the toll that Nazism had taken.

And, intellectually, he was determined to get from the Germans the highest compensation possible. But this, like the N P D, was an 'internal problem'.

Certainly he has served the Jews of Germany well. He has given them first-class representation, both domestically and in his contacts with foreign visitors. No one could more ably have presented their legal case, fought harder for their legal rights.

But I wondered when I spoke to him, and I wonder now, if this is enough. If it doesn't call for a greater involvement than he has given, a greater identification than he has made.

The Jews of Germany are more than litigants. Somehow, it seems to demean them, their suffering and their lives, to try to isolate them within the framework of Germany. It may be that I do van Dam an injustice in making this judgment of him.

I salute his achievements.

But I did not learn much from him about the Jews in Germany. I learned mch more from the men who run the branch-offices, the local communities.

4. The Managers

THERE are seventy-three Jewish communities in Germany, with the largest, 6000, in Berlin, and some as small as twenty. Only thirty-three Jews returned to Heidelberg after the war; before Hitler, there were 1200. Of the 3200 who once lived in Karlsruhe, only 165 were there in 1948 and today there are only 100.

Other cities recite similar statistics. Once large Jewish communities have been fractionized. There were once almost 200,000 Jews in Berlin. But, wherever the Jews are in Germany, they have been united. The East Europeans were long accustomed to clinging together. The German Jews learned it late. They had to.

'If we did not have each other,' said Gerd Baumann, 'We would have no one. No Jew here can afford to be a stranger to any other Jews.'

Baumann is an elderly man, almost seventy. He lives in Berlin, where he was born, and to which he returned after the war. 'I came back from Argentina,' he said, 'to look for my family. I found none of them. I did not want to go back to Buenos Aires to be a lonely man there and a stranger. Here, there are others like me.'

By 'here', he meant the Jewish Community Centre on Fasanenstrasse. This building, across the street from the Kempinski Hotel, stands on the site of Berlin's major pre-Hitler synagogue. Not all the building is new. The façade and one corner are what was left standing after the Nazi hoodlums completed their devastation on Crystal Night.

It is fitting that this building should be the heart and nerve centre of Berlin's Jewish community, for the old synagogue also served in that capacity. But it is the secular life of the Jews which binds them together today, not their religious life. And the man who is chief of the community is not the rabbi, but the community manager, Heinz Galinski.

Next to van Dam, Galinski is the most prominent Jewish figure in public life. Geography, of course, is one reason. West Berlin is a separate entity from West Germany, a state in itself. So long as the division between East and West continues, the leaders of Berlin will occupy the spotlight. But Galinski would have risen to prominence wherever he lived.

He is a marked contrast to van Dam. Galinski is neither diplomatic nor urbane. He keeps no tight rein on his emotions. He is brusque, diligent, hard-working. If van Dam is a statesman, Galinski is a working politician.

He spent years in Auschwitz and Belsen. He has his personal roll-call of the dead. These include his first wife, his mother, dozens of his family. They all perished; he survived.

After liberation, his first thought was to learn if any of his relatives might also have remained alive. He returned to Berlin where he met others involved in the same melancholy task. He quickly organized these individual efforts and created a functioning organization. From this, the Berlin Jewish community evolved. He was elected to head that group and has been repeatedly chosen since.

Like any politician, he has both followers and opponents. But all agree that he has been an effective leader. Not all agree with either the ends of the means of that leadership, for Galinski is a champion of conciliation between Jews and non-Jews. He is an integrationist, not a separatist. 'What other course is there,' he demanded, 'when there are only 6000 Jews among Berlin's two millions?'

That is why the centre is not only open to non-Jews, but sometimes appears to plan its lectures and forums, concerts and debates, exhibits and ceremonies as much for them as for Jews.

The building houses the offices of Galinski and his staff, a kosher restaurant, a library, religious class-rooms, meeting halls and an auditorium. Its doors are open.

But, seated in his private office, Galinski said that the process of conciliation still had a long way to go. 'We remain separated,' he said, 'because of memories. We remember those who betrayed the Jews for profit. We recall those who denounced their neighbours. We recall those who served as informers for the Gestapo.

There is no adult Jew who does not have personal experience of the terror or who does not mourn for someone killed. No, the Jews cannot forget.

'Nor, for that matter can many of the Germans. We know of former Nazis who hold good jobs and walk the streets. For them, wiping out the past has been easier than for us, but they must have consciences.'

His voice shook slightly. 'What do they tell their children? Our memories are bitter. Theirs must be terrifying.' He brought his voice back to normal. 'Yet, I feel that our task is to find a common ground. We try, but we have not yet come to the point of completely candid talks. Moments always come when we trip over memories.'

He slumped into his big chair, behind the big desk and lapsed into a reverie as if he, too, had just tripped over a memory. Then he straightened and his hands went to the mound of papers before him, the inevitable statistics, the numbers Jews live by in Germany. Galinski found little that was cheering in them. More than 60 per cent of the Berlin Jews are more than fifty years old. Over 40 per cent are more than 60. There are only 230 children below the age of ten. Young adults, those who offer hope for a new generation, are less than 600 and many of them are certain to leave Berlin, if not Germany.

For West Berlin is not a place which offers hope for young people. An enclave in East Germany, everything but its spirit is wasting away.

'We try to hold the young,' Galinski said. 'Most of our efforts are directed toward aiding them. But what can one do? My own daughter is now attending college in the United States. I do not believe she will return here to live.'

But, Galinski quickly pointed out, this is a matter of choice on the part of the young, not one that is being forced on them. Life for young Jews is not made difficult in Berlin, but, instead, eased. Berlin officials, beginning with the late Ernst Reuter, had made every effort to help the Jews. (*Der Speigel*, the magazine has described the West Berlin Senate as 'especially generous' in dealing with the Jews.)

And Berliners, Galinski stressed, were never as poisoned by Nazism as most other Germans. Then he said, 'Of course, there is some anti-Semitism. We sense it and feel it with some people.

It oozes like sweat out of them. It erupts in an argument or
when someone has had one drink too many. I've had it said
to me that, "Too few of you Jews were placed in the ovens."

'But this is rare. And such things happen in other countries,
even the United States. You cannot deny that. I have found that
most Germans want to create an understanding with the Jews.
You must believe that.' He looked for confirmation, for assur-
ance, at me. What could I tell him?

'Those desecrations that took place,' he said. 'They had little
meaning. There are fools and idiots everywhere. I say that there
are fewer here than in any other part of Germany. Our people
are different.'

He offered his evidence. The crowds that attend events in the
building. The interest shown by non-Jews in Jewish history. The
appearance of prominent officials and artists in the great auditorium. And, on the other side of the coin – the Jewish side –
there were young students taking religious instruction. Young
Jews who used the library continually.

'We are part of Berlin,' he said, 'that is evident. The Jews are
here and they make their presence felt. It is true, not as they
did before Hitler, but we are so few now. But the spirit is good.
The spirit is very good. That is why the N P D doesn't even exist
here.'

Now the dichotomy between Galinski, head of the Berlin
Jewish community, and Galinski, the Jew, asserted itself. 'Something must be done about the N P D,' he said. 'It rekindles old
hates. It is a headquarters for old Nazis, for men who want to
turn back the clock. And they are clever. They don't attack
individual Jews, but they attack all things that are Jewish,
especially Israel.

'It makes it hard for those of us who are older. We are the
ones who light the *yahrzeit* (death anniversary) candles. It is we
who see frightening faces in the passing crowd and hear dread
voices in the night. The N P D speaks with those voices. It should
not be permitted.'

Then, once again, the community manager asserted himself.
'But, of course, it is different in Berlin. On this side of Berlin.
A Jew has his self-respect here. This building proves it.'

But just then his eyes went past me and focused on the high
wall outside. Etched on that wall is a map – a death map. The

locations of each of Hitler's extermination camps is marked on the map. On that day, a wreath hung on the wall. It had been allowed to hang too long. The flowers were dead.

Galinski said, 'You must excuse me. I have a great deal of work to do.' I left him, thinking that he had even more work than he knew.

You have to go through an iron gate that fronts on a side street to enter the building where the Jewish community of Munich has its headquarters. The entrance is anonymous, blank. The elevator is rickety. The halls are narrow and dark. Doors are double and triple locked. Shadows dim the narrow corridors. This is a building that could house a group of conspirators – or a group of haunted men.

No open doors here. No exhibits to which the public is invited. Instead, voices are low and strangers are suspect. The air is dusted with whispers in Yiddish, in East European languages. Why not, since four of every five Jews in Munich were born in Eastern Europe.

These Jews are veteran fugitives. They fled Hitler. They fled their native persecutors. Many have fled from Communism. They came to Munich because that city was part of the American-occupied sector of Germany. To these people, America represented freedom and hope. No wonder that the camp in Foehrenwald, close by, became the largest of all displaced persons camps.

When they came, the beer halls still echoed the Horst Wessel song. The balcony above the Koenigplatz, that balcony from which Hitler so often shrilled to the throngs below, still bore a swastika. The sidewalks were uneven from the pounding of marching boots.

This is a community of the displaced persons, the D P's. Most say that their status has never changed. Once, long ago, most maintain, they had anticipated going to Israel (then Palestine) but had been prevented. As early as 1946, the *DP EXPRESS,* a Yiddish-language newspaper then printed in Munich, reported :

'The dream of emigration to Palestine has not yet been realized. The accursed German land has turned into a temporary home . . . a person cannot live without a home. What shall we do? Work in German factories, build German homes, seed German lands?'

In time, some did. Enough to make Munich the second largest Jewish community in Germany. But not one of these would tell me that he had stayed because he wanted to stay. And, even twenty-odd years later, there were but a few who admitted, soft-voiced and shamed, that they intended to remain in the 'accursed German land'. Not even these, however, would call Germany home. 'It is,' said Moritz Abusch, 'a stopping place between the camps and the grave.'

Abusch is manager of the Munich Jewish community. His office is small, box-like. The walls are bare. There is no flamboyance in either the man or his surroundings. He is middle-aged, soft-spoken. He does not dominate the community as Galinski does his. He does not set policy. He has not imposed his personality upon the community but, instead, adopted the dull, grey of the community.

Only in one major respect is he like Galinski. In his history as refugee, camp inmate, survivor.

He administers the affairs of some 4000 Jews who are alien to both Munich and Germany. And he regards those affairs as exclusively Jewish. He does not believe that it is his function to forge links between Jews and Germans. He does not believe that such links can yet be forged.

'We live beside each other,' he said, 'but we do not live together. We are still marked off, isolated, by the fact that we are Jews. That is how the Germans regard us and that is also the way we regard ourselves. Most of us are here not because we want to be, but because we had no choice.'

He was quick to add a disclaimer. 'We Jews have few problems in Munich. The Mayor of Munich (Hans-Joachim Vogel) is a fine man who does everything possible for us. The Bavarian government shows us every consideration. But this place is not home.'

And, after he speaks a time, it is easy to see that to him, as to most Jews in Munich, 'home' is Israel. No other community is so Israel-oriented. Many of the youth leaders, the religious instructors and functionaries are recruits from Israel. Some of them are frankly proselyters for Israel.

For Abusch, administering his job is a care-taker operation. He is a receiver in bankruptcy who is determined to conserve every possible asset for the benefit of one creditor. And the greatest asset is the young. And here the Munich community is better off than most others.

Abusch, of course, has figures available. Only 12 per cent of the Jews in Munich are over sixty. The average age is the lowest of any community. 'Old people,' Abusch said, 'did not survive the concentration camps and the D P camps.'

There are more than 500 children attending the religious schools. There are clubs and social organizations for them. 'The young Jews,' he said, 'have few contacts outside of school with the Germans. They stand apart just as we older Jews do.'

Almost none of the young Jewish boys accepted conscription into the German army. (German law allows such refusal.) Abusch commenting on this, said, 'How could they be asked to serve under officers who were part of Hitler's Wehrmacht?' But many of these same young Jews went to Israel to fulfil their military service there.

(In June 1967, dozens enlisted for service in the Israeli army and others signed up to work in the fields and the kibbutzim.)

'None of us,' Abusch said, 'can really accept Germany as a homeland. The wounds of the past have left scars on the present. We have not yet learned to trust. Even now, I avoid the Koenigplatz. Even now, we guard our words and our actions. It was here that Hitler found his first recruits. It was here that the N P D won its first victory. It was no accident that this happened.

'The N P D troubles us greatly. Men who were Nazis are in that party. Their newspaper is vicious. Why do they let the N P D go on? It should be made illegal. Other parties have been banned. Why not the N P D ?'

(One of the banned parties is the Communist party. This is a delicate subject with Abusch. His brother is one of Walter Ulbricht's close aides in East Germany.)

It is under the twin shadows of fear and memory that Abusch and the Jewish community of Munich live. It is a day-to-day operation, giving no sense of permanency. Abusch performs his chores.

He has his books and records to keep. There is a steady stream of people who come to see him with their problems. Two secretaries screen the callers, lock the door behind them when they enter and leave. There are contacts with city and state officials.

'As long as there are Jews in Munich,' he said, 'there are things that must be done. We have old and young, sick and well. We must provide for them. I do not know what will happen in the future. It may be that there will continue to be Jews in Munich and in other parts of Germany. It may be there will be none. If you ask me, I have no real hope for the future.'

He pushed a buzzer as a signal to one of the women in the outer office. A moment later, the door was unlocked. After I went through it, the door as again locked. Some people, waiting to see Abusch, threw furtive looks at me and then quickly averted their eyes. I was a stranger; perhaps I was to be feared.

In Hamburg, the building which houses the headquarters of that city's Jews also houses the office of I B M. A great plaque on the face of the building announces that this is the site of *Judische Gemeinde*. High glass doors reveal the reception room. There is nothing clandestine about being a Jew in Hamburg.

This city resisted the Nazis almost until the very end. Its first post-war Mayor was a Jew, as is his successor, Herbert Weichmann, who is also a member of the Federal *Bundesrat* (Senate).

Not too far away is a magnificent new synagogue that faces a broad square. Its doors are open. Attached to it are banquet halls and an auditorium. The synagogue has facilities for thousands. But there are only 1400 Jews in the city.

Some day, said Herman Singer, these facilities will be used. Singer is the head of the Jewish community, a big, broad-shouldered extrovert. His office is large and bright and his massive desk is littered with gadgets. There are a half-dozen extensions buttons on his telephone.

Singer is continually on the phone. He talks with city officials, with the old age home, with the rabbi (when the rabbi is in Hamburg). It seems that there is so much to do that time is at a premium. There is all the appearances of renascence of that ancient Hamburg Jewish community which played so large a part in that city's history, culture and business from the Middle Ages on.

But the appearance is false. Singer's efforts are more involved with decline than with growth. There are more deaths than births. The old-age homes are filled but the kindergartens are almost

empty. More young Jews leave Hamburg than immigrate to it.
The Jews of Hamburg are a mixed lot. The largest single group
is composed of Iranian Jews who came to Hamburg when the
'economic miracle' was at its most miraculous, opened different
types of businesses and have, to a great extent, prospered. There
are 400 German Jews in Hamburg and here, as everywhere, they
are the oldest Jews. In addition, there are some 400 East
European Jews.

Hamburg Jews have a long and proud tradition. Among them
were scholars, great rabbis, outstanding physicians and important
bankers. Almost all these are gone.

But Singer is a public relations man, a professional optimist.
After all, isn't Herbert Weichmann a symbol of the potential
for Jews in Hamburg? Isn't the handsome synagogue an
invitation for Jews to come to Hamburg?

When he speaks for publication, Singer never discards his
optimism. It is a necessity. But, even at his cheeriest, there are
times when he qualifies, times when he cannot help contradicting
himself. The big shoulders slump forward, the bright eyes dim.

'It is true,' he said, 'that we have nothing to fear, yet sometimes we are afraid. I have found myself looking over my
shoulder when I walk alone at night. Why? Why?'

And he provided his own answer. 'We remember.' He recalled
his own experiences in two concentration camps. His lips silently
read off the purple number on his wrist. He talked of relatives,
friends, neighbours – all dead. 'Reason,' he said, 'tells me it is
all over, that it is past and cannot happen again. But reason
also tells me that it did happen and when it happened, it was
unbelievable, too.'

But then he was the public relations man again, the community
leader. He talked of the Iranians. 'They are,' he said, 'the biggest
contributors to the synagogue. They attend services regularly and
observe ritual. They lead normal lives. They marry, have
children. Today we're having a *brith* (circumcision). You must
attend it with me. You will see for yourself.'

We went to the synagogue together. There were 200 of these
Iranian Jews in the big room. Tables were laden with food and
flowers. There was wine. And there was laughter. The only Jews
in all of Germany to whom laughter comes easy, I found, were
the Iranians.

It was hard to think of them as Jews. Their skin almost almond-coloured, their eyes bright and flashing, they contrasted so sharply with the few light-skinned persons in the room. Their voices were high and when they spoke to each other, it was in their native language.

'Of course,' Singer said, 'all the people who are in business speak German and the young people who are attending school also speak German. But many of the older people and of the women have not learned German.'

Minutes later, I discovered why. I sat down at a table with a half dozen young men. All but one were students. How, I asked them, did it feel to be an Iranian Jew in Hamburg?

They were diffident but finally one spoke out. It was difficult, but not because they were Jews, but because they were Iranians. They did not mix a great deal with Europeans, Jews or Christians. In the decade they had been here, there had been only two or three marriages between Iranians and Europeans.

'We run into prejudice,' the youth said, 'but not because we are Jewish. We do not feel that we belong here and all of us intend to leave. Most of us will go back to Iran.'

They felt, he said, no special self-consciousness about being in Germany. They knew of the horrors of Hitlerism but they had not experienced them. The concentration camps, the labour camps and the gas chambers were outside their experience. But the young man said softly, 'If I were a German Jew, I do not think I could live here.'

He translated for the others and they nodded agreement. Then, through the youth who was acting as interpreter, they started throwing questions at me. Were all the stories they had heard really true? In their classes the subject had been glossed over, sometimes not mentioned at all. I told them the stories were facts.

One of them shuddered, spoke rapidly. 'Then why did any Jews stay in Germany after the war?'

I told him that was what I was trying to discover.

Singer came to our table. The ceremonies were over and a meal was being served. He could not stay; there was too much work waiting for him in his office.

Returned, he read his messages, made repeated phone calls. Then, this done, he said, 'You see. We get along well. One week one of the Iranians reads the Torah at the services and the next week a European. All contribute to charity, to Israel. We are all Jews together. That is the important thing – that we are Jews and that we are here.'

But Singer did not want to make any predictions about the future of Jewry in Hamburg or Germany. 'How can anyone tell. After all, the future is not dependent upon us, but upon the young people.'

One of these young people came in with some papers for Singer. She was a tall, slender, blonde, a very pretty girl. Singer said, 'Congratulate her. She was married a few weeks ago to a young Israeli. She met him there when she went to visit.'

'We will be going home soon,' she said.

'Home?' I asked.

'Of course,' she said. 'Israel. My husband gets his degree in engineering soon and we will be going back.'

Did she want to go?

She wanted to very much. She had been born in Germany. Both her parents had survived the concentration camps and then settled in Hamburg. (They were of Polish backround.) But Germany had no attraction for her. She had twice gone to Israel with Jewish youth groups.

'Life is harder there,' she said, 'but better. I felt free there and I don't feel free here. No Jew can feel free here. My parents understand. They are happy that I will be going to Israel to live. In a few years they will immigrate also.'

She left Singer's office and he said, 'If I were young, I suppose I would also go to Israel. But someone has to be here.' His phone was ringing. 'There is work to be done.'

'Yes, there is work for the Singers and the Abusches and the Galinskis. There is work for a van Dam.

Budgets and cost sheets. Schools and old-age homes. Cafeterias and meeting halls. Mounds of paper work and piles of statistics.

There is always work, but there is, for none of these men, a real meaning behind his work.

It does not matter what face they put on it. Each is aware that he is dealing with a diminishing secular community. Time is against all their efforts to give vitality to that community.

But if there is little hope for the secular life of Germany's Jews what hope is there for their religious life?

5 *The Rabbis*

THERE are now fifteen rabbis in all of West Germany. If their sole task was to minister to the devout, they would be more than enough. For there are less than a thousand Jews who observe creed and ritual, no more than three thousand who give lip service to piety. The rest adhere to their faith but do not practise it.

The rabbis say sadly that the religious aspect of Judaism in Germany is a flickering flame.

As proof, there are the empty synagogues, the intermarriages (almost half) of Jews with non-Jews, the mockery made of the Sabbath.

Yet there is a fierceness about their being Jewish that dominates the lives of the Jews.

There were no practising rabbis in Germany when Hitler was defeated. Some had fled, the rest had been either killed or imprisoned. The few still alive at the time of liberation wanted no part of Germany. And when the Jewish community came into being, it was a secular one, not a religious one. And nothing has changed in the years since.

The power centre of Jewish life in Germany is the community manager. Sometimes alone, sometimes with the concurrence of the board of directors, he engages the rabbi, sets his salary and tenure. This has caused continual disagreement over the things that are God's and the things that are Caesar's. Even with the paucity of rabbis willing to serve in Germany, turnover has been frequent.

Within a few years, Munich has had three rabbis and Hamburg

mates being Chief Rabbi of the country, is the Chief rabbi of
Hesse, Rabbi Isaac E. Lichtigfeld. He is a big, lumbering man,
with a scraggly beard, flashing eyes, and a soft, almost melancholy
voice.

Rabbi Lichtigfeld fled Germany in 1933 and spent more than
twenty years in England. His English is 'British'. And he says,
'England is my country. Here, I am a stranger. But, what is
more strange than that I should be a rabbi?'

Strange, he meant, because he did not become a practising
rabbi until he was almost sixty. As a young man he had studied
both for the law and the rabbinate and, his studies concluded,
he had opted for the law.

(Traditionally rabbis have had a secular occupation as well as
a vocation. For centuries, rabbis neither asked for, nor received,
payment for teaching or dispensing the Law. Some of the greatest
rabbis have been physicians, among them Samuel the Arioch,
Sahal Albatri, Yitzhak Israeli and Moses Maimonides. Saadia
Gaon was an educator, as was Hillel, who enunciated the
Golden Rule before the birth of Christ. Rav Abba Areecha and
Samuel were jurists. Others have had humbler occupations. Israel
Baal Shem Tov, founder of Hassidism, for example, worked in
the clay pits as a labourer.)

Lichtigfeld served in the German Army in World War I. 'Unhappily,' he said, 'I was on the wrong side.' After the war, and
during the years of the Weimar Republic, he practised law. After
fleeing the Nazis, he was admitted to practice in England and
became a specialist in the Court of Appeals.

When the Second World War ended, Lichtigfeld believed that
he had a duty to return to Germany. 'I could, of course,' he said,
'have returned to Germany as a lawyer. But I knew that there
would be no lack of Jewish lawyers in Germany and that what
was needed was someone who might help restore the sense of
Jewishness both to the Jews and the Germans.

'The greatest crime of the Nazis was that they had exploited
and destroyed human dignity. It was systematic, studied and pre-
meditated. And their victims were not only those they persecuted,
but those who subscribed to their theories. This was the heritage
the Nazis left. It has not yet been liquidated.'

It was dusk and the shadows in his office became attentuated
fingers, grasping the bare, painted walls. 'Sometimes,' he said,

'I think the Jews live in a darkness in Germany from which they cannot escape. I ask myself if Jews can live in Germany. I have three children. My sons live in the United States and Canada and my daughter in Israel. I know they can truly be Jews there. I have my doubts about the ability of anyone really to be a Jew here.'

Almost reluctantly, he switched on a table lamp. He played with the papers on his littered desk. 'Paying taxes does not make one a Jew,' he said. 'It only gives the right to wear a label. For some it is enough. It permits them to call themselves Jews and so they are Jews. But being Jewish transcends a label. It is a quality, not a name.

'And yet. . .' The voice grew sadder. 'Some have asked me where their God was when they were being persecuted, tortured and murdered. When they sing *Eli, Eli, lomo asovtoni*? (My God, My God, wherefore hast Thou foresaken me?) it is from their hearts and their memories. Still, I can say they were not forsaken. They survived and their children are on this earth. In their own lifetimes, they see themselves perpetuated.

'Look at the wonder of it. From Haman to Hitler, from Pharaoh to Fuehrer, they have survived. That has meaning. And not only the Jews feel this. Over the years there have been thousands of requests for conversion to Judaism. Some, of course, from a sense of guilt, a desire to make retribution, a determination by some of the young to take the sins of their fathers on themselves.

'But many because of a conviction that Judaism has proved itself over the millenia. That it keeps some kind of fire alight in man's spirit that cannot be extinguished. Would that all those who call themselves Jews believed it so strongly.'

But more than a decade in Germany as a rabbi has given Lichtigfeld the conviction that there is no great hope for a continuing Jewry in Germany. 'The spirit must be reanimated.'

Nor does Lichtigfeld feel convinced that the present Germany is completely altered from the Germany of the past. He quickly added, however, that the policy of this government is far different and that it is being rigidly enforced. But that, he feels, is not enough.

'The German people,' he said, 'have not yet sorted themselves out. Twice in a few years they have held themselves to be the super-race. Seeds of this still remain. It is obvious in the N P D. It is in the tide of nationalism. It shows itself in the desecrations, the anonymous phone calls and letters.

'But there is hope in the younger generation of Germans. The big question with them is whether they feel as they speak. Remember, they are the heirs of a people whose crimes have not yet been totalled up for history. There are bound to be some who will not read the history books or who will tear out the black pages.'

But that – the attitude of the Germans – is only a part of the picture. 'I do not believe that the Germans will interfere with the growth of a Jewish community in Germany. I wonder, however, if Judaism can re-root itself here. The spirit of Judaism. Unless that happens, there are no Jews.'

In Frankfurt, there are religious schools and teachers of religion. There are five synagogues. There are religious celebrations and holiday observances. But these are no real promise of a Jewish future to Lichtigfeld.

'Remember,' he said, 'that under Hitler the Jews were deprived of self-respect. It is not easy to regain it. We are still trying to prove to ourselves, as well as the rest of the world that Jews are equal to other men socially, politically and psychologically. Great harm was done by Hannah Arendt's thesis that the Jews were willing victims, that they co-operated in their own destruction. There are still too many, especially in Germany, who are happy to believe this.

'This caused even now a psychological injury. Recently a Jew was voted the outstanding citizen of Offenbach. I spoke at the ceremonies honouring him. I pointed out that this had significance not because of the present, but because of the past. And I recalled that past to the audience. No Germans resented this or objected to it, but there were some Jews who felt I had erred in discussing the past.

'I understand their reasons, but I disagreed with them. The past must not be ignored. Neither Jews nor Gentiles have recovered from it. Things are not as they were before Hitler and they can never be as they were before Hitler.

'This is proved by the fact that the place where I spoke was a new, fine school that had just been opened. It is called the "Anne Frank School". I know that every child who attends it will have to learn the story of Anne Frank. Somehow, they will be aware that there was a time when children like them went, not into a class room, but into a furnace. It is important for both Jewish and German children to be reminded of this.'

As he looks back at his decade as a rabbi in Germany, Lichtigfeld finds little about which to be enthusiastic, not much more about which to be hopeful. 'In the abstract,' he said, 'I think it would have been better if there had been no Jews in Germany after the war. But the reality was that there were Jews.

'I came back and found them. They were the leavings of the D P camps, the old, the sick and the broken. There was an obligation to help them regain their dignity as humans. That is why I am here.

'My God, how could we, who were outside Germany, desert our brothers in Germany?'

But, as he sits in his office in Germany, he has faith but little hope.

And this is also true of Rabbi Hans Isaac Gruenewald in Munich.

'We teach the Talmud,' Rabbi Gruenewald said. 'We teach the Old Testament and the Law. But behind this teaching is the knowledge that we are in a country where, only a few years ago, being Jewish meant being sentenced to death. In a country where your religion made you a criminal.'

Gruenewald is another big man. He stands well over six feet, broad-shouldered and deep chested. His hair and his spade beard are grey. He looks older than fifty-odd years.

He was born in Frankfurt and educated there. When he completed his studies for the rabbinate, Germany was being governed by the Nazis. His profession had become obsolescent, his degree a warrant for his arrest. In 1936 he went to Israel, a country where there was no shortage of rabbis. He lived there for more than twenty years as a dealer in rare books and a philologist.

'After the war,' he said, 'Germany preyed on my mind. The massive problems of the Jews who were there obsessed me. So I left Israel and went to England where I studied at the Jewish College in London to prepare myself. I returned to Germany in 1960 and became rabbi at Hamburg.'

Gruenewald was one of the rabbis whose Hamburg tenure was short. He stayed only three years and then went to Munich.

'The problem of the Jews in Germany,' he said, 'is one of re-covering their Judaism. Their temporal entity was returned to them. Under the constitution of the Federal Republic, they had equality with all other German citizens. The officials have passed laws which guaranteed restitution and reparations on a fair scale. Men like Mayor Vogel, here in Munich, are men of good will.

'But Nazism broke the Jewish spirit in Germany. It was a brain-washing which affected all Germans, Jews and non-Jews alike and the results are still evident. This country is still Germany and Germany has not yet become a good place for Jews even though it has ceased to be an evil one.'

He regrets the occasional anti-Semitic acts but he has seen no evidence of organized anti-Semitism. The N P D is a potential seed-bed for that, but not yet an actual one, he said. 'It is a haven for the discontented,' he said. 'It is made up of the dissatisfied, both young and old. If there were to be an economic depression here, the young who seem to equate democracy with prosperity might well lose their faith in democracy. Then the N P D could be-come a real threat. It would be better for all Germany – not just the Jews – if there were no N P D.'

But, he stressed, his concern is not with Germany but with the Jews in Germany and here he was pessimistic on all scores. 'We are talking about a group which is disappearing. I would guess that in thirty years there will be almost no Jews in Germany. Today, only a few have any attachment to this country and they are the older German Jews. They have memories of better times as well as of worse ones.

'But for those who are middle-aged and younger, there are almost no good memories. I, for instance, try to avoid all memories of my youth. I do not like to visit Frankfurt. To me, it is a city peopled by ghosts.

'There is a feeling that the young people are far removed from the past, but I do not think this is so. The children are aware of the psychic and physical wounds which their parents suffered. They have lived the persecutions and the immolations vicariously. And, today, they live in a form of apartheid. It is voluntary, but it is *apartheid* still.'

But, above all, what concerns Gruenwald is the failure of Judaism to regenerate itself. 'The religion,' he said, 'may well disappear before the Jews themselves. To be Jewish in Germany too often means an attachment to Israel, a common past, and registration as a Jew.

'That is not enough. The true significance of Israel must not be that it has won military victories. I point out that Hitler, too, once won military victories. But too many people here react differently.'

(During the period of the Arab-Israel war, there was a torrent of requests for conversion to Judaism. Many of these came from Gentiles who had married Jews, but the larger number came from young Germans who gave as their reason their desire to join the Israeli military forces.)

'If we cannot inculcate true Judaism in the people here, it really does not matter how many people there are in Germany who call themselves Jews. They will merely be symbols and Judaism an anachronism. I am beginning to think that there is something in the air in Germany which inhibits the presence of Jewry here.'

Rabbi Nathan Peter Levinson is different from all the other rabbis now serving in Germany. He is younger than the others – in his early 40's – but the big difference is that Levinson, alone, is American-trained, a product of American, not European or Israeli Judaism.

He was born in Berlin and his family were among the last of those able to escape from Germany. This was in the spring of 1941, prior to the Nazi invasion of Russia. The Levinson family were allowed to make their way out of Germany to Poland and then to the Soviet Union. From there, they went on the Trans-Siberian railroad to Korea and finally to the United States. The family settled in Watertown, Connecticut, and Levinson finished high school there and then went to Cincinnati University before preparing for the rabbinate at Hebrew Union College.

His first synagogue was in Selma, Alabama, where he remained until 1950. That year, the World Union for Progressive Judaism sent him to Berlin. This was long before the wall had been built and for three years Levinson served as rabbi for both sectors of that divided city.

In 1953 a wave of anti-Semitism, fallout from Stalin's last, harsh, anti-Jewish campaign, swept most of the East bloc nations. With this occurring, Levinson urged the Jews of East Berlin to move to West Berlin. Many did and their actions increased the tension between the two halves of Berlin. (The long blockade was still fresh in all minds.) Even the Jews of Berlin questioned whether Levinson had acted wisely. Many thought he had not. 'I decided that the best thing to do,' he said, 'was to resign. So I did and returned to the United States.'

Back home, he served for a time in Meridian, Mississippi and then, in 1955, entered active duty as a United States Air Force Chaplain. He was stationed first in Japan and then in Germany. In 1961 he resigned from the Air Force and decided to remain in Germany.

'It seemed to me that I could be more effective as a rabbi in Germany than any place else,' he said. 'I thought there was a reason why I had come back here, that I was meant to stay here.'

He is an articulate, introspective individual. A tinge of mysticism overlays his American manner, his modern approach. He is not considered a returned German but an American, an alien, in a foreign country.

'All my orientation is American,' he said. 'I think in terms of American Judaism and the part it plays in the United States. I think of the separation of church and state and the co-operation between different religious leaders in social as well as religious matters. But there is no such situation here in Germany.'

Levinson has the title of Chief Rabbi of the state of Baden, which includes Heidelberg, where he makes his home. But, as he points out, he is not only Chief Rabbi, but the only rabbi in the state. The title, however, is important because it equates him with the heads of the Catholic and Protestant churches in Baden. 'The Germans,' he said, 'have not lost their love of titles.'

There are fewer than 1000 Jews in all Baden. The largest number are in Mannheim, about 300. There are 200 in Heidelberg. The rest are scattered, with some towns having only one or two Jews.

Levinson devotes much of his time to fostering inter-faith groups. He is the Jewish chairman of the German council of Organizations of Christian Jewish Co-operation. This group is active all over Germany, holding conferences, sponsoring lectures. 'Yet,' he said, 'I wonder if we accomplish a great deal. The arithmetic of the population makes it almost a Christian monopoly. After all, there is but one Jew to each 2000 Christians. In addition, many Jews here are not Germans and want no part of Germany. Their experience with Germans and with Christians has not been a happy one. Even the young people have a sense of separation.'

To Levinson, the condition of the Jews is still in balance. 'There remains a residue of anti-Semitism. One generation of Germans was nurtured on anti-Semitism, but their children are taught – or supposed to be taught – that such racism is both immoral and illegal. A conflict exists between parents and children. But Germans are conditioned to respect authority and so both old and young give overt obedience to the law.

'But beneath the surface,' he said, 'there is another current. Our telephone has rung at night and when my wife or I answered it, we were abused and called vile names. These calls are rare, but they do come. And I know the people who make them are sick, but I can't see that we have found a way to deal with this sickness. History proves that it is highly contagious.'

What troubles Levinson is another type of anti-Semitism, what he calls 'anti-Semitism by indirection'. He offered some examples.

'The German society against cruelty to animals attacks ritual slaughtering. No mention is made that only Jews practise this and that it has been shown repeatedly that it is not cruel. Those with long memories recall that the Nazis also attacked ritual slaughtering.

'Then there are those who come to me and remark that the bar-owners are giving the Jews a bad name. They understand, of course, but there are those who don't. And, after all, it is a shame, is it not? Yet the fact is that Jewish bar-owners are few, even in Frankfurt and Munich, and not a single bar on the infamous Reperstrasse in Hamburg is owned by a Jew.'

Hardest to bear, he said, are obsequiousness and hypocrisy. 'There is one official who rushes up to me each time he sees me to tell, again, how much he did for the Jews. What he doesn't know is that I have his dossier which shows that he was a consecrated Nazi.'

As an American, Levinson said, he is caught in a cross-fire.

When he talks of the dangers of the right-wing N P D, he is asked about the Ku Klux Klan and Birch Society. 'The problem really is,' he said, 'that the mass of Germans are both politically uneducated and politically unconcerned. There is no involvement at the personal level and the result is that too many Germans can still be swayed by emotion, not by reason. And that is what the N P D is based on. Unthinking emotion.

'And it is why I believe the N P D should be banned. I have reached this conclusion reluctantly because I believe in the right to dissent. However, dissent from the left is choked off here. That means the N P D is the only place for dissenters to go.'

But it is not the N P D which represents the greatest danger to Jewry in Germany, but the condition and attitude of the Jews themselves, Levinson believes. 'They have no faith in their own permanence,' he said, 'and even I have begun to have my doubts. The Jews here are unhappy and unsettled. The young talk of leaving Germany and the old seek to deny even to themselves that they are part of it.

'I often wonder if it is possible to have a Jewish society without Judaism. The young Jews seem so far removed from the religion itself. Our daughter is fourteen and keenly aware that she is Jewish, but not aware of it significance. She lives in a whipped cream world. She suffers no discrimination or antagonism. Nearly all her friends are Christians because there are so few Jews. What happened under Hitler – what kind of country this was – is almost impossible for her to understand.

'We will have to send her out of Germany to finish her education. We have to give her perspective. She does not get it here. And I am not sure that I have retained my own. Sometimes I laugh at myself when I think of the dreams I had when I first returned. I would help to bridge the abyss between the past and the present. I have learned that this cannot be done.

'There is nothing on which to build. The Germans will not face the past; the Jews cannot. So the question is not how to make a fresh start but whether such a fresh start is worth while. What kind of Jews will we have in Germany? I don't know. I don't know.'

Nor do the other rabbis in Germany. Not Rabbi Hans Lehrman in Berlin nor Rabbi Emanuel Schereschewsky in Cologne.

Lehrman is tall, ascetic-looking, a scholar who took degrees in philosophy and literature and who has been a university professor. He was born in Poland but was taken to Germany when he was a young child. He left Germany in 1933, going to Switzerland.

He remained there until 1949. It was there that he taught and wrote a number of books, among them a study of Henri Bergson, the Jewish-French philosopher, and an interpretation of the Jewish influence on French literature. All his writing was in French.

'I had cut myself off from Germany,' he said. 'I had no intention of ever going back. I sought to de-Germanize myself, refusing even to speak the language. To me, Hitler and the Nazis were Germany and Germany was Hitler and the Nazis. I felt that no Jew should ever again live in Germany, that no Jew should ever again give part of himself to Germany.'

In 1949, Lehrman went to Luxembourg, the miniature country bounded by France, Belgium and Germany, to become Chief Rabbi of the Duchy. While there, he met officials of the new Federal Republic and talked to Jews who were living in Germany. Slowly his adamancy was eroded. 'I did not change my mind about the old Germany,' he said, 'but I was willing to investigate the new one.'

He accepted an invitation to serve as guest rabbi in Dusseldorf. He was offered various posts in Germany.

'I slowly realized,' he said, 'that I could better serve as a rabbi in Germany than in Luxembourg. So I returned. Not to Germany, but to the Jews in Germany. They had been deprived of everything else. Need they be deprived of rabbis also?'

In the years since his return, Lehrman has seen his task as helping in the regeneration of Judaism in Germany. He accepts the vital statistics – excess of deaths over births, of emigration over immigration, of apostasy over conversions. 'Even with all these,' he said, 'I must have hope and belief that the synagogues will again some day be filled.'

Lehrman is pleased that the secular community, under Heinz Galinski, is improving relations between Jews and non-Jews, but he does not regard this as a rabbinical concern. 'Our task,' he said, 'is to inculcate Judaism into the Jews. What is the value of non-Jewish Jews in Germany? No, our work must be to give Jews a greater awareness of our faith.'

In Cologne, Rabbi Schereschewsky agreed. 'If we are here,' he said, 'if we have survived the reason must lie in our faith. The fact of survival would be meaningless if this were not so.'

Schereschewsky was born in Koenigsberg and educated in Berlin and Cologne. His primary study was medicine and he was a doctor, not a rabbi, until 1961. His was one of the first families to flee Germany in 1933, going to Israel. There, for a quarter century, he had his medical practice.

He returned to Germany to do research in Bonn and to settle some financial affairs, leaving behind his three children. He expected to return to them quickly but both the litigation and the research dragged on.

At the time of the High Holy Days in 1961, Cologne had no rabbi and he was asked to conduct the services. Afterward, he was asked to become Cologne's rabbi.

'I was not eager,' he said. 'I had already stayed longer than I had intended and I regarded myself as a doctor, not a rabbi. I had not returned to Germany with forgiveness in my heart. I had made no peace with the persecutors. But the Jews of Cologne needed a rabbi. They were displaced spiritually as well as physically. Their Judaism had to be preserved. So I stayed to do my part.'

Schereschewsky has taken into the rabbinate the personality of the family doctor. His dedication is leavened by a sense of proportion and a sense of humour. He is a believer, not a zealot. This plays a part in his relationship with the secular leaders. It is probably closer than that of any other German rabbi. He has interested himself in community affairs and in inter-faith groups.

But, after six years of service as a rabbi, he finds himself afflicted with doubts about the future of the Jews in Germany. He does not fear another persecution, another holocaust. He detests the N P D but is not frightened by it. No, what troubles him is the Jews themselves.

'I cannot help but feel that our presence here is transitory, that we are wanderers seeking Canaan. The Jews of Germany somehow do not seem to belong here. They appear to be fading away. Yet I recall from my studies that there were no Jews – not a single one – in Berlin at the end of the eighteenth century. They had either left or apostacized. Still, out of that sterility grew a great Jewish community.

'There is also the lesson of the Marranos in Spain. They were forced to deny their god. Yet, from them emerged Dona Gracia Mendes and Joseph Nassi, who reverted to their Judaism and enabled thousands of others to do so. True, they had to leave Spain to do it, but there could be a Dona Gracia or a Mendes here in Germany who can do this for the German people. Remember, it has always been easy to kill a Jew but no one has found a way to kill Judaism.

'Not even when six million are killed.'

But Schereschewsky, like all the other rabbis, knows that his task is not with the six million dead but with the thousands now alive in Germany. And, like the other rabbis, he finds himself afflicted with doubts. For these Jews who live in Germany are unlike any other Jews.

They are a group apart, a group without precedents. And every one of them is not only a problem to the rabbis who serve them, but to themselves as well.

6. The Sick

THE Jews of Germany are made up of many different parts. There are categories and sub-categories. The most obvious division is between the German Jews and the East Europeans.

The German Jews, in turn, are subdivided. There are the *illegalen*, those who through luck, ingenuity, courage or the help of Christian Germans escaped the camps.

Then there are those 'Jews' who had a Christian parent, who had been married to Gentiles, or who had been baptized. They were Jews by Nazi definition and were the last to be imprisoned, the last to be sent to the ovens or the gas chambers. Many of these died; a few survived.

A third group was almost miniscule. It is made up of those who were permitted a form of freedom because the Nazis required their services. Most of these were *consultants*, professional men, primarily lawyers, who were used to give a gloss of legality to many Nazi actions. Almost all of them were older men who had served in the German army in World War I and who had either been officers or who had received some form of German decoration.

An even smaller group was composed of those whose political, social, financial or diplomatic connections were such that they received protection from persons within the Nazi organization.

Then there are the *rueckwanderern*, the returnees, who came back to Germany after Hitler's defeat. These included older men and women unable to adjust to a foreign country; professional men, such as lawyers or doctors, who had been unable to pursue their professions in foreign countries; and writers, actors, directors and persons in the arts who had found themselves limited by language to the extent that they could not establish themselves outside of Germany.

The East European Jews are made up of three separate groups. The greatest number are survivors of the concentration camps and the D P camps. For diverse reasons, they remained in Germany after the war.

Then there are a small number who fled to Germany from the Communist East during the past twenty years.

The third are also *rueckwanderern*. After release from the camps they left Germany, some for Israel, some for the United States or England or South America, and then came back to Germany. Most say they came back for economic reasons, a few because they felt more alienated in those other countries than in Germany, and a small number who say they left Israel because of the climate.

Maon Gid said of all of them, 'We have two things in common. We call ourselves Jews and we are all sick. Ours is the sickness of being a Jew in Germany.'

Gid was born in Poland. His family immigrated to England when he was a child. He was brought up there and is an English citizen. He came to Germany in 1952 as a newspaper correspondent and soon afterward became editor of the only Yiddish-language newspaper published in Germany. It is a weekly, housed in a ramshackle building in Munich. A building which keeps its door locked and has a peep-hole. Once the newspaper had a circulation of 8000 but now it prints about 2000 copies weekly. Yet it is still influential.

Gid is slender, high-strung, voluble. 'I am like all the others,' he said. 'I suffer from torments. But I admit it and all the rest try to hide it. My head aches. My body aches. My soul – if I have a soul – aches. That is the penalty of being a Jew here. But I have one revenge. The Germans are also sick.

'The Jews are the sickness of Germany. No murderer is at ease when he has to live with the ghost of his victim. But the ghosts are not at ease either. So we spend our time making accommodations with each other. After all, it will soon be over. Time is running out. The Jews of Germany are disappearing. Jewish history will soon end here. And when that time comes, the German will feel easier.'

He waved a hand at a printer bent over a type forme. 'Look at him. He has one leg and half a stomach. Three years in the camps and a hundred scars for each year. He hates Germany, but

he lives here. He says it is his revenge. The truth is, that it is
his purgatory.' He spoke to the printer in Yiddish. The man did
not answer him.

'I asked him,' Gid said, 'when he is going to leave. When I
first came here, he told me he would be staying only a short
time. Until he got a few dollars together. Until he was healthier.
But he is still here, as I am still here. I tell you, Germany is
a quicksand for us Jews.

'We cannot escape the quicksand and we cannot escape ourselves. So what has happened is that we refuse to face any kind
of reality. We escape into a world that exists only for each individual. Each man creates his own reality. Not only the Jews,
but also the Germans. If this were not so, no Jew could stay
here and no German could let the Jews live here.

'Everybody creates his own history of the past. You will be
told – as I have been told – that not the Germans, but only a
few Nazis, were guilty of the crimes against mankind. A short
time ago we printed a story documenting that the Wehrmacht,
as well as the Gestapo and the S S, shared in the guilt for the
camps and the extermination. It was filled with facts. Facts.

'Other newspapers and magazines followed up the story. At
once all of us were victims of abuse. How dared we say that
the Wehrmacht had been guilty of being controlled by Hitler?
How could we say that Hitler's army shared in Hitler's guilt.
We were attacking the new mythology. If the Wehrmacht were
guilty, then it could mean that the mass of Germans were
guilty.'

Gid wiped the sweat off his forehead. 'And it was not only
the Germans. There were even some Jews who were upset because we had printed that story. But, then, there is even a Jew,
a member of the Munich Jewish community, who writes articles
for the N P D newspaper, the *Nationalzitung*. But there were
also Jews who worked for the Gestapo in the camps.

'Don't you see, if we face the truth it would be too horrible
for any of us. How could we face the truth and stay in Germany?
So we make up stories to fool ourselves, just as the Germans make
up stories to fool themselves.'

But why did Gid, who had no German roots, stay here?

'I am as sick as all the others. I tell myself that I am doing
some good, that I am forcing the Jews and the Germans to face

the truth. But even I haven't the real courage to do that. If I
faced the truth, I would have to go, for this is no country for
a Jew and nothing that any of us does will make it a country
for a Jew.'

The hurt he was inflicting on himself showed on his face.
'Maybe I am here as a form of retribution. When the holocaust
(this is the term that every Jew in Germany used to refer to
the Hitler period) was taking place, I was in England. I was
far away, living my own life. My people were suffering, but I
was not suffering. Well, perhaps it is my turn to suffer now.'

There was a knock on the door. Gid went to it, looked
through the peep-hole, and then opened the door. The man
who entered was short, stocky, bushy-haired. He was introduced
to me. His name was Pincus Goldman and he was the manager
of a travelling troupe of Yiddish actors.

'Tell the man about the Jews here,' Gid demanded of him.

Goldman shrugged. 'What is there to tell? This is my fourth
tour of Germany in the last seven years. (He was a Polish Jew
whose family had gone to Israel in the thirties. He had served in
the British army and later in the Israeli army.) Each time I
return, there seem to be fewer Jews who are Jews. They come
to see us and they cry and they laugh, but it seems each time
they cry less and they laugh less.

'When I first came here, they all wanted to go to Israel as
soon as they could. They were more interested in Israel than
in our songs and music and sketches. They damned Germany.
Today, they still talk of Israel, but now it is not they, but their
children, who will go there. For them, there is existence, but
no longer life.'

'It is the sickness,' Gid said. 'The sickness of being a Jew
in this country.' He pointed a finger at me. 'You will find it
out for yourself. When you talk to them, when you watch them,
when you speak to the Germans. But don't stay here too long.
If you do, you will catch it. It happens to every Jew.'

The printer looked up from his work. 'Don't pay any attention
to him,' he said. 'He is crazy.'

'Of course,' Gid agreed. 'We all are. A crazy man is one who
invents his own world, is he not? Well, that is what we are
doing. You are going to meet Jews and talk to them. If you
wish, I will take you to them. I will be Virgil to your Dante.
And you will learn that what I have told you is true. True.'

105984

I left the office with Goldman. I asked him if he agreed with Gid.

He nodded. 'I travel all over the world with my company. There are no other Jews like those who are here. They are not like other Jews. They are not even like other people.'

It could be true of some, I said. Perhaps of many. But there had to be some ordinary people who lead ordinary lives.

'There are none here. How can there be? Jews who live in Germany are filled with shame, regret, fear, self-hate. Remember, this is Germany! These people watched their parents and their children die. Their brothers and their sisters. They know that millions of Germans did nothing and did not care. And, today, they live among them.

'Don't be too hard on them. Always remember, you did not experience it.'

He left me at the next street corner. All the time I was in Germany, I remembered, when I talked with the sick people, that I had not experienced it.

7. *The Illegalen*

On September 1, 1941, all persons designated by the Nazis as Jews were ordered to wear a Star of David. At the same time, shielding a Jew became a penal offence. There were some Germans who risked their lives and freedom to help Jews.

A recent study has authenticated about 200 cases of living Jews who survived because of the courage and decency of their Christian friends and neighbours.

Berlin was the one place where a large-scale effort to save Jews was made. Records show that about 5000 Jews were hidden, fed, succoured for at least a time, by good Samaritans. But, of course, no more than 500 Jews escaped the hands of the Nazis.

In Berlin alone have the authorities paid honour to those who dared to help Jews, many of them at the loss of their own lives. Yearly the Berlin Senate issues certificates of honour to any rescuers who can be found.

An Israeli organization, Yad Vashem, has a living memorial to these rescuers, a long line of trees planted in their names in the 'Avenue of the Righteous Gentiles' on the Mount of Remembrance in Jerusalem. And the Israeli embassy in Bonn has sought out German Christians and conferred honours on them for 'acts of humanity'.

Hans Rosenthal was one of those who was saved. So were Inge Deutschkrone and her mother. And Kurt Wolff and Gustav Roth.

Hans Rosenthal lives in a ranch-style house in a new Berlin suburb, with his wife and two children. He is a brisk, dynamic man, extroverted and friendly. He is a T V and radio commentator who also has a forum show of his own over which he presides.

'I have no problems about being a Jew,' he said. 'And none about being a German. I was born here. I have lived here all my life. I married here and my children were born here.'

He was seven years old when Hitler came into power. His father was employed by the Deutschesbank. His mother and a younger brother, born in 1932, made up the rest of the family. 'Of course I don't remember much about that period.'

What he does remember is that the brother contracted polio in 1935 and was completely paralysed by the disease. That his father – 'he was the last Jewish employee at the bank' – was dismissed from his job and died six months later. ('I think now it was heartbreak.')

In 1936, the younger brother was taken from his mother and sent to an experimental hospital where his blood was used in attempts to develop an anti-polio serum. The next year the child was sent home. ('We were told that Jewish blood was no good.')

In 1940, Hans was ordered to an agricultural work camp in Silesia. When, a year later, his mother died of cancer, he was called in and told that he would be allowed to go to Berlin for her funeral. 'I was working days in the fields and nights I had to dig graves. They had told us that sometime soon we would all be allowed to go to Israel.

'I suppose I wasn't meant to be killed,' he said. 'While I was in Berlin, everyone in the camp was rounded up and sent to Auschwitz. As far as I know, none of them survived.'

In Berlin, Hans was allowed to live temporarily in the same orphanage as his brother. He was assigned to work in a factory. And told to move to a 'youth home'. He said, 'It was really a prison.' But two weeks later Hans learned that all the children in the orphanage had been sent to Maidenack. 'I have never been told what happened to my brother, but no one has ever had to tell me.'

Ironically, at almost the same time he was served with an induction notice into the Germany army. He still has that induction notice, together with the single, one-word, reason for his rejection – J U D E. He went back to work in the factory.

Shortly afterwards, he was sent to Pomerania to work in another factory and lived in a guarded hostel. His foreman, a non-Jew, took a liking to him and that, again, saved Rosenthal. One evening the foreman told him that the factory was going to be closed and that all the workers would be sent to a concentration camp that night.

'As soon as it got dark,' Rosenthal said, 'I ran away. It may be that they never knew I got away. I hid out near Stettin for a few days, but I felt I would be safer if I could get to Berlin. I managed to board a train. On the way to Berlin there was an identity check. Two police took one look at my papers, saw that I was a Jew, and started to beat me. They took me off the train at the next stop.

'It was early in the morning and we had been travelling all night. The station restaurant was just opening when we got off the train. The Krapos were both hungry. One of them said, "The hell with the Jew. Let's eat. Someone else will pick him up." He hit me on the side of the head and walked away. I waited a minute then I ran back and jumped on the train just as it started to pull away from the station.'

He reached Berlin without incident but then had to find a place to go. He went to the neighbourhood where he had been born and sought out a woman who had been friendly with his mother. 'She was a Christian, but she had always liked our family. She didn't have any children of her own, maybe that was why she was good to me.'

The woman faced a difficult and dangerous decision. The authorities had requisitioned her home and turned it into a boarding house for a half dozen factory workers – all Christians.

'She knew that any of the men living in the house could report her to the Gestapo. This was after Stalingrad and the Nazis were more vicious than ever about people who helped Jews. She could have sent me away, but she didn't. And the men who lived there knew I was a Jew, but none of them turned me in either. After a time, they began to treat me as a luck charm. Whenever there was an air raid, they'd say, "We won't be hit as long as the Jew is here." That's what I was; the Jew. But they saved my life.'

His greatest danger after that occurred after the war was over and the Russians occupied Berlin. He went into the streets wearing his yellow star. Minutes later he was arrested by Russian soldiers who charged him with being an S S man.

'I was lucky that there was a Jewish officer among the Russians. He took over questioning me and finally asked me if I knew any

c

Hebrew. All I had ever known was a prayer that my mother had taught me to say each night before I went to sleep. I could hardly get it out, but it was enough for the Officer. He believed me. He explained that the soldiers had orders to pick up anyone wearing a yellow star because the S S men who had run the Maidenack camp had stripped the bodies of dead Jews for them and then put them on, hoping to escape.'

From then on, Rosenthal said, life had been good to him. He was able to find work at a Russian-controlled radio station and was finally given a chance to become an announcer. After a time, he moved to R I A S, the West Berlin radio station, that was then under American control. He has been with R I A S ever since and is today one of their top commentators.

Rosenthal regards his as a post-war success story. As evidence he points to his home, his garden, his pretty (Gentile) wife and his two handsome children, both of them receiving 'a Jewish upbringing'. He is not aware of any special problems for Jews in Germany. 'Why should there be? We are just like anyone else. I have no hatred towards the Germans. I hated only the Nazis. After all, it was Christians who saved my life. Christians saved other Jews.

'It has never been any trouble for me to live here or to feel myself a German. I believe that only a small number of Germans knew what was being done to the Jews. A lot know that they were being persecuted, but not that they were being exterminated.'

Rosenthal readily agrees that he is among a small minority of Jews who feels this way. 'But those who cannot adjust, who suspect that the man next to them on a bus was an S S man or a Gestapo agent, should leave Germany. After all, we have to live among them. What is the use of fear or suspicion or hate?'

As a member of the Board of Directors of the Berlin Jewish community, Rosenthal has expressed this opinion often. 'I say to you that Germany is not anti-Semitic. If it were, I would know it. I have appeared on radio and T V for fifteen years and people know that I am a Jew. They have heard discussions on the Jewish situation many times on my programmes. Yet, of the thousands of letters that I have received, only a few have been anti-Semitic.

'Let us be realistic. There are too few Jews in Germany for anti-Semitism to have any political value. The German people are now building a democracy. They lived under Nazism and saw what it did to them. They know all about Communism, and they have rejected that too. This is a new and different country from what it was. A Jew can be a good German without feeling any guilt.'

He is upset that more of them have not accepted this as he has. They continue, he says, to isolate themselves instead of building an 'all-round life' for themselves such as his. He admits his life has certain anomalies.

'My wife is a Christian, a Protestant, and she has not converted to Judaism. I never asked her to. What I did ask was that we should bring up our children as Jews. That is what we have done. Birgit, my daughter, is sixteen. Gerd, my son, (named after his dead brother) is eight. Both have had Jewish education and training. Birgit had a *Bas Mitzvah* (confirmation) and Gerd will have a *Bar Mitzvah* when he is thirteen.

'I am not orthodox. I am not pious. But I am a Jew. I know that. My children know they are Jews. Ask them.'

Birgit is blonde, blue-eyed, slender and pretty. She was seated beside her father with an English-German dictionary before her, helping when there were language difficulties. Now she said, 'Of course I'm a Jew.' But when she was asked to define what being a Jew meant, she looked at her father for help. When he did not give her any, she said, 'It just means that I'm Jewish. That I'm not a Christian.'

It came out that she had no Jewish friends. The neighbourhood in which she lives, the school that she attends both have no other Jews of her age. The only times that she does encounter Jews is when she goes to the Community Centre in Berlin and this she does rarely.

'But everyone knows I'm a Jew. They ask me about Jewish history and about the Jewish religion and things like that. They don't care that I'm Jewish. It doesn't make any real difference to them.'

'You can't let being a Jew dominate your life,' Rosenthal said. 'It is important that the children know what happened in the past. It is important for me to retain my identity as a Jew. But we all have to live with the present.'

This is what Rosenthal has succeeded in doing. He has moved into the German mainstream and expects to float in it for the

rest of his life. He sees no problems for his children in doing so.
'I accept things as they are,' he said. 'After all, Jews have
problems everywhere. I think there are fewer here than in other
places. I have my wife, my children, my job, my other activities.
I lead a life without fear. I do not see Nazis around every corner.
I do not think that because there is an N P D, there will be
a return to the past. I am proof that this is a good country for
a Jew to live in.'

There is no need for him to indulge in introspection. He leaves
that to others and believes that they waste their time, but that is
their privilege. As for him, it is far more important that his
football team – the one that he manages – win the championship of Berlin.

And if it should win the championship of Germany... Ah,
that really would be something!

Inge Deutschkrone, too, is one of the *illegalen*.

Like Rosenthal, she was born in Berlin and, also like him,
she survived because there were non-Jews in Berlin who were
willing to risk their lives and their safety to provide a hiding
place for her and for her mother. It was from them that they
received the food, the clothes, and the hiding places that made it
possible to live through all the Nazi years.

'I remember them with gratitude,' she said. 'The strangers
who would slip an apple or a piece of bread in my pocket. Some
of them wouldn't even look at me. They would just brush
against me as they passed and then I would find something in
my pocket. Later, when we went underground, we were
sheltered.'

She is a slender, forthright, definite woman. A newspaper re-
porter, she has the scepticism of her profession, but no cynicism.
Her father was a Social Democratic official in Berlin. He was
in London, on state business, when Hitler came into power.
He was told to stay there; if he returned, he would be arrested
and jailed by the Nazis. Not because he was a Jew, but because
of his political activities.

'My mother and I were left in Berlin,' Miss Deutschkrone said.
'We stayed, I was told later, because so few believed that Hitler
could retain power long or, if he did, that he would carry out
the programme that he had outlined in *Mein Kampf*. After all,
the Germans have long had a capacity for self-delusion.

'When it became apparent that Hitler was in power to stay, we were unable to leave. So for years we lived from day to day, from hope to hope. After a time, you got so you never thought beyond the next minute. For years, you didn't allow yourself to have hopes, to believe that there would be any afterwards. I think now that we didn't live by our minds but by our instincts. And then, finally, it ended.'

And, with its end, she and her mother went to England to rejoin her father. 'He would not come back. Sometimes I think it was harder for those who escaped. They knew. They thought. And, if they had someone who was still there, they imagined.'

In England, Miss Deutschkrone completed her education. She became a journalist. She was given an assignment in India and spent a year there. Then she went to Israel, where she joined the Jerusalem *Morning Post*. In 1955, she was sent to Germany to become the newspaper's correspondent. Ever since she has lived in Bonn.

'When I returned,' she said, 'I was prepared to be part of a new, democratic Germany. I was a German citizen. I was grateful to those who had saved my mother and me. I remembered the apples. You know, even today, when I taste an apple, I feel a surge of gratitude. I wanted to find a Germany that I could be part of.'

But the reality she encountered made the taste of apples bitter. 'What I found,' she said, 'was that the Germans had no desire to face up to the meaning of what had happened to the Jews. Instead, they were just trying to purge what had happened from the German memory. They believe they have to fight the reality of the past. Germany needed therapy but would not take it. Instead, it tried suppression.

'I have been here twelve years and I have not become part of this new Germany because there is no way for a Jew to integrate into it. No way and no place. If the Germans have to face up to the Jews, then they have to face up to what happened to the Jews under Hitler and their own parts in it. That would be the end of suppression and the beginning of therapy. It is beyond them.'

Miss Deutschkrone has all the facts and figures about what Germany has done to offset ('not repay') the Hitler years and the Hitler terrors. She has copies of the laws against anti-

Semitism. She is aware of how many people have been convicted of breaking those laws. She has seen philo-Semitism and been its object. She has attended memorial services and heard the sincere speeches. She sees the state-built Bonn synagogue every day.

'But none of these recognizes the fundamental issue, the need to accept Jews as human individuals. Hitler lumped all Jews together; so does this new Germany. The philo-Semitism marks us now as anti-Semitism marked and branded us then. Not then, not now, are we truly people. We are still stigmatized. Different. I have learned that the Germans today cannot allow me to be a German. It would demand too much of them.

'There is no such thing as a Jewish community in Germany being part of Germany. If the Jews want to belong, they must cease being Jews. Some will, of course, make that change. The others will leave Germany. I have made my choice; I long ago gave up my German passport. I am an Israeli who is working here.'

Miss Deutschkrone drew up her bill of particulars.

'The German government realizes the value of the Jews who are here as a political instrument both in domestic and foreign policy. They need Jews and if none had stayed voluntarily, it would have been necessary for the German government to create them or import them. There had to be an antidote to Auschwitz and Belsen and Dachau.

'Some form of restitution had to be made to the Jews so as to gain credibility with the rest of the world. Read Adenauer's memoirs and you will see that he admits this. It was a counter in his diplomatic manoeuvres. He needed foreign support and was willing to pay a part of that support to the Jews. If you don't believe that was his reason, then ask what has been done to make restitution to the gypsies. They were also decimated, but nothing is said of that now. But, after all, the gypsies have no political influence anywhere in the world.

'And so there was no need to buy back respectability or credibility for what was done to the gypsies. But it was imperative to do so about the Jews.

'So money became a panacea. Money that totalled billions of marks. I'm not ungrateful. The Jews are not ungrateful, nor is Israel. Everyone of us compares what West Germany has done to what East Germany and Austria have failed to do. But we needed – were entitled to – more than money. We were entitled to being reinstated as humans.'

Her voice was heavy with emotion. Her hands were clenched so tightly, the blood had drained from her knuckles. 'People,' she said. 'If they had only permitted us to be people.' Then she laughed harshly. 'Perhaps they were right, perhaps they saw something that we did not see, that we couldn't be just people.

'But I don't think that was it. I think they were incapable of facing up to the past. It was beyond Adenauer and the C D U. It was beyond the S D P. It was beyond Germany.

'No, the politicians forgot the six million murdered Jews and only thought of the six millions who had voted for the Nazis. The dead had no votes, but those who were responsible for the concentration camps, who worked in them and fed the ovens and the gas chambers did have.

'The Jews are Germany's fig leaf, concealing Germany's shame.'

These are the emotions she feels after twelve years in the new Germany. She did not come to them overnight. They are an end product of time and experience.

'I was a different person when I came here, I was a Jew who had been protected and saved. My mother owed her life to Germans. Twelve years ago, it appeared to me that there was hope. The young people wanted to know what life had been like under the Nazis. I told them.

'Many found it difficult to believe, to relate. They had no point of reference. They had not been told these things by their parents or been taught them in the schools. Some of them broke into tears and pleaded that I tell them that it really had not been so. Then a few came back to see me and told me that I had lied. Their parents had assured them that my story was a Jewish invention. Others said they had been assured that the past did not matter, that it was all over with. And some said the Jews were getting money, so why should they complain.

'Few want to hear my story today. The past is shrouded in lies and half-truths. The Germans do not want to disturb it. They say it is all over, but it isn't over. Not for the Germans and not for the Jews. Germany hasn't survived its crisis; it has just failed to meet it.'

Since she felt this way, since it was obvious that Germany was still exacting a toll from her, why did she remain?

'I do not live here. I work here. I have asked for another assignment. Meanwhile, I report on what is happening here and my life and background give me a point of view.' Some of the crispness suddenly left her voice. 'Maybe I stay because I want to see the end of the story. My story and that of the Jews here.'

They were good reasons. They might even be the actual reasons. But I wondered. I wondered if she had not lost the will to go.

Kurt Wolff is different. He, too, is one of the *illegalen,* but he did not actually become a Jew until after the war. He was born to a Christian mother whose family had converted to Judaism, and a Jewish father who converted when he married. Kurt Wolff was baptized a Protestant.

The Wolffs believed themselves a Christian family, but the Nazis regarded them differently. The elder Wolff was sent to Dachau in 1939 and he died there sometime during the war. When he was jailed, Mrs. Wolff took her son to Bremen and moved in with a sister who was married to a German naval officer. The sister protected and sheltered them until the defeat of Hitler.

'I was fifteen when the war ended,' Wolff said. 'Slowly I learned what had happened under Hitler. My father had believed himself a Christian, but he had been killed as a Jew. I thought I owed it to him, as well as to myself, to become a Jew. My mother agreed. I was one of many who made this choice.'

(The number of such conversions is about 5000, according to available records.)

Wolff completed his education, getting a degree in engineering. 'I think I was the only Jew at the University. Even now, there are very few Jews of my age in Germany and almost everyone is the child of a person who fled Hitler. A whole generation was destroyed by the Nazis. When I took my degree, I wanted to assert my Jewishness. Germany hardly seemed to be the place to do it, so I emigrated to Argentina.'

He remained there seven years, returning to Germany in 1961. 'In Buenos Aires,' he said, 'I became part of the Jewish community, made up almost entirely of refugees from Hitler. I married there, a girl who came from a German Jewish family. Our oldest child, my son, was born there.

'Then the firm I worked for opened an office in Frankfurt and I was asked to take charge of it. I was glad of the opportunity. I felt that enough time had passed so that it would be easier for me to adjust to Germany. And I felt that the years would have changed things, that it would be easier to be a Jew in Germany.'

He returned, bought a home, prepared to live as a Jew in Germany. The office in which he sat was large and luxurious. There was no question but that he had prospered in Germany. Yet, Wolff was preparing to go back to Buenos Aires.

'I have found,' he said, 'that there is no place for a Jew here. You feel it every minute of your life. It is impressed upon you that you are different. I am a person; I do not want to be an exhibit in a national museum. That's all I want to be. A person. But they do not allow it.

'Oh, there is no open anti-Semitism except in a newspaper like the *Nationalzeitung*. What I read there angers me, but it does not make me afraid. Sometimes I feel that it is one of the few places that treats Jews as people. People to hate, but people.

'At least the N P D and its followers admit the reality of the past. The rest of Germany does not. It treats us as persons of special status but it refuses to admit what was done to the Jews. It will not face the terrible truth, maybe just because it is terrible. I cannot live in a world which denies Dachau existed. I know it existed; my father died there. And he died because someone sitting behind a desk pointed to his name and said, "Wolff is a Jew. Destroy him."

'Now, to make us forget as they claim to have forgotten, there are restitution, reparations, philo-Semitism. In this way, they wipe the slate clean. Or, rather, they break it up and throw it into a garbage heap and say it never existed.

'I cannot accept that. My father died. Millions of others died. They died without dignity. And, even now, dignity is being denied them. That is why I am leaving Germany and I shall not return. For me, it isn't that too much of the past remains, but that not enough remains.

'Tell them, tell them all, that there can be no restitution of the spirit.'

C*

Gustav Roth is a slender, pale-faced man in his late sixties. He lives in a small apartment in Berlin that has a view of the wall. He has lived in Berlin all his life, even during the Hitler years. Under the Weimar Republic, he was a minor government employee, a clerk. He has never married.

For almost six years he was hidden, fed and clothed by Christian friends. For much of that time he never saw daylight.

'My world,' he said, 'was a closet with a false back. The man who protected me was a fellow worker and, like me, a member of the Socialist party. We were alike in everything except that I was a Jew and he was a Christian. But that made every difference in those years. He could live. I could only hope to continue to exist.

'He and his wife provided for me, protected me. It was no easier for them than it was for me. Every day – every minute – there was the fear of discovery. We could trust each other and no one else. Anyone could be a spy or an informer. People sold each other very cheaply in those times.'

When the war ended and the Allies occupied Berlin, he came out his closet to try to put his life together again. 'Only,' he said, 'there was nothing. I had had two brothers and a sister, parents, relatives. I started searching for them. I never found any of them alive and there had been more than thirty. The real understanding of what had happened came late to me.

'You see, while I was in hiding, I could be sustained by hope. If I was being protected and saved, perhaps the same thing was happening to my family. At night, I used to imagine what it would be like when it was all over. I had these dreams that we would all be together again. I didn't know – couldn't have believed – that even Hitler could kill Jews like cattle.'

He had a photo album and he turned the pages. 'My brother, the oldest one. He had a store. He was married and had three children. Here is a picture of him and his family.' His voice broke and tears came into his eyes. 'I am not ashamed to weep,' he said.

There were the futile months during which he kept searching for his family and, finally, the moment when he admitted to himself that the search was hopeless. It was a period of disillusionment in many ways.

'I had thought that there were millions like my friend, men

who had not believed in Hitler and the Nazis, and I found that there had been only a few. And the other Germans resented these few. It hadn't been only the Gestapo and the S S that had conducted the terror. It was most of Germany. These people – my people, because I was a German too – had all turned into murderers and killers.

'But the really terrible thing to discover was that they did not care. In those early days no one knew how many Jews had been killed nor did they know the whole story of the camps. But they knew enough. They had seen the Jews disappear from their homes and never come back. They had taken their homes and their property. Soldiers who had returned knew. But the Germans did not care.'

As though of their own volition, his hands turned the pages of the album, turned them and turned them.

'After a long time,' he said, 'I got a job with the Americans. Later, I was returned to a government job. I was given a restitution payment. I got back my pension rights. I live on my pension now. It is enough for an old man who has few needs. If I had a family – if I had anyone – I would not be here. But, as it is, what does it matter?'

Roth has no connection with the Jewish community of Berlin. 'I was never religious,' he said, 'just a Jew. I go to the library often to read. Sometimes I run into some one I know there. We have a cup of coffee. All the people I know are old. My friend – the one who protected me – died six years ago. His wife has gone to Regensburg to live with her son. I suppose all I do is go through the motions of living.

'But I think that is all that every Jew does here. We go through the motions of living. The Jews are as much outsiders now as they were during the Nazi times. We are treated better, of course. I have an apartment now instead of a closet. But I am not part of Berlin or part of Germany. There is no place for a Jew. The place for the Jews –' He stared down at the album again. 'The place for the Jews is in an old book or the grave.

Some of us are still here, but the truth is that they killed all the Jews in Germany.'

These are the *illegalen* who survived Hitler. Hans Rosenthal has had no difficulty in accepting the world of post-Hitler

Germany. He has become part of it, evolved into a German who happens to be a Jew. With his wife and children, his work, his soccer team, and the tulips that bloom in the garden, he has found normality.

For Inge Duetschkrone, living in Germany is much harder. She is no longer a German, but an Israeli. She has made severance by passport, trying to cut every link between her and the past. But she has not succeeded. The quicksand that has engulfed Gid has also engulfed her. And she does not know if she can free herself.

For Kurt Wolff, life in this new Germany has proved impossible. He has chosen to be a Jew and concluded that he cannot be a Jew in Germany. Not on the terms he demands; that Germany give reality to the past, not denial. For him, it is an obscenity that there should be a memorial at Dachau because memorials mark death and, to him, Dachau still lives.

Gustav Roth does not live in this new Germany; he is merely there. Life, for him, is an automatic process. He eats. He sleeps. He is not listed among those killed by the Nazis, but that is only a technicality.

8. *The Consultant*

UNDER Hitler, all 'Jews' were inferior, but some Jews were more inferior than others. There were various plateaus of degradation.

It is a fact that not all Jews were opposed to Hitler and his National Socialist party in the elections that brought him to power. There were those Jews who simply did not believe what he had written or said. They believed – or made themselves believe – that this was merely election propaganda that would be forgotten once he attained power.

There were other Jews who saw Hitler as the only alternative to Communist rule in Germany. They were willing to take a chance on Nazism as opposed to Communism.

There were thousands of Jews who were in dire poverty. One third of all the Jews in Berlin were on the welfare rolls in 1933. They saw no hope in their present rulers overcoming the depression which gripped Germany.

And then there were some Jews whose pride as Germans overrode everything else. They saw their country dishonoured by the Versailles treaty, humiliated and supine under the Weimar Republic. In Hitler, they saw an end to national shame.

There were other Jews, men of importance, who were certain that the great industrial and financial powers behind Hitler – with which they were allied – would quickly put him in a subordinate position.

Once Hitler began his campaign of terror, only a few clung to such illusions. With the murder of Vom Rath in France, in 1938, and the Crystal Night that followed, even those few lost their illusions. However, some few Jews did manage to lead a better existence than others.

Among them was Max L. Cahn.

He was favoured because he had been one of the few Jewish officers in the German Army in World War I, because he had been decorated a number of times, because he had twice been wounded in combat, and because he was married to a Gentile.

Cahn is seventy-seven now, a slender, fragile man who practises law in Frankfurt. He is both a lawyer and a notary, the latter in Germany both an honour and a highly remunerative office. It was one which he held in 1933.

Also helpful to him in the Nazi years was the type and extent of his legal practice. He represented many foreign clients, especially British industrial concerns. He had an intimate relationship with the British Consul General in Frankfurt.

Cahn was not active in the Jewish community before 1933. His wife was a Gentile and his six children were all baptized.

When Hitler assumed power, Cahn, like all Jews, immediately became the subject of restrictions. He came under the provisions of the Nuremberg Laws, beginning in September 1935, and was automatically stripped of his citizenship. However, he was allowed to practise his profession, but limited to Jewish clients. Even this was foreclosed to him, as it was to all Jewish lawyers, after the Crystal Night.

'Just the same,' he said, 'I went to my office each day. I was working there when the police came and arrested me and sent me to a place of detention.'

Unlike most who were arrested, Cahn had influential friends – 'Aryan friends' – who immediately interceded for him. One of these was the Chief Judge of Frankfurt, an old friend, colleague and fellow World War I officer. Another was a high official in the Treasury Department. A third was the British Consul General. As a result, three weeks after his arrest, Cahn was 'reclaimed'.

Shortly afterward, he was appointed a 'consultant'.

'The Germans,' Cahn said, 'even the Nazis, have always had a respect for law and authority. If possible, they wanted to give a veneer of legality to their actions. Maybe they were thinking ahead to a time when they might have to justify them. This was especially true about their expropriation of assets belonging to Jews. They wanted to give the appearance of doing everything according to law – their law.

'To do this, they allowed a number of Jewish lawyers to continue to function. These were the consultants. They could represent Jews in dealing with legal matters. Of course no Aryan could retain them.

'We have been accused of being collaborationists. I say we were not. Certainly I did all I could for my fellow Jews. I was able to help hundreds of them. I managed to save some of their money, some of their valuables. I could intervene for them with the authorities. I jeopardized my safety and the safety of my family.

'Unlike many other Christians who were married to Jews, my wife refused to desert me. She was even more outspokenly anti-Nazi than I was. We lived in constant fear for our children and for ourselves. We managed to get the three oldest children out of Germany, but the others were too young and they stayed with us.

'Bit by bit we were deprived of the necessities of life. When the war came, I was no longer of value to the Nazis and they took away our ration cards for food and fuel and clothes. If it had not been for Christian friends, we would not have survived. One young boy, a friend of my oldest son, came to our house in the middle of the night with a bag of coal he had collected for us. Others brought us food that they had saved from their own rations.

'We lived like hunted animals. Our first thought was of our children, of keeping them alive and healthy. I've heard people say – some have said it to me – that we led privileged lives. We were privileged to live if we could. If we died, we would just be a few more dead Jews. We existed on scraps, on the charity of others.

'As the war neared its end, whatever use the consultants had disappeared. And so did the consultants. One by one they seemed to vanish. One of my friends warned me that it would soon be my turn. This was in the spring of 1945, not long before the end. We decided the best thing for me to do was to run away, to head toward the Allied troops who were moving in.

'I left in the middle of the night. I knew the country and was able to find places to hide during the day time and I moved only at night. For two days I was without food. I had to swim a river but I reached France. I was safe. But there was the long wait until I knew if my wife and children had survived. After Germany surrendered, I returned to Frankfurt and found them again.'

Cahn said that none of the people who knew him felt that he had collaborated, that he had been 'a cannibal'. The Jews who were in Frankfurt at the war's end showed their faith and trust in him by electing him head of the new Jewish community.

'Of course we were only a few then and we were all of German background. Today, of course, the German Jews are a minority here in Frankfurt. There are some who find it hard to understand how I and my family were able to continue to live here all those years. But I have nothing to be ashamed of, nothing to hide. People who know me, know that.'

Cahn has no problem living in Germany today. One son is a member of his again flourishing law firm. His life is back on an even keel. His entire family survived the Nazi years.

'But I have no illusions about Germany,' he said. 'The vast majority either agreed with Hitler or said nothing. Some few, thank God, were different. These were people who helped us and people like us. But there were vultures, eager to feast off dead and dying Jews. After all, for years I watched as they grabbed Jewish property, profited from the tragedy of the Jews.

'On the other hand, the present Government has done a great deal to make up for the past. It has paid millions to Israel. It has paid millions in restitution. We have a legal protection now that we never had before. In many ways, things were never before so good for the Jews. Certainly we cannot forget what happened, especially those of us who are older and lived through the Third Reich. But that is over.'

Cahn is not concerned about the NPD and whatever anti-Semitism exists in Germany. 'Look at our history. There has always been anti-Semitism in Germany. I experienced it in the days before Hitler. I think there is less now than in the past.'

Cahn does have a nostalgia for the old days before Hitler, however. The Jews he implies – though he does not say so – were different them. They were leaders in the community. They had influence and power and position. This was the Frankfurt of the Rothschilds, of the Gans family, which helped found I – G Farben, of the Weinbergs, whose banking empire rivalled that of the Rothschilds, of the Goldschmidts.

This was the city of which Arnold Zweig once said, 'I cannot conceive of Frankfurt without Jews.'

Today, the Jews of Frankfurt are primarily East European.

They are the veterans of the concentration camps or the children of those veterans. They have taken over Jewish affairs and have almost completely excluded Cahn.

'I am an old man,' he said. 'I have done what I believed was right. I do not have to justify myself. I do not have to justify myself to those who know the true facts.'

In a sense, Cahn feels that there was nothing wrong with some Jews being less inferior than others.

9. *The Survivors*

WALTER STELTZER is head of the Office of Information in Berlin. He is a decent, sincere, individual, with deep pride in the new Germany and a sense of responsibility about the old Germany. However, he wants history to be kept in balance. He wants the world to be fair to Germany.

He was the first, but not the only, German who said to me, 'Remember, a smaller percentage of Jews perished in Germany than in any other country which the Nazis controlled.'

He, and all those who made this statistical statement, were literally correct. *Only* 180,000 German Jews were killed. They were *only* one-third of the pre-Hitler Jewish population of Germany. But they were almost 100 per cent of all the Jews on whom Hitler and the Nazis could lay their hands after Hitler's mania reached the point where he called for the final solution.

Most of the others had fled, beginning in 1933.

With the exception of those few who were hidden out by Germans, or who had a greater value to Nazi Germany free than imprisoned, all were placed in various types of camps and used for whatever purpose the Nazis wished.

At the end of the war, there were a few survivors. Ernest Landau was one of these. So was his wife.

They live in a small, pleasant apartment in Munich now. Landau uses one room for his office. He is an editor, a writer and a foreign correspondent. He is quiet-spoken, a slender man with a frail build and sad eyes.

'I lost forty-two members of my family,' he said. 'Sometimes I count them off, one by one. They died, like the millions of others, because they were Jews. You know –' he raised his head – 'you rarely hear a German (like almost every Jew in Germany he draws a line between himself and the non-Jews) use the word, "Jew". It frightens them. It has too many connotations. When it slips out, they quickly apologise, as if they had used an obscenity. Why not? For years it was.

'I understand why the word should be ashes in German mouths. And, like the word, the existence of Jews is nearly always concealed by a euphemism. We are "returnees", or "Hebrewfolk".

'But, whatever they call us, we are Jews and we live in a country that can neither accept us nor reject us. So it does both. And we submit because we have neither the will to become part of Germany nor the will to leave it.'

Slowly he explained – justified – why he had remained in Germany. It was easier to speak of all who remained, not just of himself.

'In the beginning, there were so many who stayed because they needed medical care, because they needed to become whole in body and mind again. There were others who were in a state of shock, almost of paralysis. There were some who were afraid to go to a strange country, learn a strange language.

'Hitler called us "Untermenschen", sub-humans. And then the Nazis turned us into such creatures. So, when we were freed, we needed time and care to become humanized again. We had been deprived of all emotions except fear and hate, of all instincts except that of survival. We had been reduced to numbers, deprived of any other kind of identity. We needed time to re-discover ourselves. Time to heal.' Again he stopped and stared into the distance. 'But that was more than twenty years ago and I am still here. Still here.

'My wife and I would have left long ago – I swear it – if it had not been for our daughter. We married as soon as we were liberated and we had a child almost at once. It was too soon. We had been starved, mistreated, brutalized. Our bodies had taken a beating which had destroyed too great a part of them. So when our daughter was born, she was retarded. She has been in an institution all her life. There are many like her. Hitler did his work well.

'And, after she was born, we stayed because we would not leave her alone and no country would accept a sick child. That is my excuse for remaining. You can accept it or reject it.'

He held his head in his hands for a time. 'My wife lost her

parents, her family too. Who remains who did not?' He stared into the past that he had, somehow, never really left. 'Don't judge those of us who are here too harshly. We have already judged ourselves.'

He talked of the first years after the war. 'I was able to re-establish myself as a journalist. That was the time when the Allies controlled the press. They wanted writers who had no tinge of Nazism. After a while, I was Ernest Landau, a person. I had a profession. I was, as much as I could be, like other people. That was what all of us worked for. To be like other people. But, of course, we were not. We were Jews.

'Yes, we were Jews and all the others were Germans. They knew it and we knew it. And each contact between us only increased that awareness. Neither of us could forget the years of the terror. Today, it is still true. Time has not changed it.'

By reason of his profession, Landau has worked closely with government officials. Government offices are always open to him. Officials always find time for him. 'No one can fault official attitudes. If we have a complaint, it is quickly investigated. If we have a reasonable request, it is granted. Everyone tried to keep the Jews happy. It is government policy. Not Jews as part of Germany, but as Jews.'

Part of his work has involved reporting on war crimes trials and on the NPD. It has included filing dispatches when occasional anti-Semitic acts take place. 'I have found few acts of anti-Semitism, but that does not mean there is no anti-Semitism. It exists. Let me tell you a story. It involves General Harster (SS Gen. Wilhelm Harster).

'After the war, Harster was arrested and tried in Holland for war crimes. He was the commander responsible for the deaths of 55,000 Jews, among them Anne Frank. He was found guilty and received a twelve-year sentence. After serving six years, he was released and came to Bavaria. Somehow, he quickly and quietly was given a post with the Bavarian State government.

'When this was learned, there were immediate demands that he be fired. The government was reluctant to do this and kept him on the payroll until he was again indicted. They had to let him go, but they didn't fire him. Instead, he was retired at half-pay because, they said, of illness.

'Shortly afterward I learned that he had been hired by Euro-

Industry Park, one of the major shipping and transportation companies in Germany, which is located here. I went to see Anton Ditt, head of Euro-Industry Park, to ask how he could employ a man with Harster's record, a man who was already convicted of war crimes and now faced a second trial on other such charges.

'Ditt said he was aware of all the facts. That these were behind his hiring Harster. These were why he was paying him more than Harster's previous salary and, in addition, supplying him with a car and chauffeur.

' "Print that," he said to me. "It's a shame that you don't work for *Der Spiegel*. They have a much bigger circulation and more people would know that Harster was working here. The more people who know, the better for me. Let me tell you that if all Germany knew that I was employing Harster, my business would double. It would be a way of their showing how they feel. And I would be glad to have you print all I have said."

'I never wrote the story because I knew that Ditt was telling the truth. Among the people with whom Ditt dealt – the big businesses and the big industries – there are too many who agree with him. My God, look at how Krupp was allowed to start all over again and given back millions of dollars when his slave-workers were still dying in hospitals!

'So, I kept quiet and Harster continued to work for Ditt almost until the moment that Harster was placed on trial.'

(Harster was found guilty and sentenced on February 24, 1967, to serve fifteen years in prison. Figures offered at his trial raised the number of deaths for which he was responsible to 82,256. It was also revealed at his trial that the 'head price' paid informers for betraying Jews to the S S was a dollar and fifty cents. Harster continues to draw his government pension of $3000 a year.)

Landau feels that the N P D is the voice of those who want to revert to the Nazi era. 'Not all of them are Nazis, but many of the leaders are and certainly their programme is. They ask an end to trials for war crimes, to foreign aid, which is really an end to payments to Israel, and to individual restitution. They cover up their anti-Semitism with the mask of super-nationalism. They don't ever mention the Jews, only "people whom we all know". And they are allowed to function and their newspaper is allowed freedom to spread their doctrine.'

Landau sees no future for the Jews in Germany. 'There is no

incentive for them to live here. And the history of the past to
prevent it. Almost every Jew here remains afraid. Back in his
mind is the thought that what happened once can happen again.
We live with our antennae extended. Even if the danger isn't
there, what matters is that we are convinced that it is.

'That is why there are so few German Jews here. Look at them.
Most are old or their spirits broken. They have chosen to live
out their days, not their lives, here. Others are people who could
not make a living outside Germany or exist on what little money
they had. A few, like the lawyers, could not practise their professions in foreign countries. And then there are those who are
more German than Jewish. Not many, but some. And, in a short
while, they will cease being Jews.

'In some ways it has been easier for the East European Jews.
They were one step removed from the Nazis, so that the Germans
were just one of many enemies. They have memories of Pilsudski
and Beck in Poland, of the Iron Guard in Roumania, of the
Austrian atrocities.

'When they were liberated, most would gladly have emigrated,
but they were caught in a trap. Over a period of time, the largest
number did leave, but others were too sick, were caught up in
red tape. Some had married and already had children. Others
had jobs or were in business. They did not accept Germany; they
were content that Germany accepted them. They said then – they
say now – that this is only temporary.

'A Jewish community was established. Many became prosperous. They stuck to their native languages and to Yiddish and
remained faithful to their native cultures. But they have never
become part of Germany and they have taught their children
that they are not part of Germany. But all of us tell our children
that. Not that we have to, for the children learn it quickly for
themselves. Let my son tell you that for himself.'

Edward Landau is fifteen, already taller than his father. He is
quite handsome, quite shy, a student at the Polytechnic High
School, where he is an honour student. Ultimately he hopes to
study engineering.

'We're different from the Christian students,' he said. 'How can
we talk about the past, about Hitler, when their fathers were in
the German army, maybe even in the SS or the Gestapo, and
ours were in concentration camps?' Then he added wryly, 'Of

course our teachers help us avoid that. It seems whenever we come to that part of German history that deals with Hitler and the Nazis, it's always the end of the term and there's no time.'

He agreed that he had encountered almost no anti-Semitism among the young. 'One or two times someone has said something about the Jews, but it wasn't important. It isn't that that separates us. You just know that you're a Jew and that makes you different. Maybe if they didn't teach religion in the schools, if they didn't have these separate classes, it would be different.

'But the way it is, we know how few we are and that we're separated from the others. We can be "school friends" with some of the Christians, but it does not go beyond that.'

The Landaus are making plans for his future, plans with which he is in full agreement. Next year, when he finishes school, he expects to leave Germany and continue his studies in either the United States or Israel. 'I just don't feel right staying in Germany. I can't feel that I'm really German. None of the Jewish students feels he is German.'

'That is the way it is with our children,' Landau said. 'They all want a life outside Germany. I think we have lost some of their respect by staying here. They accept our reasons, but they will not make them their own. That makes them stronger than we are. Even if it costs us our children, we are proud of that strength. At least we have made them Jews.'

But the way that Landau has chosen is not the way that some other survivors have chosen. It is not the way of Imo Moscowitz, for example.

He is tall, slender, classically handsome, with deep, brooding eyes. He lives outside Munich with his wife and two children in a small private house. It is a house filled with everything except the past.

'It is only recently,' he said, 'that I have been able consciously to open the door to the past. I could not – would not think of those times. Now I can reach out and touch those memories with my mind again. I tried to deny their existence but I failed.

'For years I used to start screaming in the middle of the night and I am lost in time. I do not know what is present and what is past, what remains and what is gone. I fight. I reach out and touch my wife. I get out of bed and run to the rooms where my children are sleeping to reassure myself that they exist. If they do, then I do. And even after I see them, I have to stroke their arms, their foreheads. I have to feel them.

'Then I am reassured. They are real. I am real. I live.'

He was a child when his entire family, including a twin brother, were removed from their home in Berlin to Auschwitz. There were nine in that immediate family. More than twenty others – aunts, uncles, cousins – were also transported to Auschwitz. Of them all, only he survived.

'I think,' he said, 'it was meant that one should live to bear witness to the past. If all of us had been killed, there would be no one to prove that any of us had ever lived.'

He is a stage, film and TV director. He has done some acting and some writing. 'In this work,' he said, 'fantasy and reality are the same. That makes life easier.'

He spent seven years in concentration camps. One by one he saw the others of his family disappear. 'You did not know if they were dead. You only knew they were gone. One man saved my life. His name is Gustave Herzog. He also survived. I met him by accident a few years ago. I wept.' He turned to his wife. 'You remember, Renata?'

'I remember,' she said. 'It was in the press club in Vienna, just before your play opened.'

Renata is a Gentile. Their two children have been baptized. 'It is enough that their father is a Jew,' he said. 'Nothing can change that. Renata was willing to have our children Jewish, but I was not. If they want to be Jews later, let them make their own choice. My God, to be a Jew in Germany!'

But he had stayed on after his release. Why?

Slowly, as if for the first time assembling scattered pieces of a puzzle, he explained. He had been a child when he was sent to the camp. He was only a young man when he was liberated. 'It was all luck,' he said. 'They exterminated the young quickly because they were not strong enough to work. Somehow they missed me. Later, as I said, it was Gus Herzog.'

The years when he should have been growing up, learning, being young, he had spent in grovelling, in surviving. Each day was a contest to live until the next day.

'After a time, you begin to think that the life you are leading is a normal life. Memory of what had happened before I was in the camp disappeared. I was frightened when the day came when I was free. I had been an animal in a cage for half my life. The cage was all my world and the guards and the S S were in charge of that world. Suddenly the door of the cage was opened and I was free.

'And frightened. What did I know of any other world? I had to start another fight for survival because I had no knowledge of freedom. I have seen men who wore chains for a long time. When they were unshackled, they still dragged their legs. I was like that.

'I did not hate. Now it surprises me, for why shouldn't I have hated. But then I felt no emotion except fear. Fear of the world that was without wire fences, without guards, without routine. I had been returned my individuality but at first it was hard to be an individual. Only one thing was not changed. In the camps I was a Jew. Freed from them, I was still a Jew.'

He emerged from the camp unequipped to take up a place as a grown man. His education had ended years before. He spoke German. He had German nationality. The first days were spent in the hopeless search for any other members of his family who might somehow have survived. None had. He had to make a life for himself by himself.

'I had never thought of that while I was in the camp. All I had thought of was staying alive. So I used my glands, my instincts, my animal intelligence for that purpose. Gus had made it possible, but there was no Gus Herzog now.'

He began a course of self-education. 'I read everything I could lay my hands on. Remember, I was like a kid of twelve. Everything was new and different and exciting to me. People helped me, of course. They knew I was a Jew and a few understood what being a Jew had meant. I tried to find a place where I could fit and I decided on the theatre.

'I found that nearly all the people in it were Jews or half-Jews. Many had suffered because of Hitler. Most of the Gentiles had been persecuted by Hitler because of their political beliefs. The world of the theatre was then, and is now, made up of people most of whom never surrendered to the Nazis.'

He accepts that there is a difference between him and most other German survivors of the camps. 'They were adults when they suffered,' he said. 'I was a boy. They had begun their lives and I was still preparing for mine. They had a deep feeling of religion and I did not. This has made for a separation between them and me.'

He is not part of the Jewish community, does not observe either ritual or creed. 'Yet,' he said, 'it is being a Jew that gives me identity. Without it, I would be nothing. I am not part of Germany. What happened to me made that impossible. My God, they literally killed half of me. Remember, I had a twin brother.'

He concerns himself little with politics. Not even the N P D upsets him. 'If that is what the Germans want, it is what they will choose. If they do, I will leave here with my wife and family. It is easier for me to live and work here, to have my career, but I would find a way in some other place.

'I suppose the real reason I stay here is to keep a memory alive. Inside myself and, because I am here, inside the Germans. My nightmares are very rare now, but they will never go entirely. Go and talk to Gustav Herzog. Maybe he can explain it.'

For Gustav Herzog, the nightmares have never ceased. And they fill his days as well as his nights. 'The years in camp,' he said, 'were torture. But the years since have also been torture. I can't separate them. I can't run away from them.'

The scars of that torture, inflicted by himself as well as others, have rutted his gaunt face. They cloud his deep-set eyes. They have made life an effort of will for him.

He lives in Vienna now, travelling rarely to Germany and then only to see an editor or the head of a radio or TV station for whom he might be working. He is a writer, primarily a newspaperman, who comes from a family of newspapermen who have long been prominent both in Austria and Germany. His life has been divided between the two countries.

Half-Jewish, never a practising Jew, he has always been between two worlds. A liberal in politics, he fought Hitler and the Anschluss. 'There were more Nazis proportionately in Austria than in Germany. Hitler didn't need bayonets to take it over. He could have done it with ballots.'

Herzog spent seven years in concentration camps, five in Buchenwald and two in Auschwitz. 'I am proof of the capacity of a man to survive,' he said. Because he was a political prisoner, because he was only half-Jewish by background and non-Jewish by religion, he was low on the priority lists of the extermination camps.

For the same reasons, and because he was a public figure, Herzog was from the beginning assigned to some of the less menial jobs. Eventually, he was employed in the office of the camp commandant. 'At the end,' he said, 'I was processing lists. The lists of those who arrived – no one knew for how long – and of those who were to go – and everyone knew that would be forever.'

Life in the camps was literally a lottery. Eventually, all were bound to lose but the question always was how long would it take for an individual number to come up.

'How did any man survive seven years?' Herzog said. 'Luck. Fate. The law of averages working down to the last decimal point. Maybe God. One bitter winter night a group of us were routed out of our beds and forced to fall in in the camp courtyard. Then we were ordered to strip. We knew what that meant; we were going to be fed to the fires. Some cried. Some damned the guards. I was beyond caring. I just undressed.

'Just as we were about to be marched away, the S S commander came into the compound. He was drunk and happy. Something – who will ever know what it was? – caused him to turn on the guards and berate them. No one was to be fed to the fires unless he gave the order. He told us to put our clothes back on and return to our cells. We were saved.

'If he had had one drink more or one drink less ... If his mistress had been less complaisant ... If he had stayed with her ten minutes longer ... Any one of these and I would be dead.

'The next night another group of men were ordered out into the night. They did not come back. And night after night, others went from the cell to the crematory. It just happened that I was not one of them.

'Sometimes it seemed as if dying was easier than living. We were constantly being degraded. We would be lined up in the snow and ordered to sing. They had composed a song in which Jews were depicted as thieves, murderers, liars and swindlers. To make certain that we all sang at the top of our lungs, the guards walked among us striking at us without looking. One Jew was like any other Jew. We sang between screams. We sang as we tasted our own blood. But we lived. At least for the moment.'

It was at Auschwitz that Herzog met Imo Moscowitz. This was when Herzog were processing lists. Especially the lists of those who were to die. 'They were numbers, not people. The inventory of goods had to be kept up to the minute. So many for the fires. So many for the labour camps. So many newcomers. I was an expert at handling the lists. There were ways to change the numbers. If I were caught, I would go on a list myself, but I was already condemned. I was taking no chance.

'At night, men would creep to my bed and beg me to put their names on a death list. The old would ask to be substituted for the young. The sick, for a healthy man. A father for a son. And a son for a father.'

Herzog's voice cracked. This was his ever-recurrent nightmare. 'They made me play God. As if I had need of that torture on top of all the others. But they had no pity for me because they were beyond pity, even for themselves.'

After he was freed, Herzog stayed only a short time in Germany and then returned to Vienna. 'I was running away but I knew there was no place to run. I know now that Germany – West Germany – is probably an easier place to live than Austria. At least the Germans accept that crimes were committed against the Jews by the Nazis. Many Germans feel shame or guilt. Not the Austrians.'

Why, then, has Herzog remained in what was Hitler's Greater Germany?

'I stay because I don't have the will to leave. I stay knowing that not much has changed since the days before the war. Not for the Jews, with whom I must identify myself. We now live in another kind of concentration camp. And we see a part of the past repeating itself. Today, it is not the National Socialist Party, but the *Volkspartei*. Instead of *Der Stuermer,* there are newspapers like the *Blaue Montag* and the *Blaue Samstag*. The word, "Jew", is a malediction again.

'We have our delusions, all of us. Imo has one too. He thinks I saved his life. I saved no lives, not even my own. There were no lives to save; the Nazis had already destroyed them. In Germany, those of us who are left act like proper ghosts. We haunt the people. In Austria, they laugh at the ghosts.

'I live my life stripped naked in the cold and waiting to be marched to the furnace.'

Herzog, Moscowitz and Landau. They all are described as 'survivors'.

10. *The Returnees*

DURING the dozen years that Hitler's 'Thousand Year Reich' existed, it turned Germany into the most complete totalitarian country in history. It succeeded in Nazifying every aspect of life, political, social, economic, religious and cultural.

Every school, from kindergarten through University, was controlled and administered by people who had taken oath of allegiance to Hitler. Every newspaper and magazine was part of the Nazi propaganda machine. The radio was an instrument of government policy, with every word censored and loaded. Every court was headed by a Nazi judge and ruled on the basis of the party line. Every policeman was a Nazi stoolpigeon.

The arts had all been prostituted. Literature, music, drama, went through the Nazi pulverizer before being fed to the German people.

All forms of government were Nazi and every government official, from Fuehrer to *Blockwart* (street warden), was an instrument of Nazidom.

When Germany was defeated, the entire state crumbled along with the Nazi regime. What remained was a rubble. Whatever semblance of organization existed was manned by Nazi remnants.

The first task of the victorious Allies was the 'denazification' of Germany. A nation had been conditioned and brain-washed for a dozen years. Every instrument of communication and education had been corrupted toward that end.

In those early post-war days, it was accepted that no Nazi would hold positions of influence and power. This was the period before practicality replaced idealism. It was also the era before the Cold War, before ends and means became so entangled one could not be separated from the other.

There was an urgent need for leaders in politics, in the fields

of communication and education. A vast screening and recruit-
ment drive was begun. There were – in the American and
British armed forces – men who had fled Germany and returned
to it to fight Hitler. They were obvious choices for many of the
vacant positions. (Some of them I interviewed and their stories
will be told.)

And, in the concentration camps, there were men and women
who could be moved into military government or into civilian
posts.

Further, there were those refugees who were in many of the
Allied countries, who were persons of repute and ability. Not
all of these were Jewish, of course, but many were.

The Allies found few among the camp survivors who met
their needs and wanted to remain in Germany. (I speak now of
the Jewish survivors.) The survivors wanted to leave Germany,
their dead and their memories. Most of these were East Europeans,
unfamiliar with the German language and German society except
what they had learned in Belsen and Maidenack, in Auschwitz
and Ravensbruck.

Also, what was required was a special talent and ability, professional background. In a desolated Germany, there was no
need of tradesmen and artisans, farmers or clerks.

Nevertheless, from among the survivors a few, like Ernest
Landau, were found who were put to work in the re-education
of Germany.

It was among those who had fled Germany that a larger number of specialists were found. These included journalists, teachers,
lawyers and politicians. A number agreed to return to Germany.
Many of them were Jewish.

Another group who returned shortly after the war were actors,
writers, and producers and directors, both in the threatre and
in the motion picture field.

In the years since, there has continued to be a heavy bias towards the professional and cultural field within the German-
Jewish community. There are few 'ordinary Jews' in Germany,
few clerks and merchants and civil servants. Few labourers.

Jack Bachrach-Baker, who served with the American Military
government and is now associated with the Anti-Defamation
League of B'Nai Brith, explained, 'There just was no place for
the unspecialized Jew in Germany after the war, even if he

wanted to remain there and very few did. The German economy was non-existent. Release from the camps did not mean that a man could return to his old life. That old life was gone forever.

'No Jew could turn the clock back, return to his old home, his old job. What were once great Jewish-owned enterprises no longer existed. No, the survivors in the concentration camps – soon to be inhabitants of D P camps – had only two ideas. To stay under the protection of the Americans and the British until they could arrange to emigrate and to emigrate as fast as they could thereafter.

'That is why the core of the Jewish community would tend, in those early days, to be made up of returnees to Germany. And most of them would be intellectuals. The occupying authorities needed them and welcomed them and had work for them.

'But there was no economic or social place for the average Jew. This was long before the Marshall Plan, long before the economic miracle. Further, there really was no Germany. It was bankrupt, devastated and in the process of being dismembered. Hundreds of thousands of Nazis – probably millions – lived in it. The murderers and killers of the Gestapo and S S were walking around in civilian clothes.

'This was hardly an atmosphere conducive to get Jews to settle there, to try to build fresh new lives. They wanted to get out and, over a period of time, most of them did.'

But, also during this period of time a certain number returned. They came, some of them, at the request of the occupying authorities. Others, because they had been unable to adjust to living in a foreign country, speaking a foreign language. Some, because they had found economic opportunities foreclosed to them.

And some returned because they had high hopes for a new, democratic Germany and wanted to play a part in building it.

I spoke to members of all these groups, these *rueckwanderern*, these returnees, to discover what they had learned and how they felt after the passages of years.

11. *The Politicals*

WHEN Hitler assumed power his first act was to destroy all political opposition. His first victims were those who might provide it. He treated what opposition there might be on the right with firmness, but without brutality. Alfred Hugenberg was allowed to dissolve his nationalistic *Volkspartei* and fade into the background. The opposition on the left, however, the Communists and, especially, the Social Democrats, were bludgeoned into nothingness.

Not that these two parties had been unanimously against him or had fought him to the end. There were members of both who felt that Hitler might, after all, not be completely wrong. At one time some of his staunchest followers had been Communists or Communist sympathizers, none more so than Paul Joseph Goebbels. And long before the Hitler-Stalin pact of 1939, Nazis and some Communists had been able to make working agreements.

The Social Democrats had split over Nazism long before Hitler became Chancellor. Social Democratic votes were cast for Hitler's appointment to that post. But, within the Social Democratic Party there was a hard core of anti-Nazis, many of them of course. Jews. But the great majority who fought Hitler until the last possible moment, were motivated by ideological, rather than religious, reasons.

When Hindenburg capitulated and turned Germany over to the Nazis, a large group of his left-wing enemies knew that their lives were now endangered and their freedom even more. It was from this group that the first refugees came. It included party functionaries and various officials whose anti-Nazi position was known. It also included 'political' intellectuals.

Among these were such persons as Erich Marcus, publicity director for the German state railways; Hilde Walter, writer; and Alfred Kantorowicz, writer.

All these three have returned to Germany. All three were both politically and religiously anathema to the Nazis. None of them had any deep sense of being Jewish. Some had no sense of their Jewishness at all because they regarded Judaism as a religion and they were without religion. Each of them would have fought and fled Hitler if they had not been Jews.

Hilde Walter came back to a small apartment in Berlin. She has to remove books and manuscripts to make a place for a visitor to sit. She has to remove other books and manuscripts from her bed so that she can sleep. She is in her seventies, a bright-eyed, sharp-tongued, keen-minded woman.

'I am a German and a Jew,' she said. 'I am the first by birth and the second by grace of Hitler. He made me a Jew and I have stayed one. On my return to Germany, I realized I had to be a Jew. Not a practising, synagogue going Jew, but a Jew. It was an act of morality for me to register and pay my religious taxes.'

Her concept of the Jews in Germany is sardonic. 'We are a national monument which must be preserved at all costs. Without Jews, the Germans would not be able to live with their guilt complexes. By being here, we show them more mercy than they did us.'

She spent her years of exile in the United States. She worked for the Government, preparing broadcasts to Germany, and she was a free-lance writer. She returned to Germany because she was a German writer. That was the language in which I expressed myself best, and the Germans were the audience to which I wanted to address myself. And I am a political writer. I came back because I wanted to play a part in the post-war German world.

'I did not come back as returned Jew. I came back as a returned German. As I said, I found history had made it necessary for me to declare myself a Jew. The Germans required a Jewish presence. All right; I have helped to provide it.'

She does not believe, however, that the mere presence of Jews has helped the Germans to accept the past or understand it. 'In some ways,' she said, 'it has intensified it. It seems the

D

Germans will never forgive us Auschwitz. That is their sickness
and they desperately want a cure. But they want it to be easy,
painless. They refuse to go under the knife by facing up to the
past and their part in it.

'Recently a German professor demanded of me, "Do you
know about the Madagascar project?" '

(This was a scheme to transport all the Jews in Germany to
Madagascar. It collapsed because of the impossibility of implementing it.)

'The Professor said that if it had been carried out, there would
have been no Jews to exterminate. As far as he is concerned,
any guilt for the murders of Jews must fall on those who did
not carry out the project. His conscience is satisfied – almost. If
it were completely satisfied, he would not have to continually talk
about Madagascar. Nor tell his students about it.

'Then there are those – many of them young – who wash
their hands of guilt because "we had no part in what happened
to the Jews." They can prove they took no active part, or that
they were too young, to have responsibility. But they all make
a transference. Since they are innocent, all Germany must then
be innocent.

'Others take a different tack. They say, "I admit that we mistreated (mistreated!) the Jews, but we were not the only ones.
So did Austria and Poland and Russia and Roumania. And,
besides, didn't the British bomb Dresden?" They strike a balance;
after all, they were not the only murderers.

'But what is almost universal with the Germans is that they
identify Nazism with what happened to the Jews. At least, here,
they can demonstrate that something is being done as an atone-
ment. And it permits many of them to obscure the other crimes
of Nazism. It permits them to forget that a nascent democracy
was strangled in Germany and that it could happen again. This
time from the left, rather than the right.'

Miss Walter is one of the last of the 'Cold Warriors'. There
are more of them in Berlin than in the rest of the Federal
Republic because Berlin is still a prize being fought for by West
and East. The 'Wall' is the symbol of Berlin. The great bunkers,
filled with coal, are a reminder of the blockade and the days when
coal had to be brought to a freezing city by the planeload.

'There is too much accent on the Jews and not enough on

the basic politics of Germany,' she said. 'The Jewish community of Germany is today isolated both by history and by itself. Germany is "Judenrein" (clear of Jews) in every essential sense. The Jews have no influence on the politics or the culture of Germany. Their value is that they are a yellow light on the traffic signal. They impose caution on the Germans. In that way they have importance beyond their numbers.'

Hilde Walter is a Jew, but she has no identification with Judaism. Her relationship is cerebral, not visceral. She sees no Jewish problem in Germany, nor any problem for the Jews. They can stay or go; it is a choice for them to make.

'If the rest of the world thinks of Germany in terms of the Jews,' she said, 'it will be a great mistake. It will allow the Germans to use that as a gauge too. The real issue is not the Jews in Germany, but democracy in Germany. The Jews are peripheral.'

Alfred Kantorowicz is tall, gaunt, sad-eyed, a man of sorrows. He is an idealist who can always evoke a new ideal when an old one becomes disillusionment. The shelves of his sparsely furnished flat in Hamburg are filled with books ranging from Plato to Camus, and most deal with man's effort to attain spiritual values. That is the end toward which Kantorowicz has addressed his efforts for half a century.

'There is only one good,' he said. 'Freedom.'

In his own way, and by his own values, he has fought for freedom. Always a liberal in politics, he was an early anti-Fascist in Germany and, in 1931 he joined the Communist party. 'It became clear to me,' he said, 'that only the Communist were fighting Hitler in Germany.'

His has been the ideological Odyssey of so many of this century's intellectuals and he has touched almost every shore.

He was born in Berlin and educated there. His family was prominent and well-to-do. When he received his degree, he became an editor and theatre critic for a newspaper in Mannheim. Later he was a foreign correspondent in Paris and then returned to Berlin, where he was an outstanding critic until 1933.

'I joined the Communist Party in Berlin. My God, you could see what was happening all over Germany and you could see that the government, the political parties, were doing nothing to halt it. Except for the Communists, everyone else was compromising, appeasing, submitting. I joined them because I could do nothing else.'

Once Hitler was appointed Chancellor, Kantorowicz faced arrest. He escaped to Paris, together with a number of other German anti-Nazis and there he became General Secretary of the Association of German Writers in Exile. 'We tried, with books and pamphlets and words to awaken the world to what was happening in Germany. We thought we might succeed. We did not.'

When the Spanish Civil War began, it was inevitable that he would go to Spain to fight on the side of the government. He spent two years in the war and then returned to Paris. 'I've never been forgiven,' he said, 'for fighting against Franco. Everything else could be wiped off the books, but not that. I suppose the world has never forgiven us for being right.'

He was in France when the Hitler-Stalin pact was signed and the war began. I asked him how he could adjust to the fact that the Communists had made a deal with the Nazis.

He sighed. 'I rationalized it easily. Events, especially Munich, had convinced me that the west was more anti-Communist than anti-Nazi, that it was trying to save itself by selling out Russia. I knew the Communists were anti-Nazi, because I was a Communist. And even after the war began, that feeling was reinforced, for the French arrested and interned me. My God, they could not have believed I was pro-Hitler!'

His internment aroused writers and intellectuals in England and the United States, among them Ernest Hemingway, whom Kantorowicz had met in Spain. Pressure from this group resulted in the French releasing him, with the understanding that he would leave France. He came to the United States and immediately went to work for various governmental agencies and for C B S.

When the United States entered the war, Kantorowicz made propaganda speeches for broadcast to Germany. He was one of a group of refugees whose voices were beamed into Germany constantly. After the war, he became a teacher. But, in 1946, he returned to Germany in answer to pleas from many sources that a liberal voice was needed there.

'As I look back at it,' he said, 'I think my years in America were probably the happiest and most satisfactory in my life. I liked America and Americans, for there is freedom there. Oh, certainly, I had political differences, but only in totalitarian countries do all men think the same way. In America, I was allowed to think as I pleased.'

He went through some yellowed correspondence and found a letter from William L. Shirer and showed it to me. 'This is why I returned,' he said, pointing to two short sentences in the letter. 'People like you are needed here. Come back.'

He returned as a political refugee, not a religious one. 'I was interested not in the resurgence of Judaism in Germany, but in the rebirth of democracy. Besides, I believed in Germany. I thought that Nazism was an episode in German history, not the end product of that history. Now a new chapter was beginning. I could help in writing it. I saw no future for Germany if it moved to the right. I had one-way eyes.'

When Germany was divided, when the Cold War turned glacial, he chose to give allegiance to the Communist sector. 'Even then,' he said, 'it was apparent that the West was making no real effort to get German liberals and intellectuals to return. Men like Heinrich Bruening, or Paul Tillich or the Manns were not encouraged to come back. It was East Germany that wanted them and offered intellectuals professorships, editorships, homes.

'I found out later, of course, that they demanded a price.'

He learned this after the Hungarian revolt and the revolt in East Germany itself. The authorities came to him and asked him to write a defence of Communist actions in Hungary, a defence of the brutality that had taken place, of the suppression of freedom.

'I would not do it,' he said. 'I would not justify what had been done. I learned that I would be imprisoned for my defiance. So I fled again.'

It meant giving up security, comparative wealth, his home, his books, his position as a teacher. And temporarily, his wife.

'Many of my students helped me. They saved many of my books and later got them to me. They sympathized with me, but they could really do very little. However, what they could do they did. I am grateful to them.'

West Germany was happy to have so distinguished a fugitive from the East. And immediately set to work to get Kantorowicz to lead a crusade against Communism.

'That was beyond me,' Kantorowicz said. 'I was ready to condemn the barbarism and cruelty that had taken place in Hungary. I will always condemn the imprisonment of the human mind and the destruction of freedom. But they wanted me to go beyond that, to condemn the ideals that I still believe are inherent in true Communism, and that I could not do.'

He quickly ceased being a hero. 'Actually,' he said, 'the authorities started making many difficulties for me. I had to fight my way to the highest court before it was recognized that I was an authentic refugee. The charge against me was that I had fought against Franco.'

The years have wrought one great change in him, he said. An awakening awareness of his being Jewish has become a part of his life. 'I think it is because West Germany is the successor government to that of the Nazis and has accepted responsibility. East Germany ignores the Jewish question.

'Today, my being Jewish has become a point of reference. Mine was once a large family, but I am the only one who remains. The rest died in Auschwitz and Theresienstadt because they were Jews. I am part of them, as I am part of all the other Jews who died just for being Jews. Just as I am part of the other millions who died because of the Nazis.

'I am an assemblage of parts. Jew. German. Communist. Idealist.' He lifted his head and looked hard at me. 'Yes, I remain an idealist. I think that the old must have ideals, while the young can exist with youth alone. Being a Jew is part of the idealism that lives in me. And I spend my time trying to explain it to myself so I can explain it to others.'

His desk is littered with books and notes. File cabinets stand about. Letters lie in a disorderly pile. 'I want to tell about Germany,' he said. 'I have made my choice; I am a West German. But that does not preclude my telling what I feel about West Germany.

'It is still authoritarian, still anti-intellectual. The past has not been rooted out; only some of the underbrush has been cleared.

The major Nazis are gone, both from Germany and from power, but the bureaucrats and technicians who moved the levers and filled out the extermination forms remain. The world knows this and it knows that some have more power and influence than they had under Hitler.

'Who could have foretold that twenty years after the war a former Nazi would be chancellor. I am not attacking the man, just the fact. We are all different from what we were twenty years ago. But I see him as proof that Germany is willing to compromise with its past. About the Nazis. About the Jews.

'There is an acceptance of what happened to the Jews, but no understanding. The meaning has not penetrated and few, if any, seek either to find or explain that meaning. And not all Germans even admit what happened to the Jews. There are some who deny it, who have turned the fact into a myth when they deride.

'Who asks what was present in the spirit of the Germans that allowed this inhumanity to rule Germany? Who wants to probe and to search and to bear the suffering that must attend these? Only some of the victims and few others. What Germany lacks today are what we called "inner exiles" during the Hitler years. These were the people who could not and would not accept Hitler.

'There are no inner exiles today, none who question this easy, gold-plated transition from Nazism to democracy, as if it were only a matter of writing a new constitution, of inverting a few old laws. Don't they realize that the change must be in the people themselves, not in a document. If it is that simple, then why not a new Nazism tomorrow?'

He went to a bookshelf and brought back a small book. 'We prepared this soon after we escaped to Paris', he said. 'We called it "The Brown Book on the Reichstag Fire and the Hitler Terror". When we published it, we thought that we really understood what Nazism was. I wrote the chapter on the Jews and believed I knew the worst that could eventuate. I did not know that the condition of the Jews in 1934 was idyllic compared to what would come later.

'I did not know the German people – my people. Now I find that these people did not know themselves, which was bad, but that they do not want to know themselves, which is even worse.

When I first returned here, the young people gave me hope. From all directions, I received invitations to speak and to lecture. It was the young themselves who wanted to know, because not one of the hundreds of invitations ever came from an official source.

'Today, the invitations are few. I belong to a past that is no longer alive to them. I do not count, but they do. Who is speaking to them now? Who is demanding that they know themselves and their fathers and their grandfathers?'

He went through a mass of papers and documents. 'These invitations,' he said, 'came from the "korporationen", the duelling societies. There was a moment when even they cared. But it has been years since one of these societies asked me to speak and there are many more of them now.

'It is as if Lethe has been transplanted to Germany and everyone has been drinking from it. It is compulsory. The Jews are being obscured from the German memory and the German consciousness. I said I was the last of my family. I think all the Jews who are here are the last of theirs. There is no need to destroy them.'

But Kantorowicz, although he feels that it is a lost battle, refuses to discontinue the fight. 'There would be no honour in surrender. I will write and talk and battle as long as I stay alive. If I do, then I can say to myself that there will be others, that there must be others. I told you that I was an idealist.'

Erich Marcus, too, is an idealist. He and his wife live in Munich, in a small house with a lovely garden. Both are in their seventies and both speak with nostalgia of the years they lived in the United States, where Marcus taught German at Bridgeport (Connecticut) University and Mrs. Marcus ran a thriving fashion business.

They have been back in Germany only a few years, returning there when Marcus reached the mandatory retirement age.

'I came back,' he said, 'because I did not want to be put out to pasture. In the United States, I would not have been able to continue to work because my field of study is German and German is my primary language. Here, I have written two text books and am working on another. I have been able to do other writing.'

Marcus is a handsome man, white-haired, keen-minded. He

has a gentle sense of humour, most often directed at himself. Under the Weimar Republic, after some years as a journalist, he became head of public relations for the German National Railroads. 'I was,' he said, 'an active and vocal Social Democrat. I was still young enough to speak out loudly and often. When the Nazis came into power, I found my voice had carried. At once. I was fired from my job and informed that I had no future in Germany, except probably Dachau. I was in France a week later.'

There Marcus, who is multi-lingual, had no problem re-establishing himself. When the Nazis over-ran France, he was working as head of public relations for the French railroad system.

'I was again a political refugee. That I was Jewish was a minor matter, both to the Nazis and to me. I was Jewish by definition, rather than by religion.'

Marcus was caught in one of the periodic round ups and sent to a work camp. 'I was imprisoned as a "political", not as a Jew. It was only later that they discovered I was Jewish and I learned that I was to be sent to an extermination camp. I decided to try to escape. I didn't like being killed, but I would rather be killed in that way than in Auschwitz.'

He succeeded in escaping and then joined the Resistance in France. He remained part of it until France was liberated.

When the war ended, Marcus went to the United States. 'I did not want to return to Germany. I knew that terror of the Nazi years had been accepted by too many "good Germans". It would have been impossible without that acceptance, without the acquiescence of most Germans. They had allowed it to happen; many of them had helped it happen.

'I was a German and I felt ashamed of my nation and its people. My religion did not enter into it. If not a single Jew had been among the victims of Nazism, I would have felt as strongly.'

In the United States, Marcus met and married his wife. She is Austrian, daughter of one of the most prominent rabbis in Austria before the Anschluss. She and her first husband (who died in the United States) fled when Hitler's army entered Austria.

'My wife,' Marcus said, 'did not want to come to Germany. She came only because of me. She stays only because of me.

D*

When I suggested that we buy a house, she said, "I would not own a metre of land in this accursed country." She has found it harder to accept Germany – she has not accepted it – than I.'

The years since their return have had an impact on them. 'In a sense,' he said, 'it made us both more Jewish. I have fought against dividing people into Jews and non-Jews, but in Germany it is necessary. There is a cleavage. The Third Reich meant terror, death and torture to every Jew. Even now I feel its ghost walking.'

They have encountered few instances of anti-Semitism. 'People watch themselves,' Marcus said. 'But sometimes it shows in a casual remark, such as, "Of course you know the Jews own all the bars," or, "See that piece of property. A Jew owns it and lives off it in America." But these are pinpricks. The stab wounds come in other ways.'

The books which Marcus has written have been for young people and much of his writing has had to do with them. To gather material, he has travelled all over West Germany and interviewed scores of students. 'When I returned, I believed that I would find a new generation in Germany. I expected that the young people would be aware of decadence of Nazism, would know its rotteness. I thought they would have been taught the real facts about Nazism.

'I admit that I wanted to think so. It gave me some justification for returning. Remember, I had earlier refused to do so. But I have had some frightening moments. One young woman has risen in a lecture hall and told me that I was telling "Jewish lies". She said she had heard the truth from her father.

'Another brushed aside all that she had been told about Hitler with the flat statement that the Jews ran the schools and the government. A young man challenged my facts, saying that they were not the ones he had been taught in the University of Munich by his favourite professor. And the Professor was more worthy of trust, because he had not betrayed his country and fought against it.

'Remember, these are university students, the cream of the young people. How can anyone have complete trust in a nation when such youngsters talk in such a way?'

Marcus feels that, so far, there has been a failure in education. What troubles him is that time is not on the side of those who would give strength to democracy. He sees this failure as one of the reasons that the N P D has been able to attract young members.

'The N P D is fascist. If it were merely anti-Semitic, it would collapse overnight. But because it offers a special appeal to those who want to be led, who want to be told what to do, it is growing. We have not changed German attitudes and German concepts. The "mitgangers", the fellow-travellers, are still among us.'

Even now, it is hard for Marcus to think of himself as a Jew and weigh facts and events from that angle alone. Besides, he says, that is begging the question. 'It is not the fate of the Jews in Germany with which the world must concern itself. It is too late for that now. It is the fate of Germany.'

'Who cares about Germany?' his wife interjected.

Marcus sighed. 'I do.'

These, then are some 'politicals', persons who fought Nazism and fled from it, not because they were Jews (with none of them did that matter greatly in 1933) but because they detested all that Nazism stood for. Two of them, Hilde Walter and Kantorowicz returned for political reasons. Only Marcus returned for purely personal reasons.

Talking with them, I was struck by the fact that when they returned to Germany, they also returned to Jewishness. In this country the question of the Jews is part of the air that is breathed. Neither Jews nor non-Jews can avoid it. Hilde Walter calls herself a 'synthetic Jew', but even she has to accept her Jewishness as a point of orientation. The others accept their Jewishness as a basic reality.

All of them are troubled, questioning about the future of Germany, doubtful about – though fearing it is academic – the future of the Jews. Kantorowicz from the left and Hilde Walter from the right see democracy still on trial by the German people, though both believe it is the German people who are really on trial.

Marcus is more philosophical. He has fought long battles, but he feels that war is not over, but still continuing. But now he has been forced to the sidelines, has become a non-combatant. It is a new generation which has the decision in its hands.

All of them think as Germans, as part of the country in which they live. All are surprised, in greater or less degree, to know that they must now think and live and hope as Jews as well.

12. *The Israelis*

ADOLF HITLER intended to destroy the Jews as a people. Instead he re-created them as a nation. He is the step-father of Israel.

For centuries, the Jews had pledged each other at the time of the High Holy days, 'Next year in Jerusalem.' In 1870, the first Jewish immigration into Jerusalem was begun, two thousand years after they were defeated by the Romans. A second wave took place in the 1880's as a result of a series of Russian pogroms and a third a decade later as a result of the surge of anti-Semitism fostered by the Dreyfus case.

At the turn of this century the World Zionist Council came into being and a small, but steady, stream of Jews trickled into Palestine. Most of these were refugees from the continual, steady anti-Semitism of Central European governments. A few were idealists.

In 1917, the British Foreign Secretary, Arthur James Balfour, issued a 'declaration', which pledged Britain to facilitate the creation of Jewish National Home in Palestine. It was given to, among others, Chaim Weizmann, the scientist who had discovered a synthetic acetone desperately needed by Great Britain in the manufacture of explosives.

(At almost the same time, the British Ambassador in Washington asked the United States government to halt shipments of condensed milk to Poland because 'the large and influential Jewish element in Poland is, to a great extent, pro-German.')

After World War I, Britain was the mandated power governing Palestine. Despite continued demands that it honour the Balfour declaration, Britain avoided implementing it. Political and financial considerations, plus the vast oil reserves of the Middle East, were enough to make the declaration a virtual dead letter.

When Hitler began his persecution of the Jews, much of the world expressed revulsion, but few nations did anything more. None of the great nations of the world threw its doors open to immigration by the Jews. No country can feel pride about its policy during that period. Many, especially the United States, have reason to feel shame for their actions.

Some Jews escaped Germany and Nazi-occupied lands to Palestine. And when the war ended, the few Jews who survived saw that country as a refuge. Britain quickly made it plain, however, that not even six million dead Jews was sufficient to cause them to open the doors of Palestine to those still alive.

Palestine, like the United States and Great Britain, like many other nations, had its quota laws. If it required guns to enforce them, Britain was ready to use those guns.

But, in those post-war days, when the roll call of the dead was a daily ritual, other nations saw in Israel a solution to their own sense of guilt. And most of those other nations, especially Russia, were quite happy to work to destroy British influence in the Middle East.

The creation of the nation of Israel resulted. And, at long last, there was a Jewish homeland.

The D P camps quickly emptied. Jews from all parts of Europe hastened to this new country of theirs. They fought for it, then helped to build it. Most of them have remained there, but a few have returned to other countries. Some, even, to Germany.

In Germany today there are about 2000 Israelis. Most were born in Germany and many of them are older men and women. A smaller number are *Sabras,* first generation Israelis, who have come to Germany to complete their educations. A few have come for economic reasons. Some for mixed and confused reasons that not even they can explain. Among these latter is Jochanin Bloch, who was born in Germany.

Now forty-seven, he was taken to Palestine by his parents in 1933. He lived there until 1956. He is short, burly, bushy-haired, violent in speech, frenetic in thought. He is filled with hate, bitterness and anger, much of it directed against himself.

'You want to describe me,' he said, 'then call me an Israeli. Say I am a Zionist. That tells everything about me. I grew up in Israel, became what I am there. I fought in the war for our freedom. Israel is my country, the only one I have. The only one any Jew can have.'

But his home is now in Berlin. He lives in a small, comfortable apartment with his wife and three children. His wife is German-born, a Christian converted to Judaism. His children are German by birth. He has been in Germany for more than eleven years, makes his living there, does his writing (he is both student and professional writer) there.

'But,' he shouted, so that the echoes sounded in his living room, 'I am not a German. Who could want to be a German, part of the country of the killers, the gassers, the torturers? Not I. I came here because it is the way to become more useful to Israel.'

The words rushed out as he explained. He had studied both law and philosophy in Israel and had then been offered a fellowship to continue his studies in Berlin.

'I asked Martin Buber,' he said, 'if I should accept. I wrote Karl Jaspers to ask for advice. They, and all the others to whom I appealed, told me I should come here. But as an Israeli, not as a returnee. And as a Jew. Who can say that I was wrong to come back?'

But he was addressing the question to himself, not to me, nor to his wife who sat silently at the table with us. And because the answer still eludes him, it infuriates him. It generates, a self-distrust that he cannot conceal.

'I am not a German Jew,' he said. 'There are no German Jews. You can be either German or Jewish, but not both. Those who try to be, those who say they are, are hypocrites.'

Then the rationalization, the self-justification, began. And, again, he was shouting at himself, hoping that noise might kill doubts. 'Berlin,' he said, 'is not Germany. I could not live in the Germany of Adenaur and Kiesinger, only in the city of Reuter and Brandt. And why should I not have married a Gentile? When an Israeli marries a Gentile, he makes a Jew of her. Our children are Jewish. When we return to Israel, they will be complete Jews.

'Every minute since I came here, I have been working for Israel. I have written two books about Israel that have been widely read. I have lectured and taught. I tell the young Jews they must not live a lie – the lie that they can be Jewish and live here. I have helped many of them to learn that this is true.'

(I was introduced to Bloch by a nineteen-year-old Jewish university student. 'Please talk to him. What he says, sounds true, but, if it is, why does he stay here? How can he stay here?')

I asked him what he himself had learned in his years in Germany. What conclusions had he drawn?

'That Germany still does not understand that Nazism was not imposed upon it,' he said, 'but that it evolved from German history and the German people. Ten years ago there were those who seemed to care. Some of our suffering had rubbed off on them. They felt that they, too, had been victims.

'Today that is no longer true. Those who were born after the war refuse to accept even their historic responsibility for Nazism. They have been educated away from that acceptance. Many feel that whatever debt was owed has been paid off with money. Some of them have said they believed the Jews were over-paid.

'When I speak to a group of young Germans today, someone in the audience is sure to ask me, "Why do all the Jews go to Monaco to spend their restitution money?" or "Why are the Jews exempt from taxes that others have to pay?" A few are even crueller. They ask, "What proof have you that six million Jews were killed?" Proof! They want proof.

'Jews are not even human to many of them, are not people. They are exhibits in a museum. That makes it easy for young Germans to be anti-Semitic or neutral about Jews. They don't relate them to themselves.'

Bloch does not see the N P D, or anti-Semitic scribblings and desecrations as the beginning of a new Nazism but as a continuation of the old. 'It is part of Germany,' he said. 'It remains unchanged. There was never an internal revolt against Hitler. Don't talk to me about the generals. They were only trying to save themselves and the Wehrmacht when they saw the war was lost. There was no revolt when the Nazis were winning. And there was no generals' revolt in the early days of Hitler when they could have destroyed him.'

He pounded the table, overturning an ash tray. His wife silently straightened out the table cloth, cleaned off the scattered ashes. Bloch went on. 'Let me tell you, when the Germans today think of Hitler, they think of the *autobahns* (highways), of the 1936 Olympic games, of the "liberation" of the Sudetenland. They think of the Anschluss (Union with Austria) and not of Auschwitz.'

Bloch admits that there have been many favourable changes in Germany in relation to the Jews. As a lawyer, he hails the laws against anti-Semitism. 'But, don't you understand, it is a law, a piece of paper. The Germans accept that anti-Semitism is illegal, but none of them feels it is immoral.

'All right, the Jews have their legal rights. Should we cheer for that? Perhaps we should. It marks progress in Germany. But, tell me, do you know a single Jew who helped shape this new Germany? Is there one Jew in a position of real influence in this country? I'll tell you that there is not.

'But why talk about the Jews in Germany. Give them a little time, and they will have disappeared, become Germans. Or left this country. The only way to save the Jews here is to get them out of here. And that is what I am trying to do.'

But what about Jochanin Bloch? He came back to Germany for three years and is now in his twelfth year there. He damns the Germans, but he lives among them. He chose his wife from them.

'Moses,' he flared, 'married a woman who was not a Jew.'

Mrs. Bloch laid her hand over his.

'I will be returning to Israel soon,' he said. 'Is that not so?' He was challenging his wife.

Her free hand played with the Star of David she wore on a thin gold chain. 'We will go whenever you say,' she said.

I asked her if she wanted to leave Germany.

'That is not the question,' she said. 'I will do whatever Jochanin wishes.'

'My wife,' Bloch said bitterly, 'is tied to Germany.'

'I am tied only to you, Jochanin,' she said. 'I accepted that we would go to Israel when we married. But my family is here and all my friends and I have never known any other home.'

She did not, she told me, run into family opposition when she and Bloch were married. 'My family is not political,' she said. 'They were never Nazis. When I said I intended to marry Jochanin and convert, they accepted it.'

What about her friends, the people with whom she had grown up during the Nazi years?

'Some did not approve and they are no longer my friends. I

have never felt any different because I was a Jew rather than a Christian. But I cannot change the fact that I am a German.'

Again Bloch's fist crashed down on the table. 'No longer a German. You are now an Israeli as I am. Just as the children are. Germany means nothing to us. It tears my heart to pieces to stay here.' He raised his head and his eyes stopped glaring, softened and pleaded 'Why do you make me feel guilty. Can't you show me the pity I can't show myself?'

He stayed at the table, his head buried in his hands, as his wife went to the door with me. 'It is hard for him,' she said. 'So hard.'

And it is. Harder, by far, than it is for Dr. Paul Arnsberg. Arnsberg reveals none of the doubts which bedevil Bloch. He is calm and rational and objective about why he returned to Germany in 1958 after having spent twenty-five years in Israel. He insists – and insists and insists – that he feels no guilt about returning, that he has no trouble being a Jew in Germany.

'I do not,' he said, 'feel unfaithful to Israel or Judaism. I hold dual citizenship. Why not? The law allows it. I am not a dedicated Zionist. If I were, I would have remained in Israel. I believe those who are dedicated should go to Israel. Living here, they suffer from a form of schizophrenia. I have seen many such cases in Germany.'

Arnsberg is sixty-seven. His four children were all born in Israel. His three daughters have all 'made Jewish marriages' and are raising their children 'in a Jewish fashion'. (One daughter lives in Israel, one in France, and the third in the United States.) His son is a student in the Munich School of Economics. On graduation, Arnsberg said, he will choose whether to remain in Germany or emigrate.

Arnsberg is a native of Frankfurt, to which he has returned. He is slender, sharp-minded, a man who keeps himself under control. His statements are meant to sound as if he had made up a balance sheet, drawn its result, before he speaks.

'There is no reason,' he said, 'why a Jew should not live in Germany if he chooses. I resent Jews in Germany being regarded as different from other Jews. We are not colonials. We are entitled to equal status.'

Arnsberg lines himself up with Heindrik van Dam and others involved in running the Jewish community, on the attitude of

Jews outside Germany toward those living in Germany. 'I am opposed,' he said, 'to those Jews who use Germany as a source for sensationalism. We lead normal lives here. We have a right to be here.

'None of us has forgotten Hitler and the Nazis, but this is a new country with a new government. Of course some anti-Semitism exists here, but it is less than there is in other countries. England has its Mosley and its Colin Jordan. France has its Poujadists. The United States has its Rockwell and its Ku Klux Klan. What other country has a law against anti-Semitism?'

Arnsberg, however, did not return to Germany because of its laws against anti-Semitism. His reason was less ideological. 'I left Israel because it is a hard country for a private entrepreneur.' During his years there, Arnsberg had built up a large and profitable business as a distributor of books and magazines. (He is also a writer and journalist.) However, he said, government interference had cut deeply into his profits. 'I did not want to be a poor old man in Israel, so I liquidated my business and came to Frankfurt.

'It was not desertion, but common sense. I am certainly no less a Jew here than I was in Israel. In many ways, I am even more of a Jew here. Certainly I am more active in the Jewish community.'

He is chairman of the executive committee which manages Jewish affairs. 'Frankfurt,' he said, 'has a growing Jewish community. When the war ended, there were only about 600 persons here who were regarded as Jewish. Most of them had survived because of being married to Gentiles or because they were only part Jewish. Today we have four thousand Jews in Hamburg. We have Jewish schools, Jewish organizations. Frankfurt is one city which will continue to have a Jewish community.'

A 'Jewish' community is literally that to him. He is violently opposed to mixed marriages and does not regard the children of such unions as Jewish. Instead, ironically, he has adopted the language of the Nazis and refers to such persons as 'non-Aryans'. He resents any of them playing a part in Jewish life.

He has the genealogies of most of Frankfurt's Jewish population at his finger tips. He will say of one that he had a baptized father; of another, that his wife is Christian; of a third that he had a non-Jewish parent or grand-parent. And he will stress that he and his family have no such bar sinister.

He takes pride in his family's long local – and German – background. There remain, he said, only about sixty Jews who were born in Frankfurt before 1946. 'The important and prominent Jewish families are all gone,' he said. 'The philanthropies and the culture they supported have disappeared. Today, of course, Jews have little influence as individuals on politics or in business. It is only as a community that we exert importance or have prestige.'

He derides those who believe that Jews will disappear from Germany in a short time. 'There will always be Jews here, although the number of Jewish communities may diminish. But that will be because Jews will tend to centralize in a few cities. One must be Frankfurt, for this city has become the hub of German finance and industry, replacing Berlin. Jews have an affinity for commerce – their whole history reveals this – and so they will be here.'

More than any other person whom I interviewed, Arnsberg appeared able to divorce himself from the Hitler years. His only mention of personal loss was of a brother, who had escaped to France but who was trapped there, with his family, when the Nazis took control of that country.

He spent the period of horror in Israel, brought up his family there. Unlike Bloch, however, there is no zealotry for Israel that tortures him. He sees, as he said, nothing wrong about his having left Israel and anyone who does, he implies, is wrong.

He is content with the state of Jews in Germany. He accepts their condition. 'The Jews,' he said, 'will never again occupy their old position in Frankfurt. That is just the way things are. I find fewer contacts between the Jewish community and the non-Jewish community than there used to be. Even though most young Germans are free of anti-Semitism, there is little contact among young people with persons of different religions. But I favour that. I am not an assimilationist.'

Arnsberg has cast up the balance for himself and, as far as he is concerned, for any Jew. There is no reason why Jews should not live in Germany. A Jew has a right to live where he pleases and if he prefers living in Germany to living in Israel, that is his business.

He has armoured himself in Judaism. He believes it covers any doubts or uncertainties that he might have. But he will not look to see if there are any chinks in that armour. If he looked and found them, then life would be much harder for him.

As hard, for example, as it is for Marianne Schoenberg. To her, living in Germany – returning to Germany from Israel – is a sin. 'At night,' she said, 'when I am alone, I ask myself how God can forgive me.'

Mrs. Schoenberg is a middle-aged widow, thin and pale-faced, with eyes that are damp from weeping. She lived in Israel for seventeen years after she was freed from Belsen. She was married to a man who also lived through the torture of Belsen.

'When we went to Israel,' she said, 'it was forever. We wanted to wipe Germany out of our lives. If my husband had lived, if we had had children, I would never have returned. But when he died, I was left alone. Of all my husband's family and mine, only my brother survived. He now lives in New York and he could not understand why I should – how I could – return to Germany.

'But I did not have the courage to go to a strange country, to learn a strange language, to live in a new world. So I returned to Berlin.

'You have to understand. I was so terribly alone, a woman growing old, with no one. No one at all. Israel is young and growing and alive and needs pioneers, not broken widows. Besides, I must be honest, there were other reasons.

'I could not stand the heat of Israel, the climate. Not alone. And late at night, the time of memories, I remembered the city in which I grew up, the place where I had been young and – though this is hard to believe – where I had once been happy as a girl. I remembered the Spree and spring coming to the parks and the river banks.

'I thought I could come back. I thought I could be well again. But I am sick here too. It is a different kind of sickness, a sickness of the heart.'

She works at the Jewish Community Centre. Much of her work is with young people in inter-faith activities.

'I can only work with the young,' she said. 'At least I know that they could not have been Nazis. You see, when I came back, it was not to my memories, but to reality. I was afraid. It was an effort to keep from hiding when I saw a uniform. I saw faces that recalled other faces, that brought Belsen back to me. I had to tell myself, "No, no! That is all gone." But even now it is not completely gone.

'It is not easy, even with the young Germans. Most are eager to hear what we have to say, to learn what Judaism really is. But some say that what we tell them is not true. Some have accused us of painting their parents as torturers and murderers, of inventing falsehoods. I ask myself, what are they being taught at school? What kind of history are they learning?

'But not all is bad. We had an exhibition here of poems and drawings made in the camps by children who were exterminated. One poem ended, "The butterflies don't fly here any more." It made many of the young people cry. One said to me that he had doubted us, but he could not doubt that single line.'

Life is a continual struggle for her. 'There is no way for me to adjust. This country is Germany, and Germany is where the terror began. There is always the fear that it will come again. I read the *National Zeitung,* and it is as if it was 1933 again. How can they allow such things to be written?

'I read in the papers that a Stangl has been discovered, and I wonder how many there are, like him, who still are in Germany. And I fear that there are a great many who do not care that other Stangls are free, that murderers go unpunished. Others have that fear also. The older Jews who still remain. Nothing will ever destroy it.

'I know now that I should have remained in Israel. For me, for all Jews, the butterflies can never again fly in Germany.'

There are no butterflies for Kurt Lehmann either. He leaned across the counter of the small store he owns in Mainz and said, 'I was fourteen years in Israel. Only my body has returned here.'

Not even his whole body, for one leg is gone. That was burned or buried or just allowed to rot in Buchenwald. 'I was not even a Jew,' he said. 'I had a Jewish mother, but I was baptized and brought up as a Protestant. I never had any idea that I could be a Jew until the Nazis said I was.'

In 1937, when he was fifteen, he and his mother escaped to Holland. When the Nazis conquered that country, he and his mother were discovered. The last time he saw his mother was the night that they were captured.

Lehmann's face and eyes are far older than his forty-five years. The eyes are deep-sunk, in a face so gaunt it is almost a death's head. The skin is drawn tight over sharp cheekbones.

'In the camp, I wore a yellow star. The guards called me "Jude". Little by little, I came to accept it. And then I was proud of it. At least it explained what had happened to me.'

He was injured while working. 'They sent me to a hospital. There seemed no reason for it because I was told that when I came out of the hospital, I would not be of any use to them and that I would be killed. But before that happened, I was liberated.'

He returned, after a time, to Coblenz, where he had been born. 'Nothing was left that I remembered. My mother's family – there were sixteen of them – had all been destroyed. Not one was left. My father had been killed on the Russian front. His family were strangers with whom I had nothing in common. I think they were all pleased when I left Coblenz. I have never communicated with them since.

'They were Aryans and lived in their own world. Some of them had been Nazis. How could we talk to each other? The truth is that I have never been able to talk to anyone who was not Jewish about what happened to me. After all, every Jew shared my experiences. And no one who was not a Jew has ever been able to understand them.

'It is still true here in Germany. The Jews and the Christians have no common language about which to talk of the past because they have not shared that past.'

Lehmann went to Israel in 1948. Under Israeli law, the child of a Jewish mother is a Jew. 'But I found I did not belong completely in Israel either. Perhaps, if I had made a religious conversion to Judaism, it would have been easier, but to me being Jewish was not something religious. It was more and less than that. In Israel, I was Jewish, but not a Jew. It was something inside myself. The Israelis did not make me feel that way.

'So I returned to Germany finally. And I felt that nothing had changed in the years I had been away. The Jews can live here only with part of themselves. They are not able to live here completely. This country is no place for Jews. Just as I would say that Israel is no country for Germans.

'I have no confidence in the future. Things will not alter.

Not for the Jews and not for the Germans. Laws will not have any effect. What happened was deep inside the spirit of the people. To expect that to be overcome is like expecting my leg to grow back.'

Lehmann sees no value in catch-words, in slogans. He identifies German democracy as a phrase, not a reality. 'Maybe in two, three, generations. But it will not mean anything to the Jews. They will be gone by then and the Germans will accept their disappearance happily.

'I will stay here until I die but neither as a German or as a Jew. For me, that is the only way that I can exist.'

Returnees from Israel. The victims have come back to the scene of the crime. Some filled with guilt. Some with hate. Some cowering and some defiant. But they have returned.

I met the Steins (this is not their real name as will be explained) by accident when I went into their small shop in Mainz to buy some tobacco.

They are in their late fifties and both were born in Roumania. Both were in concentration camps. He is short, slender, with sharp features. There is a birdlike quality about his looks and his actions. She is also short, but heavy. Her hair is white.

It was she who engaged me in conversation, asking if I was an American. When I said I was, she shook her head and said, 'That is where we should have gone. To America.'

Stein said, almost curtly, 'America did not want us. What kind of Jews went to America. Rich ones. Doctors. Lawyers. Not people like us.'

I began to question them and slowly their story came out. At first it was Mrs. Stein who did most of the talking, but Stein quickly took over. It almost seemed as if he had been waiting for years for someone to whom to tell his story.

They had both been in Foehrenwald and then, in 1949, had gone to Israel. Their one child, a son, had been born there. Eight years later they had returned to Germany.

'It was no place for us,' Stein said. 'I could not make a living. I am no farmer. I have no trade. We lived from hand to mouth. Then I started to get letters telling me that things were better in Germany. That there were good times here. I was told that if I returned, I could get some restitution, that I could make a living here.'

His eyes glittered and his voice choked. 'Why, why should the Germans, the Nazis, have it so good while their victims had nothing? What kind of justice is there when those who kill go unpunished and the injured still suffer? I ask you, what kind of justice is that?'

Mrs Stein said quietly, 'That is the way the world is. Perhaps it is God's will.'

'God!' Stein made it almost an imprecation. 'Am I still supposed to believe in God?'

'You have to understand,' Mrs. Stein said. 'He lost everyone. He was in the camps for more than five years.'

'You don't have to apologize for me. I take the responsibility for what I did. I brought us back here. I was the one.' He swallowed hard. 'It was not easy. I did not tell anyone where we were going. I told them we were emigrating to Australia.' He lifted his head. 'Do you know, in all the years we have been back, I have never written to anyone, never told anyone where we were?'

'How can we tell them?' Mrs. Stein said.

'There is no one to tell anyway. They have their lives, we have ours.'

They went to Mainz because there would be little chance of their encountering people who knew them. In the ten years they have been in Mainz, they have made few friends. 'How,' repeated Mrs. Stein, 'could we tell people that we returned here from Israel?'

'Others have,' Stein said. 'Thousands of them. Why should we be ashamed?' He made a helpless gesture with his hands. 'But we are.'

Economically, they have fared better in Germany than they did in Israel. 'We make a living,' Stein said. 'It is enough.' And they have no complaints about the treatment they have received from the people of Mainz. 'They know we are Jewish, but no one has been anti-Semitic. Our son has had no problems in school except loneliness.' He shuddered. 'It is very lonely to be a Jew here.'

Mrs. Stein said tentatively, 'Perhaps when our boy has finished his schooling, we will go back to Israel.'

'We will never go back.' There was only surrender in Stein's voice. 'We will never go back. I gave up fooling myself a long time ago.' But then his voice grew stronger. 'But my son will not stay here. Any place but Germany. Any place.'

Mrs. Stein wept softly.

'If I had it to do again,' Stein said, 'I would not return to Germany. Now, I know it would have been better to starve in Israel for I could have kept my self-respect. I would not have to lie to myself every minute of my life.' He reached out and touched my shoulder. 'Please,' he said, 'if you write about us, do not use our names.'

I said I would not.

13. *The Intellectuals*

THE importance of Jews in German intellectual and scientific life was always much greater than their proportion within the population. (The same held true in German culture and economics and will be discussed later.) One fourth of the Nobel Prizes received by Germans before 1933 went to Jews, among them Albert Einstein. Six Jews who fled Germany later received Nobel prizes.

Refugees from Hitler today staff universities and laboratories throughout the world, but very few have returned to Germany.

There are fewer than 100 Jewish doctors in Germany. Before Hitler, almost every German bragged of his 'good Jewish doctor' and there were almost 6000 Jewish doctors. Those who are there now are either concentration camp survivors or those who were unable to obtain licences to practise in foreign countries. Some of these latter worked as hospital orderlies, shoe salesmen and dishwashers.

Before Hitler, there were many Jewish authors and journalists of note, 'from Alfred Kerr to Kurt Tucholsky, from Lion Feuchtwanger to Alfred Polgar,' to quote *Der Spiegel* again. Today, there is not one outstanding Jewish author, although there are a considerable number of able and respected journalists. However, not one of these journalists has attained importance within a major publishing enterprise.

The attrition among Jewish scholars began before Hitler and was made complete under him. Almost none have returned to Germany though some young scholars are now on various university faculties.

The late Karl Marx (not the author of *Das Kapital*), who published the most influential Jewish newspaper in Germany until his death and who was the foremost champion among the

Jews of rapprochement with Germany had to complain that 'no effort was made to get the intellectual Jews to return. I believe they would have come back if an honest effort had been made. None was. I do not know why.'

Alfred Kantorowicz, among many others, believes that he knows why. 'The Jewish intellectual,' he said, 'has always been anti-establishment. He has always questioned the *status quo*. His politics has normally been liberal. The German Federal Republic, especially under Adenauer, did not want questioners. It did not seek to encourage political dissent.' (Kantorowicz was quick to add that his own experience had shown that the East German government had even less desire or use for dissenters.)

Those intellectuals who have returned did so on their own. They were Jews by edict rather than commitment in most cases. They came back, most told me, because they felt that they could get greater fulfilment in Germany than in the countries to which they had fled. Some felt that they had a duty to return and work to bring about a better Germany.

All of them came back with a certain amount of optimism, about both Germany and the future of the Jews in Germany. One such is Professor Theodor W. Adorno, who teaches sociology at the University of Frankfurt and is director of its Institute for Social Studies. During the Hitler period, Adorno taught in the United States. He is half-Jewish, but to the Nazis this was more than enough.

He ranks high in the German intellectual hierarchy. Much of his work since his return has dealt with studies of the causes and effects of Nazism and the teaching of sociology, government and politics in German schools. His attitude toward anti-Semitism is detached, objective, synthesizing. The Jews in Germany, past and present, are primarily objects for study.

He makes no secret of his personal involvement, his emotional bias, but succeeds in separating this from his work.

He accepts the premise that the Jews are not a material factor in German society today. However, he does not believe this has to be permanent. 'It is,' he said, 'dependent on the growth of democracy in Germany. The best I can say is that Germany has adopted democracy as an experiment. It is still on trial with the Germans. If it works – and it can only work if another generation grows up during the experiment – then enough Jews to alter the fabric of Germany will probably live in this country.'

To Adorno, the absence of Jews is a major loss to Germany. 'It means,' Adorno said, 'a decay in the spirit of freedom. No country which has destroyed or exiled its Jews has failed to suffer this. Today, we have a lack of critical stimulation and *avant-garde* mentality. The spirit of enlightenment is gone.'

Adorno does not think of Jews in a religious sense. Heine, for example, apostacized, but was deeply committed to Judaism. 'The German Jew, as Jew,' Adorno said, 'assimilated faster than any other group in Jewish history. It was the only European country in which the Jewish dialect – Yiddish – was not spoken. Jewish consciousness was not strong. In pre-Hitler times, this was an asset. With the rise of National Socialism, however, it became a disaster.

'It meant that anti-Semitism was directed against a concept rather than a people. It turned it into an abstraction. It made it possible for the Nazis to order mass extermination with as little passion as ordering the slaughter of so many head of cattle. When the requisition forms were filled out, no one visualized human beings, merely numbers on an order form.'

In one of the studies on which he worked, Adorno took up the question of Germany 'Digesting the Past'. This has been a slogan much used in German post-war education. Adorno found it disheartening.

'By "digesting the past",' he said, 'it is generally not inferred that the past is processed in earnest and its path is cleared through lucid awareness. Instead, the desire is to relegate it to a dead file and perhaps even to erase it from memory. The gesture indicating that everything should be forgiven and for-gotten ought to be reserved for those who suffered injustice; instead it is practised by the partisans of those who inflicted it.'

Adorno has found in Germany many of the common ration-alizations. 'As if,' he said, 'human beings should not be ashamed of the argument that it really was five million Jews who were gassed, and not six million. Or the balancing of Auschwitz against the bombing of Dresden.'

Adorno, however, is not without hope. He feels that the young are showing progress. 'Among my students,' he said, 'especially among those who are working for degrees in the liberal arts, in philosophy and sociology, there is an *a priori* antagonism to the Nazis and the meaning and experience of National Socialism. But I have been told this does not hold true of those working in the fields of business and economics and even in medicine.

'Still of the seven or eight hundred students here, I would say not more than a handful are members of the N P D. There are others who are probably anti-Semitic. These would be those who have been expelled from the East and the children of un-regenerate Nazis. And their anti-Semitism, again, is impersonal for I don't think that many of them could point to an individual student and say that he is Jewish.

'There are, of course, only a few Jewish students in the University and most of them come from other countries to study here. The absence of Jewish students is obvious. Perhaps more to the faculty than to the students.'

But to Adorno the subject of the Jews in Germany is far more than a classroom exercise. He sees what happens to those Jews as determining factor in the development of Germany. It is a barometer by which one can judge if the weather is fair or foul for democracy in Germany. And his attitude is hopeful because he wants it to be, and sceptical because his experience is not as optimistic as his hopes.

Wilhelm Unger is equally sceptical but less hopeful. He is dramatic and literary critic of the *Stadt Anzeiger*, the leading newspaper in Cologne. He is also a playwright, biographer, essayist and graduate psychologist.

Bushy-browed, bushy-haired, massive-chested, he looks far younger than his sixty-three years. His English is clipped and precise as becomes one who lived, worked and taught in England for many years. 'But do not be misled,' he said. 'I am a German and a Jew.'

He already had a considerable reputation as a writer by 1933. 'Mine were among the books burned on May 10, 1933,' he said, 'when Hitler set fire to intellectualism in Germany. I thought then that I must leave Germany, not because I was Jewish, but because I dreaded living in a country where books were burned. Friends dissuaded me. They said that Hitlerism – National Socialism – was only a temporary phenomenon and that the Nazis would soon be replaced by rational men. Because I wanted to believe this, I was persuaded.'

For the next six years Unger lived in a shadow world. He

was on the Nazi proscribed list – cut off from employment – so he could not write articles for any publication. Anyone who employed him was subject to punishment. However, the editor of the Cologne *Zeitung,* the paper for which he had been working, continued to pay him his salary.

'There were many like my old editor,' Unger said, 'in 1933. They hated Hitler and what he stood for and were convinced that he would quickly be removed from power. I think, during those early days, there really was a chance for a revolt against Nazism, but it passed quickly. A miasma engulfed Germany and all Germans became its victims.'

Unger's Jewishness at that time was nominal. His three sisters were married to Christians. His parents observed none of the religious rituals. Unger and his brother were 'free thinkers'.

'I opposed Hitler because he stood for totalitarianism, for the destruction of the human mind. I believed that he was the champion of barbarism and I believed, because I wanted to, that the German people were not barbarians and would not be led by a barbarian. I continued to believe this until Hitler marched into Prague. Then I had to admit to myself that I had been wrong.

'I was kept under constant surveillance by the Nazis. The Gestapo broke into my home and searched it. They took away the manuscript on which I was working – a study of Dostoievski – and four years of work vanished. I knew it was only a question of time before they would take me, instead of my manuscripts, and that I would disappear as completely.'

He pointed to the filled bookshelves, to the pictures on the walls of his living room. 'I always collected books and pictures. The Nazis must have liked my taste. They took everything on their periodic visits. What I have now is only a portion of what I once had, but I stayed alive. I supposed that was a victory.

'When I realized I had to leave, I tried to get my family to leave also. Despite what was happening, I could convince only my brother. My sisters said that the terror could not engulf them. They had Christian husbands and Christian children. They said they would be safe. Two of them died in a gas chamber. The third died a natural death before the Gestapo could reach her.

'My father dug up his World War I decorations. He was a German. His family had been German for generations. Nothing would happen to him. He and my mother ultimately were sent to Theresienstadt. They were among the few who survived.

'My brother and I went to England. When the war started, I was declared an "enemy alien", and ordered deported to Australia. That trip was a nightmare. We were treated as Nazis, not as the victims of Nazis. The crew robbed and mistreated us. Those of us who had money quickly lost it. Our clothes were looted.

'I had some manuscripts with me. They were found and thrown overboard. Believe me, not all the insanity and viciousness was limited to Germany and the Nazis.'

Later Unger was returned to England from Australia. During the rest of the war, he worked in the German section of the B B C and with various other propaganda agencies.

'It was during those years that I became a Jew. I suppose this change in me started taking place when Hitler came into power and the extermination of Jews, just for being Jews, began.

'As I said, I had been raised in a liberal, free-thinking, non-religious atmosphere. It came as a surprise to many of my friends in Cologne to learn that I was Jewish. But, then, I was surprised myself.

'My parents, too, became Jews. It happened to them in Theresienstadt. My father, who had prided himself on his "enlightenment", returned to orthodox Judaism there and remained an orthodox Jew until his death in 1957.

'So, when the war ended, I was both a German and a Jew. I felt that it was important for me to convince the English that not all Germans had been Nazis. I had to show them that it would be an error to condemn an entire nation for the crimes of a few. I wanted the English to give the decent people of Germany a chance to demonstrate themselves.'

In 1946, the British Control Commission requested Unger to deliver a series of lectures in Germany, especially to groups of young people. He was still in Germany when P.E.N., the international writers' group held its famed convention there.

'On that trip,' Unger said, 'I convinced myself that Germany had truly changed, that it was sick and ashamed of its recent past. I found the young people eager for democracy, hungry for freedom, devoid of nationalism. I could hardly wait to return to England to tell what I had discovered. In the next ten years I worked so hard at it that I used to be introduced as "the German Ambassador of Culture".'

In 1957, Unger's father died and he went back to Germany to try to persuade his mother to go to England with him. Instead, she convinced him to stay in Germany. 'I think I wanted to go home. Besides, I had ten-year-old stars in my eyes, my memories of my earlier trip.

'They quickly began to fade. Oh, I found some hopeful signs in Germany, but now I had to look for them instead of seeing them everywhere. The students and the intellectuals still talked about democracy, but the great mass of the people were too busy making money, buying Volkswagens, gaining affluence. The urgency that drove people was not the creation of a new Germany but a fatter bank account.

'But what was more shocking was that the Germans had happily let the horrors of Nazism be forgotten. The terrors were no longer talked about. The Jewish persecution no longer moved them. If Jews were mentioned, it was to remind one that a restitution law had been passed and they were receiving a lot of money. That was enough for the Germans; it balanced the books.

'The whole history of the Nazi years was being turned into a footnote in the German history books. And the story of the Jews a line in that footnote. It was an outrage, an attack on human decency.

'Suddenly, I was more Jew than German. I registered as a member of the Jewish community. I had to identify myself, I had to say, "You cannot deny my existence". Or that of the other Jews in Cologne and Germany, in Dachau and Belsen and all the other charnel houses.

'There are about 1200 Jews in Cologne now. Only a handful compared to before 1933, and nearly all of them are strangers here, East Europeans. But we have a right to say that not only do we exist, but that we have a past that must not be forgotten. Not for our sake, but for that of the Germans, for recognition of that past is the only fertilizer that can make democracy grow in Germany.

'I became involved in various inter-faith groups. I lectured and wrote on the Nazi past. Not to make the Germans feel guilty, but to make them understand. Now, ten years later, I

E

find less and less understanding. I am told that I am wrong to bring up the past which is now long gone and better forgotten. And I cannot convince them that if they can forget, if they can disregard, if they can drive out of their consciousness the true meaning of Nazism, then the disease will run riot again.'

Unger works primarily with the younger people. 'At least, among them, if the ground is barren, it is not poisoned. But it is so difficult. A short time ago I received an invitation from the director of schools in Bad Soden, a medium-sized town near Kassel, to speak to the students there about Jews and Judaism. I accepted. When I reached Bad Soden, the director was obviously ill at ease.

' "I must tell you," he said, "that you may find the initial reaction a little strange. You see, there is not a single Jew in Bad Soden and I do not believe a single student here has ever known a Jew. What they know of Jews..." he fought for the right words – "What they know they have heard from their parents."

'A Jew was a creature from outer space to their imaginations. I must have been a deep disappointment to them because I looked like a normal person. I had neither horns nor tail.

'I tried to tell them about the history of the Jews in Germany. I mentioned the names of famous Jews and heard them gasp with surprise at each name. I told them of the twelve Nazi years. I hope some of them have remembered what I said, but I doubt that many have. There was no reason for them to remember, because, theirs is the Jew-free world that Hitler promised their parents and which their parents accepted.

'There are scores of Bad Sodens in Germany. There are thousands of young Germans who know even less about Jews than the children of Bad Soden do because they have never heard even one lecture or seen even one Jew. No one tells them. No one teaches them. No one seems to care.'

Unger feels that a great residue of anti-Semitism remains in Germany. 'That is the reason for the philo Semitism. That is a form of psychological self-bribery and it is practised by yesterday's killers as well as today's paymasters.'

To Unger, as to so many others, there is no future for Jews and Judaism in Germany. 'There could have been a future,' he said, 'only if we had returned to Germany immediately after the war. I, for instance, should have stayed here in 1947. If enough of us had stayed, had moved into German life and politics and culture, we would have forced Germany to look inward. And we would have provided a powerful impetus for democracy.

'The Germans did not want the Jews to come back. If they had, they would have asked them to return. They would have made that a national policy. Instead, Germany decided to buy peace with its conscience by using money. Today, there is a cashbox full of receipts, but the Jew is an alien.

'Today, I find many Germans who admit to having been Nazis. Right after the war, none would admit it. Ten years ago, the number was very few. Today I find that it has become almost a fashion. But, after all, today a former Nazi is Chancellor.

'All these former Nazis are reformed, of course. And they became Nazis for the best reasons. To avenge the Versailles Treaty. Because the Weimar Republic was weak and unable to deal with the economic depression. Because they felt that under Hitler Germany might realize its historic destiny of greatness.

'They want me, a Jew, to tell them that I pardon them. None of them – not a single one – admits ever to have committed an anti-Semitic act, to taking part in the persecutions, or even to have known of the existence of furnaces or gas ovens. Why, some of their best friends were Jews!

'I say to all of them that, if they were so innocent, if they have so little on their consciences, why should they have to seek a pardon from a Jew?'

Unger still retains a hope – 'a slender one' – that Germany can mature enough to accept its past. Nothing did more to strengthen that hope than the reaction of most of West Germany at the time of the 1967 Arab-Israel confrontation. The inter-faith groups in which he has been active were suddenly aroused from a torpor. Individuals called him to say that they wanted to offer money and aid because 'this is a chance to show that we remember Hitler.'

But Unger wonders if this enthusiasm will long continue.

'For a decade,' he said, 'Germany has been becoming more conservative. Each year it has reverted slightly to patterns of the past. The rise of the NPD is a sign of this. So is the continued unhappiness about the trials of Nazi war criminals. So was the fight against extending the statute of limitations for such trials. The German people want the past to be over and done with. And, since the Jews are the darkest blot on that past, they accept the disappearance of the Jew in Germany readily.

'Today I am both participant and onlooker. I am split between being a German and a Jew because I am not allowed to be both here.'

But Unger's problem is that he wants to be both. He fights a reality he does not want to accept. If he accepts it, then he will have to admit failure.

Dr. Ulrich Sonnemann accepts that reality, but it is not so difficult for him because he has set himself apart from his Jewishness. To him, religion is a minor matter. It is politics and the social organization of Germany which most concern him. It is to these that he relates when he tells of his background. 'I come from a long line of radicals. One of my ancestors founded the *Frankfurter Zeitung*.'' Then, an afterthought, 'My family was Jewish, of course.'

Now in his fifties, he spent fourteen years in the United States after his family fled Germany. He wrote, lectured, and taught at the New School for Social Research in New York. Today he lives in Munich and writes for newspapers, magazines, television and radio and is also an editor and translator.

He is a man of deep convictions and is didactic in explaining them. As far as he is concerned, he has weighed all the evidence and come up with the right conclusions.

When he discusses the question of Jews and Germany it is almost as an outsider. His first premise is that the Jews have virtually disappeared from Germany and that there is no chance of their return as a major force. He regrets this because, to him, it means that the fabric of Germany has turned dull and drab.

'The basic element that is missing,' he said, 'is independent thinking. That is Germany's biggest weakness now. It means that the psychology that made it possible for Germany to accept Nazism still exists.

'There has been no change in the conditioning of the German people, only in their circumstances. Germany is rich today; it was poor in 1932. But the people adhere to the same traditions, retain many of the same values. They still want to be led, to be told what to do. And the Grand Coalition is a force in that direction. It doesn't mean that more than eighty per cent of the people have a voice in their government, but that they have had their voices silenced.

'Isn't the spirit of democracy the right to oppose? Well, today the lone voice in opposition comes from the right, from the N P D. And they know how to use it.'

He searched through some papers on his desk and found an announcement of a meeting at which he had been the featured speaker. The subject was German-Israeli relations. 'Like all Jews,' he said, 'I am regarded as an expert. After I spoke I asked for questions. It was obvious at once that some well-primed N P D members were present.

'They asked me why I had placed the war guilt on Germany when it was "well known that other countries were equally guilty". They attacked the war-crimes trials as "sinister methods of dispensing political justice". They said restitution and reparations were "draining Germany". This is the modern way of shouting "Heil, Hitler".'

Sonnemann was dispassionate, a lecturer with a one-man audience. He had his facts and he was certain of them. This was an intellectual exercise to him. And, yet, even as he talked, his voice took on a deeper quality. 'What this country lacks,' he said, 'is a renewed moral sense. Morality was gassed by the Nazis along with six million Jews and it has not been resuscitated any more than the other victims.

'The condition of the Jews has not truly been altered. Every one of them is still an *untermensch* (a lower number). It has nothing to do with religion. It has nothing to do with Israel or sending a few anti-Semites to gaol. These serve only to repress the past, not as lessons to be learned from it. As things are, this is no country for an actual Jew. If I were such a one, I would leave it.'

All those – Adorno, Unger and Sonnemann – are intellectuals who, for various reasons, decided to return to Germany. They are only a small portion of the Jews in Germany and none of them really returned as 'Jews'. Yet, as I talked with them, I felt that none had made a true involvement in the new Germany.

Not even Adorno, who is able to stay within the confines of his scholastic world. Though he may not move into the outside world, that world impinges upon him. And he must react.

They are no 'ordinary' people, and yet, before Hitler, there was an ordinary quality to such Jews. They helped shape the culture and professional life in Germany. They were a vital and important force. Today, they are outsiders.

They have not succeeded in re-infusing a 'Jewish quality' into their spheres. Another group, the artists, have been involved in the same attempt.

14. *The Artists*

ONE of the first casualties of the Third Reich was the living culture of the German people. It was as important to the Nazis to sterilize the German mind as to destroy the Jewish presence in the country.

It began on the night of May 19, 1933. Thousands of Berlin University students marched down Unter den Linden to a square opposite the University in a monster torchlight parade and then used the torches to set afire thousands of books that had been gathered for burning. Rarely has so much light and fire provided so much darkness.

Among the works destroyed were those of Lion Feuchtwanger, Arnold and Stefan Zweig, Jakob Wassermann, Gotthold Lessing, Moses Mendelssohn, Heinrich Heine, Walter Rathenau, Erich Maria Remarque, Albert Einstein, Sigmund Freud, Arthur Schnitzler and, of course, Karl Marx. The Nazis held that all these, living and dead, were Jews and that their work had perverted the pure German spirit.

(Also burned, of course, were works of many non-Jews, but these had been tainted by Jewish influences.)

Hailing the book-burning, Goebbels said, 'The soul of the German people can now express itself again. These flames not only illuminate the ultimate end of an old era, they also light up a new.'

A few months later, Goebbels began the construction of that new era by creating the Reich Chamber of Culture. Its aim was 'to gather together the creative artists in all spheres into a united organization under the leadership of the Reich. The Reich must not only determine the lines of progress, mental and spiritual, but also lead and organize the professions.'

Following Hegelian concepts, there were created seven separate categories. These were fine arts, music, the theatre, literature, the press, radio, and films. Under Nazi guidance, these were intended to serve the propaganda purposes of the Reich exclusively. And, as William L. Shirer wrote, 'No one who lived in Germany in the Thirties, and who cared about such matters, can ever forget the sickening decline of the cultural standards of a people who had had such high ones for so long a time.'

The Jews had been important in all these areas and dominant in some of them. Jewish writers, actors, producers, journalists, artists and musicians fled from Germany. Many non-Jews refused to bend to the Nazi laws and fled also.

German newspapers, then among the most respected in the world, were either destroyed or prostituted. The Nazi press law limited control to German citizens, of 'Aryan' descent, not married to Jews. This meant the quick expropriation of the *Vossiche Zeitung*, published by the Ullsteins and probably Germany's best newspaper, of the *Berliner Tageblatt,* owned and edited by Hans Lackmann-Mosse, and of the *Frankfurter-Zeitung,* also Jewish owned.

(Today, not a single major newspaper or publishing house is owned by Jews.)

The radio, which Hitler was to turn into a tuning fork for the German masses, became solely a propaganda medium.

The theatre, the film industry, the music halls and the political cabarets were straight-jacketed and tightly policed. The artists like Max Reinhardt were expelled or fled. Hitler placed an unsuccessful playwright, but old line Nazi, Hans Johst, in control of Germany's theatre. And he chose one of his 'pure, Aryan maidens', Leni Riefenstahl, to replace such famed film producers and directors as Ernst Lubitsch and Walter Lang.

Music, too, was placed under state control and it is an anomaly that only in this field were there outstanding artists who were ready to accede to Nazi domination. Wilhelm Fuertwaengler, Richard Strauss and Walter Gieseking teamed up with a 'Putzi' Haenfstaengel to delight the music-loving Adolf Hitler.

For a dozen years the cultural and information media were an arm of Nazi totalitarianism, engaged in mass brain-washing.

When the war ended, the Allies took over these media at once. A policy of reverse brain-washing has to be instituted immediately. A system of licencing was introduced. It operated in the publishing field and in radio. It was imposed on film making. Known Nazis and collaborators were debarred from working in any of these areas.

Science and technology also provided a new, and more potent, propaganda instrument – television. The old aphorism that it did not matter who made the laws of a nation provided one could write its songs was amended to read provided one could control its T V programmes.

Beginning soon after Germany was occupied, a trickle of artists began to flow into Germany from their exile. Many of them were actors, directors and producers who had found it hard to adjust to a different language and different techniques. Men, for example, like Fritz Kortner, actor, director and producer, and Ernst Deutsch, actor. Both had gone to the United States but neither had ever felt completely at home there.

It was not easy for them to return and today, in their Munich homes, both still bear the marks of their exile. Kortner has been known to stumble on a step and address the step as 'a damned Nazi'.

In theatre and the films there is still a link to the pre-Hitler past, but this is dying – as are those who provide that link.

In television, however, a new generation has been in charge. It includes some who fled Germany as children, others who were born to their German refugee parents in foreign countries. One such is Peter Lilienthal.

Handsome, vital, he is one of the more highly regarded T V directors. His parents fled to Uruguay from their south German home and it was there that Lilienthal was brought up and educated. He wanted to become a director and the opportunities in Uruguay were very limited. But the opportunities in Germany were vast.

Multi-lingual, the language offered him no problem in Germany. Politically 'clean', his opportunities would be limited only by his abilities. He could, of course, go to the United States or Great Britain, but there he would be competing with an established group of professionals.

'I was in a dilemma,' he said. 'I had to scale the barrier which Germany represented. Hitler's Germany, the only one about which I knew anything. Almost all the Jews in Uruguay were

E*

refugees. All my youth was filled with stories of death and deprivation, of tortures and terror. I remembered when anyone receiving a letter from Germany knew it could only tell of another cruelty.

'On the other hand, my family history is a German history. I had an uncle who was an officer in the German army. His name was Dietrich Israel. I have often wondered what his life was like. How could the German part of him exist beside the Jewish part? But a German part existed in me also, as it did in all the others.

'We were raised on German music and literature. Our families had lived and died for many generations in Germany. German was spoken in our homes in Uruguay. I suppose that there is in all of us something that causes him to want to return to the place of his beginnings. And there was one important element. I could leave if I wanted to. So, I made the decision to return.'

He sat in his office, a room in the Film Academy in Berlin, a complex which houses much of the state run T V, radio and film production in that city. On the walls were awards he had received. Film and recording equipment was everywhere. An assistant was examining a roll of film. It could have been New York or Hollywood or London. But Lilienthal made it plain that it was not.

'I thought adjustment would not be too difficult. I was wrong. We are the children of the refugees and their sufferings are in our bloodstream. We know Germany only through their memories. So, even now when I look at a German, it is through the filter of their experience. I still recoil when I meet a German over forty. What was he doing under Hitler?

'It is only since I have been in Germany that I have regarded myself as truly Jewish. It is here that I have learned how much Jewish culture and history shaped me, made me what I am. Back in Montevideo, I took no part in Jewish life. There, in a sense, Judaism was only a religion. Here, it encompasses so much more. I had to become a part of the Jewish community in Berlin. But not of Berlin, of Germany.'

He searched for words to explain. 'Don't you feel it?' he asked. 'As if you were walking down a dark street in the early morning and there's someone in the shadows waiting to leap out at you? You know there's a policeman around the corner and all you have to do is call, but your voice is locked in your throat and you can't call.' He smiled apologetically. 'I'm sorry. I get carried away. But everywhere I feel the impress that Hitler and the Nazis made on Germany.

'For years, the Germans were the oppressors and the Jews were the victims. Now the two are supposed to live together and obliterate that past. Germany is a country of wishful thinking. Believe me, I know there can be no more Dietrich Israels.'

Lilienthal carefully separates the parts of himself. 'As a creator,' he said, 'I find freedom here. Artistic freedom and political freedom. In television, we can look at the past and declare our judgments. We do not have to obscure reality. Television, I feel, has been the best force in teaching democracy to Germany. That is fine. But it ignores the subjective element in me. The Jewishness.

'Beneath the creator in me is the Jew and the Jew senses that he does not belong here. There are no German-Jewish artists. The Jew has been excised. Perhaps the memory of what happened to the Jews is still too raw for the Germans to digest. So the result is that there cannot be any more Heines or Lessings than there can be Dietrich Israels.

'I am not alone in feeling this way. There are my friends, Mauricio Kagel, a musician, in Cologne, and Annie Wolff, a sculptress in Munich. They feel it too. For all of us, it is like playing a violin with a broken string.'

For Lilienthal, what exists is a bruising of the spirit, a sense of isolation. He has found no anti-Semitism. 'Sometimes I think they don't believe that we are worth hating any longer. We aren't here. We don't exist. The Jews are the invisible men of Germany.

'My satisfaction is in my work. One of these days that will not be enough and I will leave. No part of me will remain behind. In Germany, there is no place for it.'

I felt that Lilienthal had made two discoveries in the time he had been in Germany. One was about the country to which he had returned. And the other, the more important, about himself. And he had found both hard, but he had accepted them. Unlike Max Jacoby.

Jacoby, too, returned to Germany from South America. He is tall, slim, balding, emotional. All his reactions are visceral. 'To be a Jew in Germany,' he said, 'is to live a lie.' He pointed to

a gallery of photographs lining one wall of his Berlin apartment.
One of the photographs was his. 'All Jews,' he said. 'All liars.'

He stared at his own face as if it were a stranger's. 'For a Jew
to return to Germany, he must be neurotic. For him to remain,
he must be psychotic.' He tapped his forehead. 'I admit it. I *am*
crazy. But they . . .' His hand swept along the pictures. 'They
do not.'

Jacoby is one of the more successful photographers in Germany.
The pictures on the wall were to be used as illustrations in a
book about the Nazi years. 'Jews,' he said. 'If no one else destroys
us, we destroy ourselves.'

His family escaped from Berlin in 1937, using forged papers,
and settled in Argentina. Max was then twelve. In 1946 he made
the first of a number of trips to the United States to get photographic assignments. In 1956, he came to Berlin. He has been
there since.

'I was told there were few good photographers in Germany.
There was no photographic art in Germany. It was true. Now
I have a big reputation here. But I wonder when someone gives
me an assignment is it because I am a photographer or because
I am a Jew. Many people here believe there is something magic
about the Jews in art. Even being half a Jew is better than being
no Jew at all.

'Of course there is anti-Semitism, but there is also philo-
Semitism. I have profited from philo-Semitism. I tell myself that
if some Germans feel it necessary to be excessively good to me, let
them. Their need is greater than mine. They have a guilt for the
dead.'

He slapped his hand down on a table top. 'What right have
I to profit from what they owe the dead? When I profit, I am
cheapening those deaths. I am living off the bodies of my family,
my friends, the whole six million who died.'

He brooded a time. 'To the Germans, I am a Jew. Not to
myself. Oh, I'm Jewish, but I'm not a Jew. I have no contact
with the Jewish community here. I do not go to services. I
observe no religious rules. I am married to a Christian. What
kind of Jew is that?

'But the Germans don't care what kind of Jew I am, just that
I am one. That makes me different. Of course I am speaking
of the older Germans, those who were part of the Hitler times.

They drove my family out of Germany but they welcome me. The younger Germans have clear consciences. They are not anti-Semitic, most of them never were. As a matter of fact, they are not even aware of the Jews, except as a word.

'Imagine that! "Jew" to be only a word in Germany. The young have been told to treat that word kindly. It is democratic to treat that word kindly and Germany is now a democracy. I don't blame the young. I blame their parents and teachers and their government which has made the Jews into a word.

'The Bible says, "In the Beginning was the Word." But that was only the beginning. Here it is beginning and middle and end. I am a word. No wonder I eat my heart out.'

Once more his hand swept along the lined wall. 'These are Jews. Each face is a face distorted by pain. I can lie, but not my camera. It tells the truth. Every Jew here suffers from something incurable, a cancer of the soul. Look! Look!' His fingers stabbed at photograph after photograph. 'You must believe me.'

I believed him. There was no question but that he suffered from the same sickness. His self-torture was eroding him. I asked him why he stayed, why he had stayed in Germany these last ten years.

'For spite,' he said. 'To spite the Germans and to spite myself. While others died, I was safe. While others starved, I had a full belly. Or maybe it is because Jacoby, the Jewish photographer, is a success here in Germany. Publishers hire me. Galleries show my work. And, for that, I turn my back on the past.'

He lowered his head into his hands and stayed silent a time. When he raised it again, there was a tired, bitter look on his face. 'I have made a cheap bargain. Do not deny it for I know it is so. What am I doing here? What is any Jew doing here?'

He searched in a desk drawer, found some photographs. They were of an old man. 'This is the caretaker of the cemetery in Coblenz where so many of my family lie buried. I went back to the cemetery and the old man told me what it had been like. The Nazis took the headstones and used them for paving blocks. They opened graves and took rings and jewelry from the dead and threw the bones and flesh into mounds.

'And do you know who did all these things? People who had been our neighbours. People who still live in Coblenz and say they never were Nazis, say they are glad to see the Jews come back.'

There were tears in Jacoby's eyes. Tears, I knew, more for himself than for anyone else. 'And I live among those Germans now,' he said. 'I talk with them and eat with them and take their money. They accept that I have forgiven them because I am here. And inside me, there is the fear that I have forgiven them or else why do I stay? Do you understand what I mean? Do you? Do you?'

I thought that I did. Hadn't I been sent to him by people who said, 'You must meet Jacoby, the photographer. One of the best and very successful.'

The signs of his success were in his apartment. The books he had illustrated. The studies he had made for magazines. They were all there. But so was Jacoby, with his haunted look. Jacoby with his tortured soul.

'Why,' he demanded, 'did God have to create both Jews and Germany? Didn't he know they could not exist together?'

I met many persons in Germany who were entitled to pity. I had to give Max Jacoby a great deal. He has invented a torture for himself that not even the Nazis could imagine. He wants to be more than he is.

Others, like Annie and Peter Capell, have found their answer. When I talked with them, they were preparing to leave Germany a second time. Like so many who returned, they had found no peace in themselves and now they were getting ready to join a large group of double-refugees in Ascona in Switzerland.

This group, made up of writers, artists, and scholars had either been expelled or had fled from Germany during the Nazi period and then returned after the war. They had not been able to accept the new Germany. Among them are Hans Habe, the author, and Max Horckheimer, probably the outstanding sociologist Germany has produced.

The Capells intended to join them. He is a successful actor and she was, for many years both before and after Hitler, a successful literary and theatrical agent. They spent more than a decade in the United States before returning to Germany.

They describe themselves as 'Hitler-made Jews'. Capell said, 'We never thought of ourselves as Jews until Hitler told us that we were. It has been impossible for us to think of ourselves as anything but Jews since.'

He smiled ruefully. 'You know, all during the years we were in the United States, we also thought of ourselves as German, as belonging in Germany. There wasn't much question in our minds but that we would return when Hitler and the Nazis were defeated. Good as the United States was to us, and happy as we were, it seemed only natural that we should go back.'

During their years away, Capell said, they were cut off from what was evolving in Germany. 'In a sense, what we imagined was that when we came back, the calendar would have reverted to the times before Hitler. We had no idea of the deep changes which had taken place, of the impact of National Socialism on the minds and attitudes of the people. So, when we returned, it was to a strange Germany.

'There still were in Munich many people whom we had known, who had been our friends. These were people who had been anti-Nazi, who had befriended the Jews, who were anti-Fascist. We thought that we could pick up with them where we had left off. It was a shock to find that we could not establish communication with them.

'Some of them said to us, "Oh, you lucky Jews. There you were, safe in America and getting rich, while we were suffering bombing and invasions." We – we – were lucky!'

The Capells, and others like them, refer to themselves as 'rimmigrants'. They are neither German nor alien. Few have reverted to German citizenship. They tend to stay within their own circle, both professionally and socially.

'We found,' Capell said, 'that to become German, we would have to erase the past. Not just what happened to the Jews, but the whole meaning of Nazism, which transcended even what happened to the Jews. For we discovered that too many Germans have done that, pushed the memory of evil out of their consciousness. It is as if it never had been.

'So many Germans take it for granted that all their obligations have been repaid by the Federal treasury. They are the same Germans who regard our exile as a long, happy vacation.'

Mrs. Capell agreed. 'In Germany, people like us are what

Orwell called "non-persons". I grew up in Munich, was educated here. My family was German. Then Hitler came and everything was changed and we had to leave. He took away our personality. We thought it would be different when we returned, but it wasn't. The Germans had grown accustomed to thinking of us, to treating of us, as if we were abstractions.

'It isn't anti-Semitism. It's a denial of existence. No laws can change that. No official solicitude. It makes it easy to erase the past. There is no understanding of what happened to people like Peter and me. Even worse, there is no understanding of what happened to those who were killed. But, above all, the tragedy is that the Germans refuse to admit their own part in all that happened by acting as if nothing had happened.'

Capell said, 'Leaving Germany makes us feel as if we are purging ourselves. Germany has been a place to make a living and nothing more. But it has not been enough. It is a country that has lost its soul and we must leave it to retain ours.'

Maria Mattray, however, stays in Germany. She, too, is a Hitler-made Jew. another 'rimmigrant' from the United States. Blonde, petite, handsome, she was at one time an actress but now is a successful television writer in Munich. It is a field in which she entered after returning to Munich from the United States.

'Every once in a while,' she said, 'I have to leave Germany so that I can breathe. There is a sense of suffocation here.'

Miss Mattray specializes in documentary films, many of them dealing with the Nazi years or touching on such problems as the rise of nationalism in post-war Germany.

'I am a political writer,' she said. 'German television devotes much time to political subjects. It is the most potent instrument for democracy that this country possesses. It is the one way to get through to the German people. The schools have not succeeded. The newspapers have not succeeded. Only a few of the magazines have come close.'

Each of the German *Laender* has its own television corporation. However, many times the different corporations exchange programmes, so, while there is no national television, many programmes are shown nationally.

'I did not know how deep Nazism had penetrated when I came back. I thought that it had touched only a few, that the great mass of Germans had accepted it because they had to accept it. I underestimated how effective the Nazi indoctrination had been and how willingly the great mass of Germans welcomed it. I have learned since.'

The learning came when her name first appeared on an anti-Nazi television programme. 'I got phone calls, letters. I was wakened in the middle of the night and when I answered the phone, I was greeted with obscenity. The favourite expression was "Jew-whore". The station and all the people concerned with the programme were also victims. I was told it happened every time such a programme went on the air. I have since learned that this is true.

'Then the *National Zeitung* and *Soldaten Zeitung* (the right-wing newspaper) took up the attack. It didn't use the word, "Jew", of course, because that would be a violation of the law. But it attacked me as a traitor to my country, as an alien who was certainly in league with the Communists. I got a dose of super-refined Goebbels treatment from them.'

She described her feeling as one of alienation from the Germans. 'I cannot accept them on their terms and they are unable to understand mine. I was never a Jew, but it isn't a matter of being Jewish. I have found that the word "Jew", has lost its specific meaning anyway. To many Germans it is anything that says to them that they must exist with a knowledge of their past. And this they do not want to do.'

She sees no signs that Germany will return to Nazism if, by that word, is meant virulent, general anti-Semitism and persecutions. 'That would be pointless because they would run out of victims so soon. But what I do fear is a return to an intellectual brutality. To an intellectual primitivism. That possibility exists. We have seen how terrible a brutalized Germany can be. So far, Germany has not done enough to make its re-emergence impossible.'

Max Reinhardt was a symbol of pre-Hitler art in Germany and Austria. Under his direction, the Salzburg Festival became a world theatrical centre. His productions in Berlin were major international events. When Hitler came into power, Reinhardt had to flee Germany. He went to the United States, where he became an American citizen. He died there in 1943.

Today there is another Reinhardt in Salzburg, his son, Gottfried Reinhardt. He has been living there for twelve years and producing and directing motion pictures, both in Germany and in Austria during that period. Ironically, he lives in a *schloss* which was once occupied by Martin Normann, Hitler's deputy, who is believed still to be alive, and the Number One 'most-wanted' Nazi war criminal.

During recent years, Gottfried Reinhardt has directed a number of Festival productions in Salzburg.

He is broad-shouldered, thick-chested. His hair is thick, though grey. His eyebrows are bushy. The most apt adjective to describe him is 'sardonic'.

'During the period,' he said, 'when I am busy directing, it is "Herr Professor, this," and "Her Doctor Reinhardt, that." But all the rest of the time, it is, "That Jew, Reinhardt." The Austrian character has not changed since the days when people threw things at my father and shouted, "Jew, Jew" at him.

'It is far worse here than I have found it in Germany. I cannot speak for the hearts of the Germans, only for their actions. There, at least, anti-Semitism is both concealed and illegal. I have no doubt that it exists, but it is not so visible.'

Reinhardt believes that Jews are an atavism in both Germany and Austria. 'Those who are here are fighting the inevitable. There is nothing to show that Jews are really wanted, that either Austria or Germany is ready to accept them as ordinary citizens. It does not matter that both countries are suffering because of a lack of Jews. They think that is a cheap price to pay.

'Look at the theatre! Almost everywhere it is barren. Music suffers. If it were not for the Jews, those few who remain, it would be marked for death too. Even here in Salzburg.

'Another example is medicine. In the old days, Jews dominated that field, but today there are none. And Vienna, for example, which used to be renowned for its doctors and its professors, has lost its renown.'

To Reinhardt, the Nazi party with its banners has disappeared, but not Nazism. Like many, he places the blame on the occupation forces, especially the Americans. 'There was no real attempt to get rid of the Nazis, only a surface one. There are men in important positions, both in Austria and Germany, who were long-time party members. Right here, I am often taunted by a man who delights in telling me that he was a Nazi as early as 1932 and is still one. And he is a government official.'

Reinhardt admits there is a contradiction between what he believes and his staying in Austria. 'Maybe I stay because I enjoy suffering. No, the truth is that I stay as a gesture of defiance. My presence here says that they haven't driven us all away or destroyed us. Every time an old Nazi sees me, he's reminded of what the Nazis did. And reminded that they lost.'

The world of art and culture has been de-Nazified. But it continues to exist in a Germany and an Austria which is still contaminated by Nazism. Neither those who suffered under Nazism – the older ones – nor those whose parents did, like Lilienthal and Jacoby, can escape the past or the present.

It can give to some of these people success, but the success is an exacerbation of the spirit. It can drive a Jacoby into self-hate. It can drive the Capells out of Germany a second time. It makes a cynic of Reinhardt.

Once all these could only have been described as 'artists'. To-day, they must be described as 'Jews'. And all of them now accept the new designation. None, not even Jacoby, would seek to deny it. And none finds it easy to be a Jew.

15. *The Court Jews*

FROM the time of Joseph in Egypt, there have been 'court Jews', men close to the seats of power who used their influence on behalf of their people.

Moses was a court Jew. So were Nehemiah, as adviser to the Persian king, Artaxerxes I; Samuel, in the court of Shabur I; and Chasdai ibn Shaprut, during the Spanish califate. Samuel ibn Nagdala served two successive Emirs for twenty-eight years when the Berbers ruled North Africa and Southern Europe. The great Moses Maimonides served in the court of Saladin.

These early advisers were important in diplomacy, trade, finance and domestic affairs. Later the influence of the court Jews became restricted to financial affairs. Ferdinand and Isabella, of Spain, who launched the Spanish Inquisition, offered Don Isaac Abravanel any reward if he would convert. Abravanel refused to apostacize and fled, penniless to Naples, where he later became financial adviser to Ferdinand I.

The Mendes and Nassi families served as advisers in Spanish courts from the 12th Century. During the Inquisition they converted to Christianity, following the precept of Maimonides that martyrdom for one's religion, while noble, was not mandatory. He wrote:

'If a person puts to us the question whether he is under obligation to surrender his life... we must in all conscience, and in accordance with the precepts of Judaism, reply "No".'

But, having saved their lives by conversion, the Mendeses and Nassis then escaped from Spain to Venice and reverted to their ancient faith. It was as Jews that they were then exiled from Venice, and, as Jews, that they were welcomed in Turkey where, first Suleimann and later Selin II, put the financial affairs of the Turkish Empire in their hands, especially those of Joseph Nassi.

These court Jews acted both for the rulers and for their people. For centuries they were a buffer between persecution and the Jews. Among them were the great banking houses of the Montefiores, the Rothschilds and the Warburgs.

There is, again, a representative of the Warburgs in Germany. This is Erich Warburg who is back in Hamburg, surrounded by reminders of his family's past in Germany. There are pictures, scrolls and medals in his rich dark panelled office. Kaisers and presidents have acknowledged the importance of the Warburg family.

Erich Warburg is conscious of this. He is slender, of medium height, elegant, a cosmopolitan, an internationalist. His is the internationalism of the board and of the drawing room. His is the world of captains and kings, not foot soldiers and the dispossessed. He is a *grand seigneur,* descendant of a long line of *grand seigneurs*. He is also a Jew.

He is deeply aware that he is part of that German Jewry which regarded itself as an élite among world Jewry. He has a deep pride in that special Jewish background. After all, he is an example of how high a Jew can rise in a non-Jewish world.

And an example of how precarious being a Jew – even a Jew named Warburg – can be. When he speaks of his German background, it is with pride. But he is now an American citizen. And he believes that 'it was a mistake on the part of the Jews that they did not return to Germany after the war. One cannot solve a problem by turning his back on it.'

Yet Warburg did not return to Germany until 1956. And, when he did return, it was not to Germany but to the bank which had borne his family's name for generations. And, in many ways, his was a return to the past, not to the present. Because that past does not exist, Warburg lives a life of many contradictions.

He has, for example, little patience with those who believe that the Jews will disappear from Germany in a short time. He finds it inconceivable because 'Germany is the heartland of Europe and Jews will always be here.' But the Jews he meant were the bankers, the financiers, the industrialists.

He condemns the anti-Semitism of the Nazis and of Hitler, their persecutions and killings, but, as a reasonable man, he adds, 'Remember there was a violent amount of anti-Semitism in all

Central Europe. It reached its height under Hitler.' Nor does
he believe that there has been a basic change in the attitude
of the Germans toward the Jews. 'But that is immaterial because
if you have no Jews, anti-Semitism has no target.'

Still, he is greatly troubled by the fear that there may be a
revival of active anti-Semitism in Germany. He sees its germs
dormant, but not dead. But he worries not only about changing
German attitudes and German concepts, but about the Jews
themselves.

'I worry,' he said, 'about the kind and quality of the Jews who
might come to Germany. The Jews here must have both courage
and tact. They must not make the mistake of blaming the children for the sins of the fathers. I believe that Germans should, and
must, feel shame but not guilt.'

His ideal is the ancient Jewish colony of Hamburg and its
environs which produced great rabbis, great scholars, great
financiers, great industrialists. It was a community which prided
itself on learning and culture, whose representatives were at home
anywhere in the world. A community far different from today's,
which is dominated by the Persian Jew and whose leaders were
chosen, not by families like the Warburgs, but by the whole
community.

It was not like that in the old days.

His is a strange pride in his Judaism. His eyes light up when
he talks of the beautiful, richly-woven Torah Mantel (cover) for
the sacred scrolls which his family bought years ago and which
today still encloses those scrolls in the new Hamburg synagogue.
But it is hard to tell if his pride lies in its symbolism or its artistic
value.

The Mantel was saved on Crystal Night by a devout Jew
and hidden by him in his home until he was taken to Theresienstadt. (Warburg did not know the man's name.) The man took it
to Theresienstadt with him and managed to keep it secreted
there. When he was taken from the camp to a furnace, he passed
on the cover for safe-keeping.

All but 10,000, out of 250,000 men, women and children who
were sent to Theresienstadt, perished. But the cover remained
unfound, a symbol of a Judaism that could not be destroyed.
And when finally the few remaining survivors were freed,
one of them had the Mantel. (Again, Warburg did not know

the man's name.) This man walked from Theresienstadt to Hamburg and on the first night that services were held in Hamburg, the cover was again about the Torah.

'Can you imagine,' Warburg said, 'that later there were some people who wanted to replace the cover with a new one?' These 'some people' were the new Jews of Hamburg.

They have no memory of the largesse and philanthropists of the past. They know no more about them than Warburg knows of the men and women who protected the cover and lost their lives. Warburg knows his family bought the cover. The new Jews think of the thousands whose deaths sanctified it.

He is not callous or unthinking. It is simply that once the Jews of Hamburg were the concern of his family over whom the Warburgs laid a protective layer of paternalism. It is hard for him to accept that Hitler changed all that.

He is upset because Hamburg has no rabbi of its own, but is served by Rabbi Levinson. His thoughts go to finding a rabbi who would fit into the Hamburg tradition of the past. 'I am thinking,' he said, 'of asking the present Chief Rabbi of Denmark, who is retiring, to come here.'

In the old days, a Warburg would have automatically arranged for such a rabbi and would, of course, have provided any necessary funds.

Warburg is unique among the major Jewish figures in business and industry of the pre-Hitler days in that he has returned to Germany and re-entered a traditional family enterprise. Yet, in one sense, he is an example of why they did not return.

Before Hitler, the bank was 'the Warburg bank'. It bore the family name. Today, however, the bank is called 'Brinckman, Wertz and Co.' Those are the names of the two Aryans who finally bought the bank from 'the Family' when Hitler decreed that it must be sold. Once, the name 'Warburg', gave stature, strength and history to the banking enterprise. In the new Germany it would be an anachronism.

So the name Warburg has disappeared, as have the names of Ullstein, Mosse, S. Fischer, Karstadt, Tietz, Rathenau and Ballin from the enterprises which these Jewish families once owned and operated. And Warburg's bank, like the Duetsche, Dresdner, and Commerz banks, all of which were Jewish-controlled, is now controlled by non-Jews.

Yet he maintains, 'It is economic conditions which will determine whether there will be any future for a Jewish community
in Germany. If men can prosper, they will ignore the past.' It
is quite easy for him to argue from the particular to the general.
For him, it is necessary.

Warburg is untroubled by the philosophical problems which
weigh heavily on many others. He does not equate the treatment
of the Jews with the permanency of democracy in Germany for
after all, two Kaisers and their Chancellors honoured Warburgs.

The fact is that the Warburgs were exceptions before Hitler
and they are exceptions now. The persecutions, the tortures, the
deaths of millions of Jews were sad, unhappy, corrosive incidents
in history, but they were not – not for the Warburgs – a personal tragedy. If they too lost much, they also saved much. Erich
Warburg did not tell me of any of his family who died in either
oven or gas chamber.

If any German Jews were fortunate from 1933 to 1945, he and
his were among them.

Still, none of this prevents him from truly feeling his own
Judaism. He is proud that the Torah is enclosed in the *mantel*
that his family bought, but it is difficult for him to accept that
a Persian Jew reads from it at the Sabbath services which
Warburg does not attend.

Yet he feels that he has a task, as a Jew, in Germany. 'Someone,' he said, 'must be here to guard the ramparts.' He has girded
himself for that task.

He does not recognize that he is an anachronism. The Jewry
of which he was a part was murdered by Hitler. He is a
stranger in his own house. His kind of court Jew is obsolescent
in Germany.

Not, however, the type represented by Ulrich Coron. Coron is
a product of post-Hitler Germany, not a relic of pre-Hitler
Germany. Where Warburg is naïvely a German Jew, Coron is a
Jew who happens to be in Germany.

Coron has attained importance because Germany is divided in
two, because Berlin is split. He has attained importance because
a new kind of Jew now lives in Germany, one who has few
links to the past and even those few links are fetters of the spirit.
His is not one of the famous families of German Jews, intertwined with German history.

But in today's Germany he plays a far more important role than does Warburg.

He is a giant of a man, well over six feet tall, and massively built. Now in his late sixties, he still gives the impression of great physical strength. He was born and educated in Berlin, studying mineralogy and petrology. As soon as Hitler became Chancellor, he went to France. His mother, a widow, refused to leave. 'She said she was born in Berlin and would die there.' Coron's younger brother stayed on to look after his mother.

When the war began in 1939, Coron entered the French army. After the fall of France, he joined the Maquis and fought with them until 1944 when he was captured.

'I was,' he said, 'with a Communist group. I had false papers which did not list my religion as Jewish nor reveal that I was a German. That was how I escaped the furnace. I was sent to a forced labour camp for political prisoners. It was hell. Torture, starvation, beatings. It stopped one inch short of murder.'

When Coron was freed, he weighed less than 100 pounds. 'I had only a spark of life left in me,' he said. 'But I also had a raging fire of hatred for the Germans and the Nazis. It was these that kept me alive. It took more than a year, but I finally recovered.'

Released from the hospital, he asked the Red Cross to find out what had happened to his mother and brother. 'I didn't expect that they had survived. I wanted to find out the date of their death so that I could say Kaddish (prayer for the dead) for them.'

For two years there was no word. Coron had established himself in the oil distribution business and was doing well. Suddenly he received word that both his mother and brother were alive. They had believed him dead just as he had believed them dead.

'I wrote at once,' he said, 'sending them money to join me. I could not believe that they would stay one day longer than necessary in Germany. My hate for Germany was as strong as ever; I expected them to share it. But my mother wrote back that she would not leave. Instead, she asked me to return. She was then over seventy and she wanted both her sons with her.

'Of course I went to Berlin, but I was sure that I could

convince my mother to leave. I refused to speak a word of German all during the trip. I would not touch a German hand. I would not look at German faces because, if I saw one I recognized, I would be tempted to kill.'

There was no question but that he meant it. We were seated in the ornate lobby of a great hotel, but for a moment he was transported back to the labour camp. The brown eyes which an instant earlier had been compassionate with memory of happiness, were bitter now with memory of pain. He was aware of it, for he said, 'I have tried to forget, but, of course, I cannot.'

A reason he tried to forget was that when he rejoined his mother and brother, he discovered that they had been among the *illegalen*. 'They were alive,' he said, 'because old friends and neighbours had protected them. They had been hidden out, passed from hand to hand. People stinted themselves to feed my mother and brother. It was then that I first accepted that I must draw the line between the saviours and the slaughterers.

'But there had been far more of the latter. All about me was evidence of the Hitler years. Relatives and friends were dead. Strangers lived in their homes, owned their businesses, slept in their beds. There were no Jewish children, no Jewish young.'

Coron had been raised a devout Jew and had continued to be one after he became an adult. 'It was a part of me,' he said, 'and when I returned to Berlin, I saw that it was possible for Jews to live as Jews again. They could walk the streets as free men. The synagogues were open. My brother told me how, on the day of liberation, the few remaining Jews in Berlin gathered together to pray in a burned-out, gutted building. How, a day later, the Jews made plans to start life again.'

But Coron wanted no part of Germany. 'My mother, though, was a fierce, proud woman,' he said. 'She would not leave. And she wanted me with her after all these years. So I stayed.'

It was here that he became a new kind of 'court Jew', an essential Jew. He went into the oil business in Berlin. And the sole source of oil supplies was from the East, from the Communist countries. In those days, the Cold War was being waged. The Berlin blockade had just been eased, but tensions were great between East and West. In order for Coron to stay in business, he had to get oil. He went to East Germany to see if he could find a source of supply.

'I was told,' he said, 'to call at a certain government office. As I entered, I was greeted by name. I turned and saw a fellow ex-prisoner in the labour camp. Men who have suffered together always retain a bond and there was one between us. He told me about some of the other prisoners – all Communists, of course – who were now in positions of influence in East Germany and other Communist countries. Then he wanted to know what had brought me to East Germany.

'When I told him, he was delighted to help me. "Coron", he said, "we will make you a wealthy capitalist. At least we'll know we're not making some Nazi rich."

'I have encountered many other ex-prisoners since. Nearly all of them are married to Jewish women. They explained that they wanted to be certain that the mothers of their children had not been Nazis or connected with the Nazis.'

Coron's ex-campmate kept his word. Coron did become wealthy. And, with his wealth, he became the new kind of court Jew. He was important to the authorities because he represented a source of oil. This gave him influence.

He also became important to the Jewish community, because this was the period before restitution laws and reparations. It was a time when Jews depended upon international relief and private charity. Coron, and his brother who became his partner, helped create the post-war Jewish community in Berlin.

'But,' said Coron, 'I knew that I could never again become part of Germany. I had been one of the hunted. I had seen so many captured and slaughtered. I remembered the cruelties. And I knew that the killers were still walking around. They wore white shirts instead of brown ones, but the same bodies were inside the new shirts.

'I was an alien in Germany just because I was a Jew. When I prayed, my prayers had to be for those who had died. And in those who were living, some part had also been killed by the Germans. So I still cannot believe that there is a new Germany because I have experienced the old one.'

Coron shrugged. 'I want to be fair. I want to be honest. Maybe there is a new Germany. But there is also the N P D. There are the desecrations and the swastikas. Aren't these part of the new Germany too?'

Coron has been spending much of his time in Austria since

the death of his mother in 1960. He bought a home in Vienna. 'Don't ask me why,' he said. 'In many ways, Germany is better today for the Jews than Austria. It has recognized its obligations, paid restitution, helped Israel. It has banned anti-Semitism. I have met Germans who feel shame for the past and who talk of their guilt. But no Austrians have talked that way.

'No, the Austrians remain openly anti-Semitic. They have a nationalistic right wing which uses anti-Semitism as a political plank. Still, the fact is that it was an accomplice, not the perpetrator of the terror. But what does it matter where I live? My only homeland is Israel.'

Since he feels that way, why does he not go to Israel?

'Because,' he said, 'I am of more value to Israel here. I raise money for Israel. I help Israeli students who come to study. I recruit young men, strong men, who can help build Israel and arrange for them to immigrate. And, because I am wealthy and because of my connections, I have influence with many officials. Believe me, it is not "Coron, the Jew," for whom they do favours, but "Coron, the oil man."'

'I use Germany as Germany used the Jews, as a means toward an end. No Jew owes Germany anything.' He stared out the big picture window that faced the wide street. 'When I first came back, there were no big, new automobiles, no fancy stores, no crowds. It was all litter and debris. Today, all is changed but one thing and that thing is the Jews.

'We are not different from what we were. We are still the victims. Time has not altered that. And so we must live in our own way, separated from Germany. We are no longer Germans. I do not think that we can ever again be.'

Coron and Warburg. The past and the present. The first wears Savile Row clothes and the second a *yamulka* (skull cap). One lives in a nostalgic world and the other in a harsh one. The only likenesses they have is that they are of German background and each is a court Jew in his own way in Germany.

16. *The Once and Former Jews*

WHEN the first Nuremberg law was enacted in 1935 (to be followed through the years by thirteen more statutes, each progressively more severe), it created an anomaly. It did so by raising the old question, 'What is a Jew?' It also provided its own answer: a Jew was whoever was so defined by Nazi edict.

Over a period of time, this made Jews of persons who had been Christians for two generations, individuals who had long since put aside even the memory of their origins. (This was a severe blow to both the Catholic and Protestant churches for it negated the proselyting efforts of the church, based on the doctrine of *nulla salus extra ecclesiam* (there is no salvation outside the church).

The laws separated husbands from wives, parents from children. They pauperized all persons of 'Jewish blood'. This, of course, was one of the basic reasons behind the laws. Nothing evidenced this more clearly than the instructions given by Reinhard Heydrich, second-in-command of the S S, for the 'spontaneous demonstrations of Crystal Night'. Among these were:

'As many Jews, especially rich ones, are to be arrested as can be accommodated in the existing prison camps ... Upon their arrest, the appropriate concentration camps should be contacted immediately in order to confine them as soon as possible.'

And: 'The business and private apartments of Jews may be destroyed but not looted.'

By Crystal Night, the term, 'Jew', was as elastic as the Nazis wanted to make it. Swept up in the mass arrests were many who had, until that moment, believed themselves exempt from the Nuremberg laws. But even earlier, there had been many of these 'Nuremberg Jews' who had foreseen the future and fled Germany.

Thousands of mixed marriages were ended by divorce, with the Jewish partner, in many instances, seeking to safeguard a Christian wife or husband and any children. There were also instances where Christian partners took advantage of an opportunity to end a marriage.

The Nazis directed their efforts primarily at those 'Jews' who were wealthy and important. Bankers, industrialists, publishers and members of the various professions were the primary targets. Poor 'Jews' (there were many of these) were the victims of cruelty and imprisonment, but they were low on the list of priorities.

These 'Jews by statute' were shown little more humanity than those who were Jews by birth and conviction. They were sent to concentration, extermination and labour camps. However, they were granted one concession. Under ordinary circumstances, they were not to be sent to ovens or gas chambers until the supply of other Jews had been exhausted. In many camps, however, commanders had no time for such technicalities and lumped all 'Jews' together.

The more fortunate, and wiser, converts and children of converts fled Germany. Nearly all immediately cast off their Nuremberg identity.

When the war ended, however, there were some thousands of Nuremberg Jews in the camps. After liberation, some of them were among the 5000 of these who asked for conversion to Judaism. As Rabbi Lichtigfeld saw it, 'They felt that if they were not Jews, they were nothing.'

And, again after the war, a number of those who had fled returned to Germany. Among them was Hans Wallenberg. A member of a prominent and wealthy family, he was in the publishing business before 1933 and, on his return, became an editor in the book division of the Axel Springer publishing empire. (Springer now controls what was once the Ullstein publishing enterprises. He is, of course, not Jewish.)

Wallenberg, in his late sixties, is stout, balding, forthright. 'I come,' he said, 'of a Jewish background, but I long ago converted to Christianity. Some of my relatives are Jewish and some are Christian. We feel no sense of separation because of that difference.'

He left Germany in 1933 and went to the United States, where he engaged in his profession. When the United States entered the war, Wallenberg was commissioned. He served for a time with the occupation forces in Germany and then chose to remain in Germany.

The choice has been a satisfactory one. His large, opulent office in the vast Springer building in Berlin is lined with book cases. Good pictures hang on the wall. The furniture is massive and expensive. Wallenberg fits well into the decor. Like the room, he has style.

'I never,' he said, 'have concealed or denied my background. That would be foolish and pointless.' And, as he talked, he showed that he had not forgotten his past or sought to disassociate himself from it. When he speaks of Jews and Judaism, it is from the inside, if only just inside.

Yet he has separated Jews from the Jewish religion. He knows the two are not concomitant; his frame of reference is himself. Just as his thinking and attitudes go from the particular to the general. In many ways, he is a part of the past, like Erich Warburg. That was an ideal state and its like will not be seen again.

'The Jews,' he said softly, 'are fading out of Germany. It is a great loss but nothing can be done about it. The loss is everywhere. In politics, in science, in education, in culture, in *belles-lettres*. Remember that before Hitler Jews made up less than one per cent of the German population, yet they won a quarter of the Nobel prizes awarded to Germans. (Six German Jews were awarded Nobel prizes after fleeing Hitler.)

'No place is the loss greater than in the field of culture for its own sake.' He lifted a manuscript from a pile on his desk. 'This is a history of art. Once it would have been written in Germany, by Germans. In order to have it written now, it was necessary for us to go outside Germany to those who fled from here and have not returned. This is a specialized field, but what happened in it is symptomatic.

'I do not believe that there will be any future return of Jewish scholars to Germany. Those who intended to come back, did come back. They were a small minority and included almost none of the first rank. Those stayed in the United States, in Israel, in England and even in South America. The umbilical cord to Germany has long since been severed.'

He rose from his desk and went to the bookshelves. As he walked along them, he tapped the spines of book after book. 'This was written by a former German Jew, and this one, and this one.' His finger kept tapping as he walked. 'Some countries complain of a brain drain. Germany suffered a torrent, not a drain, of loss.'

He returned to his desk. 'It is not talked about, but we have begun to accept the disappearance of Jews from Germany as inevitable. But no one, I think, has made a real study of what this will mean. What will it do to the structure of Germany? Take politics, as an example. Those German Jews, in the days before Hitler, who involved themselves were primarily liberals. They generated new ideas and concepts. They were the catalysts who caused change. No one is doing that now.

'And I do not hear any voices raised pointing out this loss.

'The Jews,' he went on, 'imposed a tradition of pure scholarship on Germany. Far out of proportion to their numbers, they were teachers, researchers. If they did not create the tradition of German scholarship, they gave it spirit. Germany lacks that tradition now. Just as it lacks scholars. Each year the lag between Germany and other countries grows. There are those who deny it and point to how well Germany is doing materially.

'Well, some day they will learn that scholarship is at the heart of growth in gross national product. All they have to do is look at the United States and what it spends on research, on education, on cultural fields.'

For Wallenberg, this is the true Jewish problem and it involves, not the Jews, but the German nation. It is why, for example, he is pleased that there is 'less anti-Semitism in the Federal Republic than in any other Western country,' and yet is troubled by that very fact.

'Philosophically it is a sign of growth, a sign of change in the national character. But it is also a sign of the disappearance of the Jews from Germany. Of Jews from the consciousness of Germany. Even the NPD does not trade on anti-Semitism, but on German nationalism. If they tried to use the Jews as the Nazis did – as a whipping boy – only a psychotic, senile few would go along with them.

'The Jews are today an enclave in German society, a small pocket of strangers. They serve a number of purposes, none more important than to remind the German people of what Hitler did to the Jews. But even this has another side. Just because they are reminders of the past, the government and the people are made uneasy. They are reminded of German responsibility. If there were no Jews, this reminder would disappear.'

Here Wallenberg reverted to what he saw as the core of the problem, Germany's need for Jews. 'I am no sociologist. I am a writer, an editor, an amateur of knowledge. But I know that every culture needs a cross-fertilization of ideas or it grows inbred. This is the danger that Germany faces and which almost no one discusses and studies.

'It is easier to go along as we are, to have a policy of philo-Semitism that ignores the disease and treats the symptoms. If things continue as they are, Jewishness must vanish from Germany. And, not long afterward, the Jews in Germany.'

This was the considered opinion of Hans Wallenberg, who once was a 'Jew' because Hitler decreed that he was and who ceased being a Jew when Hitler's voice no longer spoke.

Hitler also made a Jew of Hans Reiner. 'It was his loss,' Reiner said. 'In those days, I was as ready to become a Nazi as anything. I was out of a job. My family had no money. I didn't care about politics. All I wanted was someone who'd make it possible for me to support my wife. Besides, I was a patriot. The Fatherland had been betrayed and it must rise again.'

Reiner is a lean, sardonic individual. His leathered face bears a duelling scar. In his sixties, he has not attained serenity with the years. He runs an appliance store in Bremen. All the time we talked, it was to the accompaniment of tape-recorded music. His favourite composer apparently was Mahler.

'My father's family was Jewish,' he said, 'but he converted to Catholicism when he married my mother. I was raised a Catholic. I even took it seriously for a long time. But, by the time I went to the University at Marburg, I'd stopped. But, if I was anything, I was a Catholic.' He laughed. 'So was Hitler, wasn't he?'

Reiner never completed his university education. 'It wasn't just the big depression. I never cared much for studying. That was my father's idea. I guess he never got over being Jewish even if he became a Catholic. Anyway, I left the university and went to work. That is, I worked when I could. And I got

F

married. To a Catholic, of course. Her father had a little money and that helped.'

Then came the Nuremberg laws. 'Someone, I don't know who, denounced my father. He was a teacher and he was fired from his job right away. He couldn't believe it. He went to the priest to get proof that he wasn't Jewish, but they just tore up the paper. Then he did something a good Catholic should never do. He committed suicide.'

Reiner listened to the music a moment. 'How would you like to wake up in America one morning and find that you were black? Well, that's what I felt like when people began calling me a Jew. It made me want to crawl inside my skin and hide. It was like having leprosy. The people I knew – the men I had worked with – even my wife...' He cocked his head again so as to hear the music better. 'Yes, even my wife.' He shook his head. 'You know, I could understand how she felt.'

He waited on a customer and then returned. 'I didn't know what a Jew was,' he said. 'I never knew my father's parents. All I knew about the Jews, I'd read in the *Beobachter* (the Nazi newspaper). Anyway, after that, it kept getting more difficult. My wife's family finally gave me the money to go to England. Before I left, I told my wife to divorce me. I didn't expect ever to come back.'

He reached England in 1938 and was there when Hitler invaded Poland and the war began. 'In England,' he said, 'I'd been helped by some Jewish organizations. I told them I wasn't a Jew, but a "non-Aryan". They said they were helping a lot of non-Aryans. I was grateful to them, but I didn't feel I was one of them.'

In 1940, Reiner was sent to Australia, together with a shipload of 'enemy aliens'. In Australia, he enlisted in the army. 'A lot of us did,' he said. 'It was either that or some form of internment. I decided it was hard to be a Jew. Hitler had driven all of us out of Germany and the English and the British seemed to think that we were potential spies. Even in the army, we were treated differently.

'For the first time in my life, I had an intimate contact with Jews. I found they weren't different from other people, but that they were treated differently. Jews became human beings to me.

I stopped thinking about what Hitler had done to me and started to realize what he was doing to others.'

The music had stopped momentarily and while he waited for it to recommence he lit a cigarette. When it began again, he sang along with it in a good baritone voice. 'It's from *Das Lied von der Erde*. Mahler was Jewish, wasn't he?'

I said I didn't know.

'It doesn't matter. It's just that I think in those terms now. Anyway, I came back in 1950. I had never felt at home in Australia. I'm a German and it's only here that I have a feeling that I'm part of the people. But, do you know, I found things had not really changed. Not about the Jews. They were outsiders still. They remain outsiders.'

He chuckled. 'You know something? I registered as a Jew. I'm still registered as a Jew. I pay my taxes as a Jew. But I've never been inside a synagogue. I wouldn't know what to do if I went there, except to wear a hat. I suppose I'm one of the few Catholic Jews that there are. Well, why not? In a few years there won't be any Jewish Jews in Germany.'

He chuckled again as I started to leave. He winked and said, *'Shalom aleichem'*. His face broke into a smile. 'A man has to adjust,' he said. 'Especially a Jew.'

Horst Mandel was also a Jew by edict, but he was a Jew for a very short time. And only by edict.

He is tall, handsome, urbane, a highly successful manufacturer of women's clothes. His luxurious offices occupy half a floor in a new, modern building just off the Kurfurstendam in Berlin and his work rooms and factory occupy three full floors.

He is a second-generation Christian, though one of his parents was born a Jew. Before Hitler, the family was in the manufacturing business and for much of the Hitler period were treated as 'Aryans'. During the war, Mandel was in charge of a factory that manufactured gas masks.

Toward the end of the war, when the Nazis were gripped by frustration and the knowledge that they were losing, Mandel was removed from his post and placed in a concentration camp. 'I was there only a short time,' he said, 'and then I was liberated by American troops. I and my family suffered very little compared to what happened to others.'

While Mandel accepts that his imprisonment stemmed from

his Jewish background, he never has regarded himself as a Jew. Nor does he have any sense of Jewishness. 'Being called Jew,' he said, 'did not make me one. That was only another aspect of Nazi fanaticism.'

To Mandel, present day Germany is completely different from Hitler Germany. He said bluntly that he knew of no anti-Semitism and added, as so many others did, 'There are so few Jews that it has lost any political or economic value it ever had.' And, to prove the latter, he said that before Hitler the clothing business was dominated by the Jews – 'at least ninety per cent owned by them –' but that now only a small percentage of the business, and that in small units, was Jewish owned.

The young people, Mandel said, were free of anti-Semitism. To prove his point, he called into his office his son, in his middle twenties, and his secretary, a pretty young woman of about the same age. Both were, as he explained, examples of post-Hitler education and conditioning.

They concurred with Mandel. There was no anti-Semitism. But, said the secretary, she felt that philo-Semitism was being overdone. 'Why,' she asked, 'can't Jews be treated like everyone else?'

I made the point that they had not been treated like everyone else under Hitler.

'Are you sure about all those stories?' she asked. 'Isn't it possible that they have been exaggerated?'

I reminded her that Mandel had been placed in a concentration camp. And that he had been one of the fortunate ones. Besides, had she not been taught the history of the Nazi years in school?

Young Mandel said cautiously that the subject had been treated 'very objectively'. I pressed him to explain further.

'Well,' he said, 'they taught us that a number of persecutions took place and that a large number of Jews were forced to leave Germany. Of course, since it was only a period of twelve years, not much time was devoted to it. But we know all about what happened. We've seen it on television and read about it in the magazines.'

'My family thinks that there has been too much on television,' the secretary said. 'It's all over now and we ought to be allowed to start fresh.'

Mandel nodded agreement. 'What good does it do to keep bringing it up all the time? It all took place before these two – 'he motioned to the young people – 'before those two were born or when they were babies. They had nothing to do with it, so why should they be made to feel responsible?'

But hadn't his own experiences, what he had lived through affected him?

He considered this, then shook his head. 'It happened and then the war ended. It was a terrible period, of course, no one can deny that. Terrible. Especially for the Jews. But I wasn't a Jew, so it was different for me.'

Not even Hitler had been able to make a Jew of Horst Mandel, or to give him any feeling of kinship to the Jews. He was glad the 'terrible period' was over and that now he could give all his attention to business.

For Franz Bodenheim, however, the terrible period still continues. I met him in the Jewish library in Berlin, a tall, white-haired, uncertain man in his early fifties.

'My whole world,' he said, 'was suddenly inverted. I knew my Jewish background, but I had never even remotely considered myself a Jew. If I was anything – I never paid much attention to religion – I was a Protestant. When it happened, I was a student. Suddenly I was not even allowed to go to school. My friends would no longer speak to me.

'After that, it was a nightmare. I was sent to Dachau and then to Buchenwald. There I was made to wear a yellow star. I told them I wasn't a Jew, that I had never been a Jew. I wasn't anti-Semitic. It had never mattered enough to me for me to care one way or another about Jews.'

He ran a thin blue-veined hand across his forehead. 'For four years I was in the camps. I expected to die in Buchenwald. But I did not. I was lucky. And each day I was there, I was called a Jew, told I was a Jew, treated as a Jew. I tried to fight back, but it was useless. I finally began to believe that I was a Jew. If I were not, then why was I in Buchenwald? That was the way it was in the camps. They turned you into whatever they wanted to make you.'

When he was released from Buchenwald, he returned to Berlin. 'I didn't know what I was any more. I had almost been destroyed physically and mentally. I weighed about ninety pounds.

It took more than a year before I was strong enough to be
released from the hospital. And now I had to find myself again
because I didn't know any longer who I was.'

Again the thin hand wiped sweat from the forehead. 'You
know, it was not possible. Not possible to find out who I was.
I was a stranger to what was left of my family. When I
saw them, I remembered that they had been free, had been fighting and working for the Nazis, while I was in Dachau and
Buchenwald. I had become a Jew to them the day that I was
rounded up.

'They were not – are not – evil people. That's just the way
things were in Germany in those days. Maybe it is the German
way. To do what you are told to do. To believe what you are
told to believe. After all, it happened to me. They told me I
was a Jew again and again. And, after a time, I suppose I
became one.'

Bodenheim now works in a book store. He received a sum of
money from the government as compensation for his years as
a prisoner. 'You see,' he said, 'this government treats me as a
Jew also. It treats me well, where the Nazis treated me badly, but
still as a Jew. Do you wonder that, at last, I have accepted that fact?

'As a Jew, I wanted to find out more about the Jews. That is
why I come here often. I read the books. I listen to the conversation. I want to find out what it is that makes me like
all the other Jews. But I have not yet found out. I do not believe
that I ever will.'

These are four whom Hitler made 'Jews'. To Bodenheim and
Reiner, it was cataclysmic. To Wallenberg and to Mandel, it
was almost incidental. Of the four, the only one who has made
a conscious acceptance of his 'Jewishness' is Wallenberg and he
has been able, by some form of alchemy, to transmute it into
a cultural inheritance.

Reiner, with his mordant outlook, has transformed himself
into a reverse Pangloss for whom everything is for the worst
in the worst of possible worlds and he finds a bitter satisfaction
in it. He is far more fortunate than Bodenheim.

All four of these are of German background. All four have
an attachment to Germany, its history and culture. Whatever
relationship they have to Judaism is peripheral, though the
effects, in at least two cases, are traumatic.

There are in Germany, however, Jews of a far different type and background, Jews who are there because they are Jewish. These are the *Ostjuden*, the Jews who were transported or fled there from Eastern Europe and who, today, make up the majority of Jews living in Germany.

17. *The Pinakothek*

THERE were more than 200,000 East European Jews in Germany when the war ended in 1945. Almost all were still there, in displaced persons camps, two years later. (Some would remain in such camps until they were closed in 1952.)

In 1950 the number of East European Jews was swelled by refugees from the east who were fleeing the harsh, repressive, anti-Semitic measures that Stalin was taking against all the Jews in lands under Communist suzerainty.

Nearly all these Jews left Germany as soon as they could, with the vast majority going to Israel as soon as that country was established. The few thousands who remained were augmented by about 7000 Jews who returned to Germany during the 'economic miracle'.

These East European Jews were alien to all Germans, including German Jews. Their culture was Yiddish, not German. For centuries they had fought to preserve their identity while the German Jews had been seeking assimilation.

The economic level of the East European Jew was lower than that of the German Jew, with far more artisans and working men than industrialists or professionals. Their education level was lower as well.

The German Jews had long been schizoid about their co-religionists to the East. On the one hand, the Germans believed that they were culturally superior. On the other, they acknowledged the ties of a common faith. As a result, for decades the German Jews would do almost anything to aid the East European Jews except allow them to come to Germany to live.

So, when Czars and Cossacks, Russians and Poles, perpetrated atrocities and killed in pogroms, the German Jews were always quick to offer financial aid and seek to arrange for emigration of these other Jews in any direction except to Germany.

Hitler, however, had not let geography determine the manner in which he would treat Jews. German and East European went to the same camps, the same gas chambers and the same ovens. And, in the process, he decimated the Jews of all the lands he overran with his armies.

And, after the war, history, by a freak, made Germany a country which not only tolerated Jews, but needed them. The Federal Republic had to demonstrate its democracy, its 360 degree turn from Nazism. Since the tortured and murdered Jew had been the most visible symbol of Nazism, the Federal Republic had to put its Jews in a showcase.

And the only Jews available in any sizeable numbers were the East Europeans. And to Adenauer's government they were as manna. It did not matter that they were sick and poor and virtually unlettered. All that counted was that they were Jews.

Today, the East European Jews are a large majority in Germany. They dominate every major Jewish community except that of Berlin and even there they are approaching a majority, for they are younger than the German Jews. Most of them have adapted quickly, but some of the older East Europeans still wear stiff-brimmed black hats and long black coats. Some still wear earlocks.

More than eighty per cent of the Jews in Munich are East Europeans. Dr. Hanns Lamm, a high school vice-principal, and an officer of the *Zentralrat,* who described himself as 'one of the few (Munich) Jews who returned,' called the local community 'difficult'. This was because 'the best elements in the displaced persons camps went to Israel.'

For Lamm, these new Jews have not made sufficient of an adjustment. One reason has been the language difference. Another has been clannishness. 'In sum,' he said, 'it might be best to describe the Munich Jewish community as a transplanted *shtetl* (settlement) without the cultural values of a *shtetl.*'

There are those who see the new Jews differently from Lamm. Among them is Kurt Cohn, a German Jew, who owns the Pinakothek cafe, named for the famed art museum only a short block from the cafe. The Pinakothek is club, settlement house, library and meeting place for many of the East European Jews in Munich.

Cohn is a big man, with a fringe of spikey red hair on an

F*

otherwise bald head. He is gaunt-faced, hollow-eyed, and the eyes are always seeking the shadows. Born in Hamburg, he fled to Belgium in 1936. When the Nazis invaded that country, Cohn enlisted in the Belgian army. 'By that time,' he said, 'I had lost two sisters and a brother to the Nazis. They had not been able to fight. I had the chance.'

When Belgium surrendered, Cohn joined the small Belgian resistance movement. He took his wife and infant daughter into the back country where they were looked after and protected by Belgian Christian patriots. A family passed off Cohn's daughter as their own.

After Hitler's defeat, Cohn was employed by the occupying authorities. He had a college degree, a working knowledge of English, and his Jewish background as qualifications. He was employed in relief and rehabilitation projects for a number of years. 'I applied for a visa to the United States for my wife and my two children (a son was born after the war),' he said, 'and in 1952 I was told that I would soon receive it. I didn't intend to return to Europe again, so we went to Germany to straighten out some business affairs.'

Within weeks of his arrival in Germany, he became ill. An examination revealed that he was tubercular. His visa was invalidated.

After more than a year of hospitalization, he was released and went to work for the International Relief Organization, applying for another U.S. visa at the same time. He was refused the visa when X-rays showed that he still had a spot on his lung.

'So,' he said, 'I found myself in Germany. In Germany where I had sworn I would never live again. And doomed to stay there.'

Shortly afterward he bought the Pinakothek. Both food and liquor are supplied to patrons, but that is not why they fill the place each night. It is because the East European Jews have made this a Jewish oasis in a German desert, a place that is all their own.

Yiddish, Russian, Polish, Czech and Roumanian are all spoken here. Card players sit at their table, some playing *skat* and others *klob yosh*. Others manoeuvre chessmen while kibitzers mutter. Men, sucking boiling hot tea through lumps of sugar held between their teeth, read newspapers in a half dozen languages.

Here are older men, in black hats and kaftans and some younger ones in flowered sports shirts.

'We are all lonely men,' Cohn said. 'Each of us over forty has had his life broken and has never been able to knit it together again. We are lost, estranged. None of us has confidence in himself, so we get together. We seek out our own kind. Here, no one flinches at the touch of a stranger. After all, a stranger could have been a killer.

'We live here, but people like us – ' he waved a hand to encompass those in the room – 'people like us have no lives. The only Jews in Germany who have lives are in the old folks' homes. Today is possible for them because they have lost their yesterdays, because they no longer remember. But for us, there is only memory. And every memory of Germany is bitter.'

Why, then, do they stay?

Cohn had an answer. 'We are the dregs. We are the sick, the broken. We all settle for one thing – an existence. It is possible for us to make a living here. There are pensions and restitution payments. These are enough to take care of us here. Some do better. Like Rubinstein.'

Rubinstein was a short, slender, bitter man. His narrow face was lit up by glaring brown eyes. He was combative, derisory. He had been born in Warsaw, spent time in Auschwitz, then in Foehrenwald. Finally he had emigrated to Israel, where he had stayed for twelve years, and now he was back in Munich.

'Why did I come back? A stupid question. To make a living. Is there any other reason for a Jew to live in Germany? What do I do here? I drive a taxi. My own taxi.

'I couldn't get a job driving a taxi in Israel. The taxi business is government controlled there and all the drivers belong to Mapai (the governing party). I was too radical for the Mapai, so I could not get a taxi to drive. I had a wife and three daughters. Was I supposed to let them suffer for my politics?

'Israel . . .' His hands tightened about his glass. 'All the time I was in the camps, I dreamed of going to Israel. What else was there to dream about? My family were all dead. Murdered. My friends were all dead. There was only Israel about which to dream. And finally I was there and it was different from my dreams.

'You think it was easy to return to Germany?' His voice

cracked and he fought for control of it. He took a long swallow of his tea before he spoke again. 'It was like coming back to hell,' he said. 'Hell. And yet Germany provides easier entry for Jews than other countries do. Of course, that is because no other country owes so much to the Jews. So they really are giving us nothing, only returning part of what they took from us.

'Every day I drive Germans in my taxi. There are two kinds, those too young to have been Nazis and those who got fat on anti-Semitism and Jewish bodies and plunder from the Jews. Sometimes I hear them talk about it and I want to choke them with my bare hands. I have told this to some of them and watched the fright come into their eyes. And the hate. Believe me, there are many who still hate us.

'But I make a good living, enough for my family. I am able to save. When I have saved enough, I will return with my family to Israel. There my daughters can be Jews. It is impossible for them to be Jews here.

'There are many returnees from Israel here and they have all come back for the same reason. To earn and save German money and go back with it to Israel. There is no reason why we should be ashamed of this. It is a small repayment for Auschwitz and the gassings and shootings and starvation.

'Do you think that any Jew wants to live in Germany? Do you think any Jew really does live in Germany? If you do, you are a fool. Now, leave me alone.'

Rubenstein stomped away, throwing one last, glaring look over his shoulder.

'He feels guilty,' Cohn said. 'We all feel guilty. We tell ourselves that things have changed and that it is no crime to live in Germany now, but we do not believe even ourselves. The Nazis are gone, except maybe in the NPD, but the feeling against Jews is here. My son has a Christian friend who received his notice to serve in the army. And he said to my son – to my son – "I won't serve. I hear they let Jews be officers now."

'Soon I will be sending my two children away to Israel. It will be hard for their mother and me, but it would be harder for us if they stayed here. Foehrenwald is too close. Ask Eisenberg?'

Zolman Eisenberg looked up at the sound of his name. He was a heavy-set man, with deep-set yellowed eyes. They were abstracted, distant, eyes that looked beyond me even as we were introduced. His short beard was a yellow-grey.

He had been born in Minsk. When the Germans captured it, he had a wife and three children, a mother, two brothers and one sister. 'And cousins and aunts and uncles,' he said. 'We were a family,' he said.

But then the Nazis came and the Jews of Minsk were slaughtered or sent away. 'And after the war,' Eisenberg said, 'there was no one, nothing.' The yellowed eyes stared into the distance. 'I told myself that there had to be someone. That, if I had survived, they must have survived also. I began my search in Foehrenwald. I asked the Red Cross. I asked the Joint Distribution Committee. I asked the Americans. Every time I meet a stranger who was in Auschwitz or Belsen or Natzweiler (the famous medical experiment camp), I ask. Someone has to know.

'That is why I stay in Germany. Because I am sure that some day some one will be able to tell me. They cannot all be gone. God could not have been so cruel. You believe that, don't you?' He besought the far distance with his voice and his eyes.

'I have nothing to do with the Germans. They tell me that the young are different, but I know none of the young. I know only those who came to Minsk, only those who were in the camps. I tell myself there is no need to be afraid of the Germans for what can they do except kill me? I have suffered worse than death. But I stay because it is only in Germany that I can learn about my family. Otherwise, I would not be here. This is still a graveyard where a Jew is forced to dig his own grave.'

For the first time he focused his eyes on me. 'Ask for me,' he said. 'Ask for me wherever you go. About the family of Zolman Eisenberg of Minsk.' He got up from his chair and walked away. His eyes were searching the distance again.

A man had picked up the English newspaper I had laid down. But he had not read it. Instead, he had listened as Eisenberg had been talking. Now he said in English, 'See. I am an American, like you.' He reached into his pocket and took out a blue passport. 'I have been away to Israel and then came back. Then I went to the United States and now I am back.'

His name was Samuel Cradinsky. He was forty-six and had been born in Lomza, Poland.

'In 1940, when they took my family away, I escaped. They

did not find me until 1943 and then I was sent to Oswiescim (Auschwitz). After I was liberated, I came to Germany. I was in Foehrenwald for a time but I found work. I made some money and went to Israel. I fought in the 1956 war. Then I came back to Germany.

'I felt unclean here. I knew it was not right for me to be here. It wasn't anything that the Germans did. It was just that I was in Germany. I got my American visa and went to the United States. I made good money in the United States. I became an American citizen.' His hand slid over his passport. 'It is good to be an American. I bought a car. I had a nice apartment. Why, then, did I come back here?'

He looked about the room. 'To remind myself. To remember. Americans do not know about Oswiescim. They do not know about Foehrenwald. And I found that I was forgetting too. So six months ago, I sold my car and quit my job. I gave up my apartment. And I came back here to Munich. I have enough money to last me some time longer. And all I do is come here and sit and talk to people like me.

'I know that I am living off my own vomit. This is no country for a Jew. It will never be a country for a Jew. We know this, so we exile ourselves to this restaurant, to our locked rooms, to the gemeinde. We exist because we have each other and our memories that we can bear because we can share them.

'Soon I will go back to the United States. I can live a life there. Here, I live a past. Maybe I will find the strength never to return again.'

He put his passport back in his pocket.

A customer came in, nodded to Cohn and sat down wearily at the next table. His name was Simon Potocki. Cohn said that he was a Lithuanian, a former inmate of Belsen and Foehrenwald. He was a baker, working in a shop close by. His hair was snow-white. I would have guessed his age as more than sixty. I found out that he was forty-one.

Why had someone so young – he was just past twenty when the war ended – stayed on in Germany?

'At first,' Potocki said, 'it was because I was looking for any of my family who might have survived. There had been five children, my parents, aunts and uncles, cousins. I could not believe that they were all dead. Even now I cannot believe it, though

I know that it is so. Then I got a job. I kept thinking I would stay only a short time and then leave for Israel.

'But after I started working, I could not find the strength to leave. Something had happened to me in the camps. I had lost the power of decision, the ability to act. If someone had come to me and said, "Potocki, here is your ticket, you are going to Israel," I would have gone happily. But I could not do it by myself.'

He smiled a grotesque smile. 'Time passed. I had a place to live. I had work. I lived in a world that was half-dreams. I talked with the living and with the dead. Oh, yes, I talked with the dead. I still do. With my mother and father and brothers and sisters. They say, "Mourn for us. We are dead but you are still alive." And I add to myself, that I am alive in Germany.

'And the horrible thing is that I have accepted this. I live here. I speak the language. I deal with Germans each day. I should hate them, but do you know something? I have lost even the power to hate. That was also destroyed in Belsen. All that was left me was a body, a shell.'

A waiter brought him a plate of soup and he took a mouthful. 'I go from day to day,' he said, 'and that is all. I have not married. I ask nothing. I want nothing. I am not even sure that I want to keep on living, but to end my life would force me to make a decision and I cannot do that.' He went back to his soup.

Cohn said, 'There is no hope for the Jews in this country. Our only future lies in the cemeteries. Not even the richest of us can buy anything else.'

18. *The Rich*

It was part of the Nazi mythology that all Jews were rich. This was as far from the facts as other parts of Nazi mythology. At the time that Hitler came into power, more than twenty per cent of all the Jews in Germany were receiving welfare payments, more than 31,000 in Berlin alone.

A large number of the prosperous Jews were able to escape from Germany. They lost wealth and property, but they saved their lives and avoided the extermination camps. It was the poorer Jews who fed the ovens. They had neither friends nor influence to enable them to get visas and passports. Or to bribe Nazi officials.

Very few of the prosperous Jews have returned to Germany. Erich Warburg is an exception. So are the banker, Feuchtwanger, in Munich and Rosenthal, the manufacturer whose porcelain has a world-wide reputation.

Today, the great majority of Jews in Germany are either lower or middle-class financially. Restitution money, pensions and social security support more than one-fourth of them. (Almost all of these are German Jews.)

There are fewer than 10,000 wage-earners among the Jews and more than 7000 of these are self-employed as small businessmen or as artisans or in the professions. Fewer than 400 are labourers. About 1000 are civil servants, employed in government offices or as teachers.

The East European Jews had no capital except the clothes on their backs and relief packages. They took any kind of work, went into any kind of business. Some of them got their start in the post-war black market.

Some have prospered more than others. Three who became quite wealthy were Arthur Brauner, the major film producer in

Germany, Emil Januscek, a clothing manufacturer, and a man who asked not to be identified by name who is now in the construction business in Munich.

Brauner is a Pole, Januscek a Czech, and the third man a Galician.

The German motion picture industry, which Hitler and Goebbels had converted into a propaganda machine, was a shambles when the war ended. There were no studies, no producers, no directors. The Allied Control Commission was alert to prevent the Nazis from gaining control of the medium. For a short time there was no industry at all and then Arthur Brauner emerged as the new titan in the field.

Brauner is forty-eight, balding, dark, dynamic, controversial. He is a pacer, unable to sit quietly in a chair for more than a moment. Words cascade from him. He talks volubly, but as much to conceal his thoughts as to reveal them. He has a highly developed sense of self-protection.

He lives on Koenigsalles, in one of the finest residential districts in Berlin. Brauner quickly tells visitors that it was once the home of the Mendelssohn family and that a grandson of the Kaiser lived only a few doors away.

He is a mixture of vanity and ingenuousness.

Both he and his wife are deeply involved in the Jewish community of Berlin. They have four children, the oldest a boy of twenty, the youngest a girl who has just had her first birthday. 'I am a father, a husband, a Jew,' Brauner said. 'That is the way to describe me. I am very conscious of my Jewishness. It motivates my life. Even during the worst times, I made up my mind that some day I would tell the world what it was like to be a Jew.

'It was then that I decided that I would make motion pictures.'

This is a deep and revealing insight into Brauner's character. During those 'worst times,' he was a fugitive in Poland, barely twenty, living off the land. His chances of survival were tenuous. His knowledge of motion pictures was limited to his having seen a few. Yes, he insists, that while living like a hunted animal, running from enemies who were all about him, he determined what his future would hold, determined that he would have a future. To him, capture and death were not inevitable, but impossible.

'Once two soldiers caught me as I was preparing to swim a

river. I knocked one down and evaded the other. I ran into the forest and stayed hidden for twelve hours while they searched for me. Then my chance came and I jumped into the river and swam across. For six years I outwitted the Gestapo and the German Army. I outwitted the Ukrainians, who hated the Jews even more than the Germans did. I never had any doubts. I was always certain that I would survive.'

Shortly after the war ended, Brauner appeared in Berlin. There was no problem about his being allowed to go into the movie business, but there has always been a mystery about where he obtained the capital. It has long been rumoured that during his flight he found a hidden Nazi horde and it was with this that he came to Berlin. Brauner ridicules this. He says that the money came from his parents.

'They were able to secrete some articles of value before the war. After they retrieved them. It was from selling these that I was able to finance myself.'

Why did Brauner come to Germany?

'I was going to make pictures,' he said. 'I knew that I couldn't go to Hollywood. There I would be laughed at. But there was no German movie industry. I had as good a chance as anyone. Besides, I had a deeper reason. I wanted revenge against the Germans. I wanted to show that they had not destroyed all the Jews. And I would force them to see what they had done to the Jews.'

Brauner, thus, was one of the very few East European Jews who deliberately chose to live in Germany. Even now he finds it hard to decide if altruism or self-interest motivated him more.

'I had a mission,' he said. 'Forty-six members of my family and sixty-two of my wife's family were killed by the Nazis. More than a hundred people! Just think of that. Today, when I look at my children, when I hear their voices, when I touch them, I get sick inside at the thought of what would have happened to them if they had been born twenty-five years earlier.

'I was determined that I would do something to keep alive the memory of the Nazi years. And, to be honest, I also had a driving ambition. I wanted to succeed. I wanted to be somebody.'

Success did not come to Brauner at once. His first picture was a propaganda picture – a message picture. It was well received by the critics but it found only a small audience. Its anti-Nazi message caused mob attacks on the theatres where it was played. Hoodlums broke the windows of those theatres, frightened away some who might want to go to see the picture.

'It proved that there were far more Nazis left than people would admit. It was evidence to me,' Brauner said, 'that the war was not over.'

The picture almost bankrupted Brauner. He found himself deeply in debt. 'I sold off some property. My wife and mother even sold their fur coats. I gambled everything that remained and made another picture, a musical comedy and that made me solvent again. In the years since, I have had more successes than failures.'

Brauner scorns the idea that he is a German. 'No Jews can be Germans. If we have a home, it is Israel. That is where our duty lies. That is where our love must go. It is our obligation to defend and aid Israel.'

The surviving members of Brauner's family are all in Israel. Brauner takes a patriarchal interest in them, helping them to set up businesses, assisting in the education of the young, providing money when money is needed.

He takes a cold-blooded view of anti-Semitism in Germany. 'I have received hundreds of threats and anonymous letters. It could be I am a target because I am one of the few identifiable Jews, but I know others who have been threatened and cursed. Rabbis. Businessmen. Any Jew.

'However, there was only one really difficult period. That was the terror that began about Christmas, 1959, when swastikas appeared all over Germany, when cemeteries were desecrated, when hooligans scrawled "Jude" on doors and walls and sidewalks. For a few days, even those of us who knew better, feared that we would see Storm Troopers again.

'About forty or fifty of us Jews in Berlin held a meeting to decide if we should stay or leave. We decided that we must stay. We would not be chased out. We would not allow a few hoodlums to do what Hitler and his gas ovens could not do — destroy Judaism in Germany. We were determined that this time we would fight.

'The German government and German public opinion put an end to that outbreak. But it confirmed what we felt; Nazism still remained in Germany. The hate was still there. And it remains. Far less of it among the young than among the old, but not all gone. Not so long, for example, as there can be an NPD which uses anti-Semitism to gain votes and power.'

(The NPD has launched a nation-wide boycott of Brauner's spectacular version of the Niebelungenlied. Not, the NPD declares, because Brauner is a Jew, but because he is not a German and has distorted one of the most holy of Teutonic myths. Brauner, the NPD newspaper charged, has 'debased our country and our gods.'

(The boycott has been effective. The picture has done badly.)

'This, as I said, is no country for Jews,' Brauner said, 'but Jews must remain here. We have to offer ourselves as hostages so that the Germans are prevented from burying the past. We must make ourselves known and felt.

'This falls on those of us who lived through the years of the great terror. The younger generation feels removed from it. Even my own son thinks of the past as something that belongs only to his mother and to me, not to him.

'I tell him that he must never forget what happened to the Jews. I tell him of the Warsaw ghetto, of the Ukrainian pogroms, of those who are dead. He has to know – every Jew has to know – that life was not always lived in a grand house on the Koenigstrasse, with cars and servants. It was lived in Auschwitz too. That there was a time when not candles, but Jews, burned on Friday nights.

'He has no right – none of us has the right – to live except as Jews. For what else were our lives created and saved?'

Brauner is a strange mixture. He is part zealot and part bookkeeper. He is truthful when he speaks of remaining in Germany because he wants to assert his Jewishness. But he is also there because he believes it the one country where he can continue to live his dream – to be an important motion picture producer.

The past weighs heavily upon him. The dead are always with him. But a large part of him is divorced both from the past and the dead. That is the part which drives him to make more pictures, make more money, flash his name large on the theatre screens.

It is these mixed parts – these mixed drives – that give him no peace.

Nor has the man from Galicia found peace. 'Call me Itzhak,' he said.

I encountered him in the dark, narrow hallway that serves as a waiting room in the office of the Jewish community in Munich. He and his wife were waiting to see Rabbi Lichtigfeld. He was a small man, slightly built, his face drawn, the skin stretched taut, almost to the tearing point, over his cheekbones.

His age? 'I've lived a thousand years,' he said, 'but I am forty-eight. I spent seven years in camps, five in Auschwitz and Buchenwald, two in D P camps. I lived a year in every day, so that I am not a thousand, but several thousand years old. I am a very old man.'

The rabbi came into the hallway and called Itzhak into his office. His wife's eyes followed him. 'He is a good man,' she said. 'We came here to give some money for Israel.' (This was during the Arab-Israeli crisis.) 'If we had sons, we would gladly give them.' She kept her eyes on the closed door.

While we waited for Itzhak to return, she talked a little about herself. She exhibited the tattooed concentration camp number. She had spent years as a prisoner. 'I want to forget,' she said. Her home had been in Lvov. She never wanted to see it again.

Itzhak rejoined us. 'The Rabbi said it was all right to talk to you. Come with me and I will tell you about myself.'

When we reached the street, a car was waiting outside, a young woman at the wheel. 'My daughter,' Itzhak said. He helped his wife into the car. 'Let us walk,' he said. 'I walk whenever I can. You would understand if you had ever been imprisoned, if you had ever known that one step too many, one step in the wrong direction, could mean your death.'

We walked for about a quarter mile and came to a site where an office building was under construction. The girders were up, the foundations had been laid. He pointed. 'That is mine. I am building it.' He threw me a sidelong glance. 'I am also building respectability. For a long time I was not respectable. I owned bars.'

Rabbi Lichtigfeld had talked to me about the bar owners. They troubled him because they reflected on the Jewish community. He had shown me a letter which had appeared in the most important Jewish newspaper. It had read:

'You probably cannot imagine how often Jews are being slandered and talked about because of these bars. People immediately generalize and apply it to all Jews ... I ask you, why are these places financed by Jewish capital and run by Jews?'

I told Itzhak about reading the letter.

His answer was half-bitter, half-ironic. 'I did not approve of Auschwitz. What in hell do I care about the Germans? Damn them.'

We stopped at a restaurant and went in for coffee. Itzhak looked out the big window. 'You drive out that street,' he said, 'and you get to Dachau. Beyond Dachau is a fine picnic place. You see Germans, stuffed with sausage, drive past Dachau every Sunday on their way to eat more sausage.

'When I was liberated, I prayed to get out of Germany. I wanted to go anywhere, but I was too sick. We were the ones who remained. The discards. The years in the camps had rotted our guts, weakened our hearts, spotted our lungs. For years we had been starved and beaten and taunted with the ovens. Our lives had been spent thinking, fighting, cheating to stay alive. Each day was a contest between us and the furnaces.

'And always there were the Germans, guarding us, beating us, breaking our spirits and our arms and legs. And promising us that it would not be long before they killed us. Now I am supposed to seek their approval.'

He looked at the table next to ours. A group of middle-aged German women were having a mid-afternoon snack. Their plates were piled with pastry. Each was a contented looking *hausfrau*.

'I wonder,' Itzhak said, 'where they were during the war? My wife was a labourer at Krupp's. She was a young girl, barely fourteen, when she was taken there. She was an old woman of eighteen when the war ended. She cannot bear to speak of that time. No one can stop her thinking of it.

'Now the Germans smile at us and give money to rebuild the synagogues they burned and pillaged. The government says it is against the law to be anti-Semitic and sends a school teacher to jail for breaking that law. It sends money to Israel.

'They want us to believe that the German people are changed inside. To believe that a people who enjoyed hurting and maiming and killing are changed because there is a law that says be nice to the Jews. But that law does not change what happened to us, what we learned. But how many Germans really care what happened to us?

'I am not talking of those who died. The dead are beyond help and revenge. Besides, the Jews are not really vengeful people. I speak of those who survived, like me. Now they want to deny us the life they forced upon us.' His eyes swept the long street. Nothing – no one – escaped them.

'How do you think people like me survived? We were intelligent and cunning and lucky. We cheated and lied and schemed. We did not survive because of morality. Morality was a luxury and you paid for it with your life. We paid with everything else, but we saved our lives. Nothing more. Sick and penniless, but alive.'

He lifted his coffee cup and stared at it. 'Who could have believed that the time would come when I would have real coffee with cream? That I would have a full stomach. That I could stand up in Germany and say, "I am a Jew?" In the camps we had no dreams because our minds were as broken as our bodies.

'When we were liberated, our battle to survive was not over. The gas ovens were cold, but the grave-diggers were still working full time. Jews kept on dying. Death is death, in a furnace or a hospital bed. I was not going to die.

'I became involved in the black market. There were packages from the Joint (the Joint Distribution Committee), packages from UNRRA. There was coffee and cigarettes and canned food that the Americans gave us. And there were the Germans, begging for these as we had been begging for life only a short time before. We didn't put them in gas chambers. We sold them the food and the cigarettes. We didn't send them to slave labour camps; we just took their money. On balance, didn't they get the best of it?

'We dealt in contraband, but we were contraband ourselves. We were also illegal. And unwanted. Especially by the Germans. We were a reminder that they had lost. Sick, beaten and broken, we were the victors. Everyone of us was a knife sticking in the German heart. There were good Germans, but how could we tell the good from the bad? We had no experience with the good ones. We did not love our enemies; we hated them.'

He insisted on paying the bill. 'Believe me, the one thing I have is money. Let me use it.'

We walked some more. Near the central railroad station we came to a show window filled with pictures of half-naked women. Juke box music came through an open door. A big sign advertised continuous entertainment from noon till dawn. 'This place is mine,' he said. 'I have four such bars, but I no longer run them. I have rented them on a concession basis.' He laughed. 'To good, Christian, Germans.'

A group of American soldiers were looking at the window display. 'I learned English,' he said, 'from boys like that. From the American and English soldiers. Of course they were our customers. People like me didn't want to speak to Germans, trade with Germans. I ran an honest place. I did not cheat.

'I have been condemned for running bars. Tell me, since when is it a crime to own a bar in Germany? The beer halls where Hitler and his men gathered to plan the destruction of the Jews are still open in Munich. No Jews ever owned them. There is not a single Jewish bar owner on the Reeperbahn in Hamburg, but no one mentions that. No it is only we East European Jews who are at fault.

'What did they want us to do? I did not need a college degree to open a bar. I did not need much money; just what I made in the black market. I suppose I am not a very nice fellow. A nice fellow would have opened a hotel like the Four Seasons or the Continental and he would have gained the respect of the Germans.

'He could have such good Germans as Von Thadden of the NPD as a guest. Or those fine Germans who grew rich under the Nazis by using Jewish slave labour. Or those smart Germans who put their money in numbered bank accounts in Switzerland and are now spending it while the money deposited by murdered Jews still sits in those banks.' He spat. 'I like it better this way.'

We passed some other bars. 'Most of them are now run by Germans,' he said. 'We were not proud of our business, so as soon as we could we left it. Not to gain the approval of the Germans, but as a mark that we had passed beyond owning bars. And, to be truthful, because most of us had grown well-to-do. But the main reason was our children.

'It is hard to explain to them what happened to us. Hard to tell them. We want to save them the pain we suffered. But, at the same time, we are cheating them a little. Still, my daughter is now able to say that her father is in the construction business, that he owns a fine office building.'

He swung his head toward me, his eyes blazing. 'Tell me, is owning a bar worse than profiting from rendering human fat into soap? Is selling liquor less respectable than selling steel from a foundry where Jews were used as fuel?' Some of the fire went out. 'Or is it simply that owning a bar if you are a Jew from Galicia is disreputable? It is not the bar; it is the Jew.'

We waited for a traffic light to change and he looked into a shop window. 'I came out of the camp in rags,' he said. 'Today I have my suits made for me. I once sold single cigarettes and today I deal in hundreds of thousands of marks. It seems that things have gone well with me, eh? That Germany is a good country for a Jew? It is true; it is better than a ghetto. But we are in Germany and none of us is part of Germany.

'How can we trust them? It has all been too easy. Press a button, and the Germans hate the Jews. Press another button, and they love the Jews. But people are not buttons. I speak boldly, but I am not really brave. Down deep, there is fear. A part of me is still behind the barbed wire, for Germany is still a camp for the Jews. The difference is that the cruel guards have had their orders changed. Today, they are told to be kind.'

He drew a long breath. 'Let me tell you something. Each night I pray to God for forgiveness because I am here. I cannot forgive myself.'

Nor can Emil Januscek find peace. He is a heavy-set, slow-speaking, introspective. An invisible weight appears to make him bend; he is never without this load.

Januscek is in the clothing business and the business has brought him wealth. His firm has a luxurious office and a vast showroom in a modern, post-war building on Berlin's Hardenbergstrasse. His private suite is luxurious, but furnished with taste. As is the board room into which it leads, with its large leather chairs and great, long oak table.

Januscek is an edgy man. He chain smokes, drinks dozens of cups of coffee during the day. It is as if he must tauten a spring within himself in order to relax. His face is seamed and his eyes have the wariness that I learned to recognize as the brand of the concentration camps. He spent fifty-seven months in Dachau and Auschwitz. 'Then,' he said, 'I was liberated. That is a false word because none of us has ever really been free again.'

He was born in a part of Czecho-Slavakia which became German and is now Russian. This does not matter to him. 'People – Jews – like me,' he said, 'are part of no country.'

He is in Germany because he could not get a visa to leave it. 'Just before the war ended,' he said, 'I saw an opportunity to escape. I got out of the camp and thought that I had made it until I ran into a group of S S men. They had been at the camp and they, too, knew that the war was lost, so they had changed into civilian clothes and were trying to go underground.

'One of them recognized me and knew that I had recognized him. So the group opened fire on me. They left me for dead. I almost was. I was found and removed to a hospital. I was there for months and when I was released the doctors certified me as eighty-five per cent disabled. Today it has been reduced to seventy-five per cent. I am still not healthy enough to get an immigration visa.'

He lit a cigarette on the butt of the one he had been smoking. 'Those S S men shot me, knowing the war was lost. And then other Germans moved me to a hospital. How can one understand the Germans? One night they came into the barracks to take some of us to the ovens. I was one of the group, but a guard saw I was sick and called the camp doctor.

'I had typhoid. So, instead of killing me, they sent me to a hospital. I was treated well there. I was cured. Then I was returned to the camp. Did the Germans want to kill only healthy Jews? Was that why every other member of my family was killed? We were a healthy family, healthy enough to die. All twenty-nine of them.'

He told the story of the immediate post-war days that others had told.

'There were many like me. We had nothing. Yet none of us ever thought of suicide. In a normal world, broken people like us might have considered it. But we knew that all we had was life and we were determined to cling to it. Life, the idea of life, dominated us. We wanted to assert it, to pass it on.

'I wanted to marry and have children. I wanted to show that this Jew was indestructible, because he could pass on his seed.'

He met a woman and fell in love with her. She was a Christian Scientist. (Christian Scientists, like Jews, were anathema to Hitler. They were imprisoned, tortured, killed, sent to labour camps.) 'I was deeply, profoundly, Jewish, desperately conscious of being a Jew. It gave meaning to the years of torture. I explained this to my wife before we married. She understood and converted to Judaism.

'We have had only one child, a son. When he was born, people told us that we should not have him circumcised in case the Nazis came back, in case Germany turned against the Jews again. My wife and I told them there could be no better reason. Our son had to be marked as a Jew. It was imperative to us.'

Januscek picked up a picture of a boy in a skull cap, wearing a prayer shawl. 'His Bar Mitzvah picture. He knows what it means to be a Jew. He was the only Jewish student in his school and one day he came home with his face battered. At first he would not talk about it, but finally did. A boy who was four years older and much bigger, had attacked the Jews, mocked them. My son had fought him. He told me, "I had to, Papa." Of course, he had to.

'We have all encountered a few instances of anti-Semitism, but they are rare. But none of us knows how many there are like that boy in my son's school, who feel as he does but do not give voice to their feelings. But I do not let that dominate my life. However, this remains Germany and it is an alien country to me because I am a Jew. I am also a Czech, but that would not matter if I were not also a Jew. It is being Jewish which separates me from the Germans. And I am still separate after twenty-two years.'

During those years, Januscek's business has grown large and important. He manufactures women's dresses and raincoats, both for domestic sale and for export.

'I am rich,' he said. 'Sometimes I ask myself if what I have is worth the price I have paid. Once I was negotiating a deal in New York and all that remained was to sign the papers.

It was then that the man with the pen in his hand asked me where I lived. I told him it was Germany.

'He threw the pen away. He said, "Even if I could make a million dollars on this deal, I would not sign. Not one penny of mine will go to Germany." He pulled up his sleeve and I saw the number on his wrist. How could I say that he was wrong?

'There have been times when I have lied about where I lived. I've said it was Austria or Switzerland because I could not bring myself to say that I lived in Germany. The Germans butchered my parents and my family. And I live among the butchers.

'Tell me, have I sold my character, my decency, for money? Have I allowed myself to be bought? That thought haunts me. It is the reason I refuse to take one penny of restitution from the German government. They keep sending me papers. They tell me that there is money due me for my years in the camps, for my wounds, for my disability.

'But I will not sign a paper. I have written to tell them to give the money to charity, to send it to Israel, to use it for the poor. And the answer is always that, before anything can be done with that money, I must sign for it. They want a receipt. I will not give it to them. Never.

'Somewhere the murderers of my family, of the millions of others, still live. As long as I refuse to sign, they will not be free of guilt.'

His hand shook as he lit another cigarette. 'And yet, I wonder if they have not already won. I am here.'

For Januscek there are two Germanys, the one official and the other made up of the German people. Toward the first he bears no malice nor ill will. 'I have been to Austria, to East Germany, to other countries. None of them has made the effort that West Germany has to compensate for the past. None of them has admitted responsibility. Here, restitution has been attempted. Israel has been given indemnities. There are special laws to protect the Jews.

'But the government, is impersonal, a machine. It has no emotions, only policies. It is people who have emotions, and the German people still have not proven themselves. There is still hate.

'You see it in the N P D. It preaches hate. Hate of the Jews, hate of Israel, hate of democracy. And there are those who would use that hate. Did you read where the head of the farm owners' association – the whole German agriculture – has threatened to merge his organization with the N P D because he wants a higher farm subsidy than the government is allowing? Hitler, too, promised more money to the farmers.

'Do you wonder that all Jews remain afraid here? The German people have no faith in themselves. If hardship comes, they will turn to another Fuehrer. And the new Fuehrer will look for scapegoats again and, of course, he will find the Jews.

'Yes, I suppose I have corrupted myself by staying here. All of us who are here have done this to ourselves. But it is not too late. Not too late yet. If I do not leave Germany, I will make certain that my son does. I tell you this, I will not allow him to live in Germany.

'If Germany gets a new Fuehrer, he will not have young Jews with which to stoke his fires.'

Brauner, Itzhak and Januscek. They have all become wealthy in Germany. They produce pictures and manufacture clothing. Two stayed in Germany after the war because no one else would accept them. The third because he had a dream of revenge.

All three are haunted by the fear that only Januscek was able to put into words – the fear that they had corrupted themselves, sold out for money. And all three console themselves that if they have corrupted themselves, it has been for the sake of their children and that these children will atone for them.

What are the children like?

19. *The Inheritors*

THE Nazis, systematically and with premeditation, immolated a generation of Jews. These were sacrificed in the name of both Nazi ideology and Nazi economics.

Extermination of the Jews was, of course, Nazi creed, but, at the same time, the extermination had to be carried out to the greater glory of the Third Reich. Jews who could work, who could produce, were kept alive so long as they had any economic value. But children had none. And so they were killed.

When the war ended, there were fewer than a hundred Jews under the age of twenty in Germany. Nearly all of these had been *illegalen*. In some instances, Christian families had taken them as infants and brought them up as their own children.

As both Emil Januscek and Ernest Landau told, the men who were freed from the death camps had an urge to propagate, to create fresh life. They had to assert that some vitality remained in their shrivelled bodies. Time has shown that their physical and physiological abilities were not equal to that psychic drive.

The Jewish birth rate in Germany is half that of the rest of the country. Only 4500 Jewish children who have been born in Germany since the end of the World War are in the Federal Republic!

They are dispersed among more than 25,000,000 Germans who have been born in that same period.

Only a few of these children are of German Jewish background. The primary reason for this is that nearly all the German Jews were past the age of bearing and raising children. There are exceptions, Jochanin Hoch and Hans Rosenthal, for example, but both married non-Jewish women.

It is the East Europeans who have had the children, the youngsters whom their fathers so proudly introduce as 'my

Kaddish'. As those who will pray for their parents when those parents die. And, if there is to be a continuing Jewry in Germany, these few thousand children will have to create it. They will have to stay in Germany, marry in their faith, and raise their children in that faith.

The Jews have always cherished their children, but never more than is the case in Germany today. A large part of Jewish communal funds is devoted to the young. There are kindergartens, religious schools, youth organizations and summer camps. And there is a continuing battle between the leaders of the various Jewish communities and proselyters from Israel for the future of these young.

The community leaders fight more with their heads than their hearts. They have a vested interest in seeing that the young remain in Germany. Some sincerely believe that this is important to Jewry. But I did not speak to a single local community leader who did not say that if he were young the chances were that he would be going to Israel.

It is an uneven battle. The Galinskis, Abusches and Singers bear the honourable wounds of the past. But it is the past. The young, exciting, zealous religious teachers and youth leaders who have come to Germany from Israel offer the promise of the future.

Hans Hochwald is one of these. Born in Italy, he studied in Switzerland and then went to Israel where he completed his education. He is multi-talented, speaking seven languages fluently, a graduate of both the Talmudic School in Switzerland and the School of Social Work in Israel. In addition, he is a graduate of a music school and a cantor.

There is fire in Hochwald. Dark, flashing-eyed, bearded, he is a young prophet, preaching that salvation today lies in Israel. 'My task,' he said, 'is to intensify Jewish consciousness. There is a constant danger of assimilation in Germany and I believe it is my duty to prevent this. Jews do not belong in Germany. They belong in Israel.'

Hochwald uses every means to inflence the young people of Munich to think in terms of emigration. And of their Jewish heritage. He encourages the study of Jewish history and law. He supervises religious instruction. He edits a 'young people's page' in the German-language newspaper. He teaches music and has formed choral groups. He encourages a drama society. And he even has coached a soccer team.

Because of the East European background of the young people, he feels his work is easier in Munich than it would be, for example, in Berlin. 'The East European Jews,' he said, 'are more orthodox. They have a far stronger religious feeling. . .'

He denies that he is anti-German. 'I am pro-Israel. I think in Jewish terms. I would work as hard to proselytise for Israel in the United States or in England. Jews belong in Israel. I know that the German government has made reparations to the Jews, but that is only a partial payment for what the Germans did to the Jews. I can never forget that while this is not Hitler's Germany, it is the Germany which produced Hitler.'

Hochwald said that his work is made easy for him because the young Jews feel no ties to Germany, are eager to leave Germany at the earliest opportunity. To prove it, he invited me to a meeting of the dramatic club which he had organized, a meeting which was devoted to a reading of the play, 'The Oppenheimer Trial'. (This was a dramatization of the hearing at which J. Robert Oppenheimer lost his security clearance.)

The group met in a ramshackle building at 13 Georgenstrasse which houses one of the Munich synagogues. (The building is in sharp contrast to the synagogues of other German cities, which are new, modern and shining.) The club room looked like an old class room, but instead of a desk, there was a long table about which twenty young people were gathered.

A huge blackboard was covered with stories and pictures of Israel. The Israeli flag was hung in the room. The young spoke as much Hebrew as German among themselves.

Of all these children and young people – their ages ranged from fifteen to twenty-one – not one was the child of two German Jews. Three, however, had a single German-Jewish parent. All the others were children of East Europeans.

They were bright, almost cocky. They paraded their attachment to Israel.

Hochwald had even been able to inculcate into these young people that touch of arrogance which is obvious in Sabras (Israeli-born Jews), an outward sign that they truly believed they were the chosen people. They stayed well within the bounds of politeness while we talked, but gave the impression that it was because they had been told to stay within those limits.

They suffered my questions. The first one asked was how many of them (all but two had been born in Germany) intended to remain in Germany. Not one would admit that he expected to stay after completing his (or her) education. Two, one of whom had been born in the United States, said they hoped to emigrate there. One boy intended to go to England. All the others said they would be going to Israel.

It was quickly evident that none of these youngsters felt any attachment to Germany. They were only there physically and thought it obvious that they owed no allegiance. During the evening, as they talked of their parents, of the past, it was in relation to Hitler's Germany, not the Federal Republic.

For nearly all of them, the country of allegiance was, and had to be, Israel. None of us was aware (this mass interview took place in late April, 1967) how soon that allegiance would be put to the test. For the record, three of this group, including one who had earlier opted for the United States, did go to Israel. Four others registered to go and were waiting for transportation when the war ended.

David Wassertein, twenty-one, a medical student, explained why he would leave as soon as he was a qualified physician. 'I'm not at home here. I don't feel safe here. It isn't a physical fear, but a psychological one. I'm not afraid of what the Germans might do. I'm afraid of what they did. The idea of Germany appals me.'

The others joined in agreement. They said this was no sudden decision, but one that all of them had long had. It explained their choice of studies. The courses they were taking included engineering, biology, chemistry, agronomy and business, as well as medicine. 'Israel,' said Jack Schiff, 'needs young, educated people. Well, Germany owes us an education. They're not doing us any favours, just paying off a debt.'

Sima Berkowitz, sixteen, pretty and intense, broke in. 'Don't you understand. We have no feeling about being born in Germany. That was an accident. If there had been no Hitler, we would have been born in other countries. Are we supposed to feel indebted to Hitler because our parents came here from Auschwitz and Dachau and Theresienstadt? Do we owe Germany any gratitude for that?'

Feder Abraham, nineteen, is an engineering student. He said,

G

'This just happens to be the country where we live. Not our country. We don't want to be part of Germany and the Germans don't want us. We know. We've grown up here. We're separated from the Germans with whom we go to school. There's a wall between us. In class we never get over the wall, just talk through it. Outside class they have their world and we have ours. Even in class, we are strangers.'

All of them agreed that the teaching of recent German history in the schools was deliberately slanted against telling the full story of the years between 1933 and 1945 and the fate of the Jews during that period. 'We know what happened,' Feder said, 'but the others don't. Our parents have told us about the camps and the tortures and the deaths, but their parents tell them nothing. And the books and teachers don't tell the truth either.'

(In Bavaria, a textbook that is in use is *Aus der Deutschen Vergangenheit – About the German past*. It devotes seven lines to the treatment and persecution of the Jews and then adds, 'hundreds of thousands of the imprisoned Jews lost their lives.')

There is, the young people said, little active anti-Semitism. 'They just treat us like specimens in a zoology class,' Feder said. 'They are neutral about us.'

David said, 'Ten years ago there was more anti-Semitism. When I first started going to school, some of the students called me "that Jew". It doesn't happen now, but somehow I feel they still think of me as "that Jew". I have tried, but I cannot trust them. I keep waiting for an attack because I am a Jew.'

Didn't they feel that if they left – if all the young Jews emigrated from Germany – that it would be a victory for Hitler? That he would have succeeded in driving all Jews from Germany?

Gisela Strauss, almost eighteen, answered for the group, 'Do you mean that Hitler should force us to stay here? That would be no victory for us, but for him. The real victory is to get what we can from Germany and then use that knowledge to go to Israel and make Israel stronger. Hitler said he would destroy all Jews, but Israel is the answer to that. None of us will stay here as hostages.'

Did they really mean all these things? Would they leave the ease and comfort of their lives for the harsh, wearing, difficult life of Israel? Weren't they romanticizing? Weren't they reacting to the proselyting abilities of Hochwald?

They reacted with scorn. Jack Schiff said, 'I have a ten-year-old sister. She reads everything she can about Israel. Every time there is a television programme about Israel, she watches it with tears in her eyes. This is what we believe, what we have been taught. My sister does not even know the cantor.'

A pretty, dark-haired girl who had come in late, said, 'You're an American. You don't understand about us. You never were awakened in the middle of the night by your parents screaming in their dreams. You don't have to look at the concentration camp numbers on their wrists. You don't have to listen to the weeping.

'I never had grandparents or uncles or aunts. They were all killed. By the Germans. Who says it could not happen again? Why should we stay here? What do we owe them?'

Her name was Eva Winter, she said later, and she was studying chemistry. Her father was German, her mother Austrian. 'But I am an Israeli. My parents want me to leave here. They tell me it would be a sin if I stayed.'

A man who had come in during the discussion (he was Jack Schiff's father, I learned) spoke for the first time. 'It is a sin even for the parents,' he said.

His son rushed to his defence. 'You had no choice,' he said. 'You were in the hospital for a time and then in a D P camp.' He turned on me. 'You Americans don't understand. You were safe and free. The war hardly touched you. It was a terrible thing, but it was happening to someone else. You have no right to judge us.'

The others nodded their agreement. I was an outsider. I had no right to make a judgment.

As if this was a signal, Hochwald suggested that they go on with the reading of the play, the business of the night. When the reading was finished, David Wasserstein said to me, 'Is it true that this happened to Oppenheimer because he was a Jew?'

I pointed out that both Lewis Strauss and Edward Teller, who had pressed the fight to revoke Oppenheimer's security clearance were Jews.

'You get so,' David said, 'that you think that anything bad that happens to a Jew is a sign of anti-Semitism. You can't help it here in Germany.'

Did this, I asked, mean that he believed even the young were anti-Semitic in Germany?

The others joined him in saying that they didn't know. 'We can only feel,' Eva said. 'None of us has Christian friends. None of us knows a Christian well enough to ask him, to really understand how he thinks. If you want the answer to your question, why don't you talk with Christians?'

Hochwald suggested that they conclude the evening by singing a Hebrew song. In a moment, they had forgotten all about me, were singing with bright, lilting notes. They were in a world that excluded me, that excluded everyone but themselves.

The meeting then broke up. I talked a moment with Hochwald. I asked him if he didn't feel that he was limiting the future for these young people? If he would not be helping them adjust better if he allowed them to make peace with the world in which they lived?

'It's not a world,' he said, 'in which they have a part. They can't ever fit into Germany. I'm not talking about the past; I'm talking of now. Even those Germans with the best will in the world would be happier if there were no Jews in Germany, no reminders. The Jews are the albatross they're wearing. Can't you see that?'

'Even the young?' I asked.

'Even the young,' he said. 'You'll find that out.'

It was only a few days later that I had the chance. I met with a group of student leaders at the Free University of Berlin. The meeting had been arranged by Dean Hartwich and he brought me together with four young men, three of whom had spent some time in the United States, two as exchange students and the third on a working vacation.

Joachim Lenz, an economics major, had been in San Luis Obispo, California. Ekkehardt Wesner, also an economic major, in Bradenton, Florida. Harold Preuss, studying English and history, had been in Kingston, Tennessee. Christof Conrad, a third economics student, had been to Israel.

Anti-Semitism was an abstraction to all four. They even had difficulty defining it, finally agreeing that it was a combination of hating Jews and committing harmful acts against them. 'But why look into that in Germany?' Joachim asked. 'How can there be anti-Semitism in Germany when there are no Jews?'

'I do not believe,' Ekkehardt said, 'that I have ever met a Jew. If I did, I didn't know it.'

Hartwich slowly rolled up his sleeve. A tattooed concentration camp number was revealed. 'I suppose I'm a Jew,' he said. 'I had a Jewish parent.'

The young men needed an instant to adjust. They had been born either during, or just after, World War II. It was the first time that any of them had been so close to the Hitler years. Even Christof, who had been to Israel. The Israelis were strangers; Hartwich was not.

Christof broke the silence. 'Then you can tell us. Are all the stories they tell about the camps true?'

'They're true,' Hartwich said. 'Weren't you taught that?'

The boys said they had been taught very little about the Hitler era and almost nothing of what had happened to the Jews or the full extent of the Nazi persecutions.

(All four of them had received their primary and secondary education by 1960. Until that date – until the violent outbreak of anti-Semitism that took place – all authorities agree that the German schools had played down education in this field.

(Norbert Muhlen, in his introduction to the study, *Education for Democracy,* wrote: 'The third term of Germany's democratic education set in with the 1960s – almost on the day, in fact, on which the decade began. Swastikas painted by hoodlums, morons, and other Nazis on Christmas Eve of 1959, triggered a shock of recognition among the German majority. In the months that followed they felt that the time had come for them to build barriers against the approach of a new catastrophe and the main barrier was to be political education. Since that time, Germany has witnessed an impressive effort to build this barrier.' Muhlen wrote in 1961. The evidence that I have gathered questions how 'impressive' that effort has been.)

Harold said, 'There are newer, younger teachers now. I suppose they don't find it as hard to teach about the Nazi years as the older teachers. After all, many of my teachers were teaching under Hitler.'

Hartwich asked if any of the four saw any evidence of anti-Semitism, or knew of any anti-Semitism.

The quick answer was, 'No,' and then Ekkehardt said, 'Of course there is anti-Semitism in Lower Saxony where I come from.

It's among the older people and the conservatives. A couple of years ago my father accepted an invitation to go to Israel with a group of industrialists and many of his friends were shocked.'

Christof said quietly, 'My father was a Nazi. He was a member of the Motor S S, not the intelligence or police units. On his day off from the chemical factory, he had to serve as a chauffeur for the S S. He was put in prison for four years by the British for that. They didn't believe that he was just a chauffeur.'

Did Christof believe that?

'A boy has to believe his father, doesn't he? He has to trust and respect him. My father thought he was being a good, patriotic German. He followed orders he was given. I know he isn't anti-Semitic now. He knows I am pro-Israel. He approved when I went to Israel.'

'There is anti-Semitism in the United States,' Harold said. 'I met anti-Semites when I was in Tennessee. I read about the Birch Society and this American Nazi, Rockwell. I think there is less anti-Semitism in Germany than in any other country. And what there is, is individual, not organized.'

'In that case,' Hartwich asked, 'What about the N P D?'

'The N P D isn't anti-Semetic,' Joachim said. 'They don't preach doing harm to the Jews.'

'But they want to stop reparation payments and aid to Israel,' Hartwich said. 'They want an end to war-crimes trials. Aren't all those anti-Semitic?'

The boys considered that. Finally they agreed that such ideas were probably anti-Semitic. 'But,' Joachim said, 'The N P D isn't the National Socialist party. It doesn't preach imprisoning the Jews or killing them.'

'Neither did Hitler in the beginning,' Hartwich said. 'He preached nationalism and economic benefits and anti-Communism.'

Harold got the point. 'That's what the N P D talks about too. But nobody listens. There can't be more than thirty students here who belong to the N P D. There are that many Maoists.'

'The N P D,' Ekkehardt said. 'is just a group of old Nazis and expellees from the East. It doesn't have any policy or programme. They said they want to make it possible for German women to be free to walk the streets again. Does that mean they want to make all German women street walkers?'

This was apparently an 'in' joke at the University.

Christof said, 'I believe there are many more students interested in improving relations between Israel and Germany than in the N P D. That was why we went to Israel.'

'But some who went,' Ekkehardt said, 'weren't so interested after they came back. You know that.'

'Only a few,' Christof said. 'Some things happened. We found that the Israelis weren't ready to accept us. We know they have reasons for resenting Germany, but why should they resent us? We're a new generation. We didn't have anything to do with the persecutions.'

'And we're ashamed of them,' Harold said, 'but we don't feel personal guilt about those things. How can we? We didn't do anything to the Jews. We were hardly born then. And none of us is anti-Semitic. Don't they realize that?'

Hartwich asked, 'How often do you think of those persecutions? How much influence do they have on you?'

'Not often,' Harold said. 'They're over and things are different now. Of course, when there is a television programme or somebody bears swastikas, we have to think of it.'

Joachim said, 'I suppose the truth is that we only think about it when it's forced on us or at a time like now. Mostly what happened is just part of history. It's not part of our lives.'

'But it's part of the lives of all the young people in Israel,' Christof said. "They remember it all the time and they talk about what happened to their families. I suppose the same thing is true of the Jews here. Everyone of them must still feel he's a victim.'

Joachim said, 'I'm wondering if there can't be a passive kind of anti-Semitism, not thinking about the Jews, not caring about them, being unaware that they exist. Is that what's happened to so many of us?'

That brought the others up short for a time. They looked to Hartwich for a cue, but he was staring down at his wrist. Finally Ekkehardt said, 'But we know we're not anti-Semitic.'

'What about –?' Christof asked. He explained this was one of the group who had gone to Israel. 'He bought something in Israel and told everyone he had been cheated. He said, "Well, we all know that's the way Jews do business," and a lot of people agreed with him. Let's admit it. There is still anti-

Semitism among us even if it doesn't show often. And this is at the Free University. No place in Germany is more liberal.'

'Now that I think of it,' Ekkehardt said, 'you hear a lot of talk like that in the country and the small towns. You don't pay any attention because the word "Jew" just slips out. You don't hear it, though, from the educated people.'

'But there are a lot more of the others,' Joachim said.

(Only 17 per cent of West Germans between the ages of fifteen and nineteen attend school full time. Only 6 per cent of working-class West Germans received higher education. The figures for the United States are 66 per cent and 30 per cent.)

'We can only speak for ourselves,' Ekkhardt said. 'Students in German universities are to the left of the general population. We are always in opposition. Later, of course, we change.'

Did Ekkhardt expect to change?

'Yes. Now I'm to the left of centre. When I get my degree and got into my father's business, I expect to move to the right. That is, in economics, for instance, not in respect to such things as anti-Semitism, though.'

'Then,' Hartwich said, 'you regard anti-Semitism as an instrument of politics?'

All four boys disagreed. Anti-Semitism was a moral issue. But they would not accept that it was a major issue. 'It's personal,' Christof said. 'It doesn't play a part in Germany today. It's a bogey-man that's left over from the past.'

'The truth is,' Joachim said, 'that it's the rest of the world that makes anti-Semitism an issue. Here in Germany, it hardly ever comes up. We're back where we started. There just aren't any Jews in Germany.'

I said that it seemed to me they were brushing off the question.

'But we aren't,' Christof said. 'We're just telling you the way it is. This matter of Jews and anti-Semitism isn't part of our daily lives. If we don't meet the issue, it's because the issue doesn't come up.'

The others quickly affirmed this. 'We don't have to run away,' Joachim said, 'because there's nothing to run away from. That's the simple truth. In our lives, there just aren't any Jews.'

Hartwich glanced down at his wrist and then rose. He had another appointment.

Christof stayed with me until a taxi arrived to take me back to my hotel. 'I've taken more interest in the Jews than the others,' he said. 'Maybe it's because of my father. But what we've told you are the facts. We really live in a world without Jews.'

And, in a sense, they do. I felt they were young men of good will. That they were decent and fair-minded. And honest. They were neither pleased nor unhappy about their Jew-less world. They just accepted it.

On the other side of Checkpoint Charlie, in East Berlin, I also found acceptance, but an acceptance of a different sort.

G*

20. *The East Germans*

WHEN the Germans surrendered, a large proportion of the Jews who were still alive were in territory which ultimately became the Soviet-held sector and later fell within the boundaries of the German People's Republic – East Germany.

As these survivors were liberated from the various camps, they began an exodus south and west, to the American, British and French sectors. They had a number of reasons. Many of them had been turned over to the S S and the Gestapo by Russians, Poles, Hungarians, Roumanians when the Nazis invaded those countries. They felt no gratitude to those who had sent them to servitude and death.

In addition, these Jews had a conviction that they would be better treated by the Western Powers. There would be more food, better shelter.

Russia made no attempt to halt this early exodus. The survivors were not valuable booty. Caring for them would be costly and onerous. The result was that only a few thousand Jews remained in the Russian sector. And, in the next few years, many of these made their way west.

In 1949, when actual division of Germany into two separate states took place, there were about 8000 Jews still in the east. Then, in the early 50's, when Stalin adopted Hitler's use of anti-Semitism as a political weapon, the head of the East German government, Walter Ulbricht, was quick to follow suit.

As a result, most of the Jews in East Germany sought to make their way to the West. There was a steady flow until the Berlin wall was built and the last relatively easy exit to freedom was closed.

Today, there are about 1500 Jews still in East Germany, more than a thousand of them in East Berlin. More than three-fourths of these Jews are over sixty. There are only seventy who are less than thirty. Such Arab countries as Egypt, Syria, Iraq, Lebanon, Algeria and Libya have more Jews than East Germany.

From a Hitlerian viewpoint, the blood stream of East Germany is almost pure.

Since its inception, East Germany has done very little for those Jewish refugees within its borders, and no more for the native Jews who were victims of the Nazis. Neither reparations nor restitution have been given them. Ulbricht and his government have explained that this would be discrimination against other victims of Nazism.

Today there is no known opposition to this policy. Earlier, however, there was. When it was announced, Paul Merker and Erich Jungmann, both Jews, were members of the Communist Party Central Committee. They spoke out. Shortly afterward they were both removed from office. A trial was held at which they were publicly disgraced and they were given prison sentences. Neither has been heard from since. They simply disappeared.

So, too, have Jews – as Jews – disappeared from all of East Germany except for a symbolic few. These few are displayed to the world as signs that East Germany does not practise religious discrimination.

It is for these Jews that synagogues are opened in East Berlin, in Dresden and in Leipzig. It is for these that *matzoth* are baked for Passover.

One year's vital statistics tell the story of the East German Jews. There were fifty-six deaths in East Berlin and eighteen in other communities. There were three births. And one Bar Mitzvah.

Ulbricht, like Tomas de Torquemada, gives the Jews a choice between apostasy or extinction. But, instead of the cross, he offers them the hammer and sickle.

And, like Torquemada, he gives rewards to those who choose the new faith. Albert Norden is propaganda minister for East Germany. Gerhardt Eisler is head of television and radio. Alexander Abusch, whose brother is director of the Jewish community in Munich, is an executive assistant to Ulbricht. Friedrich-Karl Kaul is chief legal apologist for the régime.

Arnold Zweig and Anna Seghers, now old and their writing days far behind them, are public monuments.

There is one rabbi for all of East Germany, Edward Singer, imported from Budapest in 1965 when Rabbi Martin Riesenburger died. He conducts services in East Berlin's Peace Temple which has room for 200 people, but is never filled.

There is a cantor in Leipzig.

There is a community organization in East Berlin, headed by Heinz Schenk.

The East German state supervise Jewish activities. And damns the Jews. All during the Arab-Israeli crisis in 1967, East German television, radio and newspapers poured out a hate-Israel vituperative. East Germany, like the Arabs, equated Israel with Nazi Germany and Moshe Dayan with Hitler. Norden and Eisler directed the propaganda.

In East Germany there are no Jewish schools, no Jewish religious education, no Jewish youth groups.

But, then, what need is there for these when twenty-five Jews die for each one who is born; when only one boy in all East Germany has a Bar Mitzvah?

This new Inquisition is far more effective than the old one.

I talked to one who has grown up during it, the tourist bus guide on the severely limited tour of a few selected East Berlin sights.

Ulrich (which is not his name) is in his middle twenties, dark, heavy-set, bushy-haired. He speaks a pedantic English, self-taught, he told me, by aid of an English grammar and a German-English dictionary. His first words to the load of tourists were a stilted greeting and an announcement that he, and the two soldiers standing beside him, must make a quick search to make certain that none of us had brought any newspapers, books, or other possible reactionary propaganda on board.

This speech, like his descriptive commentary later, came from him automatically, like a playback on a tape recorder.

We visited the beautiful Pergamom Museum, circled about the few rebuilt, renovated streets of East Berlin, heard priase of the German People's Republic and condemnation of West Germany and the United States. He pointed out, but did not comment on, the monster billboards that called for aid to North Vietnam.

His words had heat, but no fire.

Almost at the conclusion of the tour, we were driven to the Berolina Hotel, East Berlin's answer to West Berlin's Hilton

Hotel. All passengers on the bus tour are always taken to the hotel not only to admire it, but also to buy souvenirs or coffee or beer.

I asked Ulrich if he would have a beer with me and he accepted. The beer, he said, was very good. It was a copy of a Czech beer and approximated the original because the water of East Berlin was superior to that of West Berlin.

While we drank, he asked what I was doing in Germany and I told him. He made no comment. Then we talked about the theatre and I said I wanted to attend a performance of Brecht and asked if I would have any difficulty.

He assured me that all I needed to do was take the U-Bahn and come over, making sure I had my passport, obeyed the currency regulations, and didn't stay in East Berlin overnight. He got a copy of the weekly tourist guide and looked up the performances. I said I thought that I'd be coming back on Thursday. He remarked that he was free on Thursday and, if I wished, he would be happy to go to the theatre with me.

On the way back into the bus, he handed me his card. It had his telephone number. He did it out of sight of anyone else. He said it was not necessary to be surreptitious, but he preferred to be careful.

On Thursday, we had coffee after the theatre. He brought up the subject of my visit to Germany. How was it progressing? What was I learning? Then he said, 'My family used to be Jewish. My father and mother died in Auschwitz.'

A few minutes later we started to walk down Karl Marx Allee. 'I was one of the *illegalen*,' he said. 'My father was a Communist long before Hitler. I was hidden by one of his old comrades after they took my father and mother away. He said I was his son. Of course, he was not a Jew.'

'And you? Are you a Jew?'

'I do not believe in religion. Here, Communism is the only faith. No one has any other religion. Oh, there are still some Evangelicals (Protestants) and a few Catholics. But that is only among the older people. Just as it is with the Jews. I have never met a young Jew. Some young Christians, but never a young Jew.'

After some silence, he said, 'All Jews are Zionists. They are allied with the imperialist countries. Israel is a tool of the United

States.' He spoke now as he had on the bus, a tape-recorder playing back.

'The Nazis said all the Jews were Communists.'

He took one of my cigarettes, refusing the full package as he had a number of times before. 'The Jews are well-treated here,' he said. 'I know an old man. He is over seventy. He was a friend of my father's. He is a Jew, but no one bothers him. He would tell you that himself.'

'Could I talk to him?'

'I asked him if he would talk to you. He said he wanted to be left alone. He said he had no complaints. He gets free medical treatment. He has a small pension. He does not want any trouble.'

'Is he afraid to talk to me?'

Ulrich nodded slowly. 'Yes, he is afraid, but that doesn't mean he has any reason to be afraid. It's just that he's old. He was in Auschwitz. He was tortured. He lost his wife and three children. But it was the Nazis who did that to him, not the Communists. Here, no one mistreats the Jews.'

'Then why have they all left East Germany?'

'All right, they are afraid.' His emotion made his voice quaver. 'It is true you can't be a Jew in East Germany. (This was the only time he used this term.) Even if you want to be, you can't. That's the way it is. Don't ask me if it's right or wrong; how do I know? Anyway the Jews have all gone. But we don't have any Nazis here.' He waved his hand. 'They're all on the other side.

'My family is all dead. The Nazis killed them because they were Jews. No one bothers me. The Jews are just like everyone else here.'

'Only,' I said, 'they are not Jews.'

'What do I know about being Jewish? How should I know anything? I don't think I should see you again.' He grabbed my hand, shook it, and walked quickly away from me. I was left standing alone on Karl Marx Allee.

I called his home the next time I was in East Berlin. His wife said, 'Ulrich asked you please not to call him again. He said you would understand.'

On the next Friday night I went to the East Berlin synagogue. There were seventeen men there. All old. There was no rabbi. A bearded patriarch, with a thin, reedy voice conducted the services.

When I entered the room, every head turned toward me. There was a sudden stillness. The group appeared to coalesce, as if in self-defence. After a time, they took up the serious again. But something alien and frightening had come into the room. These old men were unable to speak the prayers that were second nature to them.

Finally the services ended. I had bought three prayer books in West Berlin because I had been told they were unobtainable in East Berlin. Now I offered them to the old man who had conducted the services. He drew away from me, from my extended hand.

'Please, please, leave us alone. You don't understand.' His eyes sparrowed about the room. 'They will ask where these came from. They will want to know how we got them, who gave them to us.' He took it for granted that I knew whom he meant by 'they'.

The others were gathered in a little knot. I could catch their eyes, but not hold them. There was no hostility, no unfriendliness in that quick meeting. Only fear.

I left the synagogue, the prayer books in my pocket. Outside, I darted looks in all directions. Their fear had been contagious. What if my coming here caused harm to seventeen old men?

I searched out an official of the Jewish community in East Berlin. He was polite and evasive. Like his opposites in West Germany, he also had statistics. 'We are not maltreated,' he said. 'We receive the same pensions as other victims of Nazism.'

(Actually, East Germany calls these pensions awards to 'fighters against' and 'persecutees of' fascism. The word 'Jew' is not mentioned.)

He would not compare the treatment of Jews in East Germany with their treatment in West Germany. 'That,' he said, 'is a matter of politics and I will not discuss politics.'

Nor would he, for the same reason, talk about the attitude of the East German Government toward Israel. No, all he would do was repeat the statistics. It was only as, frustrated, I prepared to go that he broke down only a little. 'My God,' he said, 'do you realize there is no new generation? In a little time, there will be none of us left. None of us.'

Gunther Grossmann said the same thing about the East German Jews. Grossmann in his mid-sixties, is an apathetic man, physically and mentally. His skin sags. His eyes are cached behind deep sockets. He served his time in Auschwitz. More than thirty members of his family, among them his wife, two children, his parents, two sisters and two brothers, were killed by the Nazis. One brother left Germany in the early Hitler period for Brazil, where he still lives. A familiar story, except that Grossmann was twice a victim.

Today, Grossmann owns a small shop in Frankfurt, but he has been there only a few years. After liberation, he went back to Leipzig, where he had been born and where his family had long been in the fur business.

'I wanted,' he said, 'to make some connection with the past. I wanted to belong somewhere. I felt like a piece of paper that had been blown about in the air. I wanted to drop to the earth, to attach myself to something solid. My home was gone. I had no family. I walked down streets I had known as a boy, but they were not the same streets.

'I looked at every person I passed, hoping it would belong to someone I knew. And when I saw others searching my face, I knew they were also Jews who had returned.

'That was all we had left. That we were Jews. It gave us identity. It was all that we had that gave us value. Not that we had shared so much, but that we were alike now. So we slowly formed a community. A Jewish community.

Grossmann remarried. His wife was a Polish Jewess who had survived Maidenack. 'I cried the first Friday night that she lit candles in our home. Home – it was only a room, but it was ours. It was a sign that we were re-entering humanity.' The first of their two children was born there.

'I tried to establish a business, but I found that no man can really have his own business in East Germany. It belongs – you belong – to the state. But I could have adjusted to that. When I was young, I was a Socialist. No, it was not politics which was my new burden. It was that I learned that they wanted not only your business, but you, to belong to the state.

'They told you what to do, what to think, what to believe. And there was no room there for a person to be a Jew.' His eyes came out of their hiding place and glittered.

'It was not the same thing as under the Nazis. No S S. No Auschwitz. But it was still persecution. Like the Nazis, they were determined to kill Judaism, to kill the Jew inside each of us. The Jews would be allowed to live, but not their religion. Jews could exist if they denied their existence as Jews, if they denied their God.

'They wanted no rabbis, no cantors, no synagogues, no Hebrew teachers. They suffered the old and broken to remain Jews, but they intended to bury their religion with them. And they denied our young and our strong the right to be Jews.

'So my wife and I knew we would have to run away again. Other Jews realized the same thing. We would not give to Ulbricht what we had denied to Hitler. In those days – it was more than ten years ago – it was still not too difficult. It had to be planned. One had to be careful.

'Finally we escaped, leaving behind much more than we could take with us, but we brought our Jewishness and the same candlesticks that my wife had used on that first Friday.'

In Frankfurt, he went back into the fur business. 'I make a living,' he said, 'but what is more important is that I can live here as a Jew. No one watches to see who enters a synagogue. No one reports that my children are getting a religious education and that my son had his Bar Mitzvah. The "jahrzeit" candles can burn in a window. Here, a Jew can be a Jew.'

Grossmann is a member of the Jewish community, participates in its affairs. He is active in raising money for Israel.

'It is better – far better – here than in East Germany,' he said, 'but it is still Germany. There are reminders. One day somebody wrote "Jude" on my window and painted swastikas on the walls. They said it was the act of some hooligan. But who taught that hooligan? Was it his father? Was it a teacher who had been important under the Nazis? Was it something he read in the *Soldatenzeitung*?

'The policeman behaved properly. The government behaves properly. West Germany accepts the right of each of us to be a Jew. It is far better than it is in East Germany. But all Jews remain strangers even here. I was born in Germany, but I am not a German Jew. There is no such person.'

He shook his head sadly. 'I should not have stayed in Germany. Not in either Germany. I know it now when it is too late. But at least here I can feel that I can live like a Jew. In the East, that was forbidden. There we still run and hide.'

And for the few remaining Jews in East Germany, life is a matter of running and hiding. Ulrich, the tour guide, has to run from himself and hide from the faith of his fathers. The old men in the synagogue and the community manager are fleeing, but fleeing like rats in a maze, unaware of what path to take and uncertain that there is a path which would lead even to temporary freedom.

An impersonal machine is at work in East Germany to extirpate every vestige of Judaism. It is not as bad as the Nazi racism, for it uses the velvet glove rather than the bayonet, but its end is the same. It is a sad compliment to the Jews that no totalitarianism, whether of the left or the right, feels it can afford their presence.

21. *The Officials*

THE Jews comprise only one-twentieth of one per cent of the West German population. They have a miniscule importance in any aspect of West German life (and none at all, of course, in East German) and no place is their importance less than it is in politics. And yet, the Jews – past, present and future – dominate much of the foreign and domestic policy of the country.

The symbol of this importance is the clause in the German Constitution which equates the preaching and advocacy of anti-Semitism with sedition and treason and makes it a Federal crime. Men are in prison for having committed it.

The Federal government, the *Laender* and West Berlin all have departments which deal with internal relations with the Jewish community and, in the first case, with foreign relations, which means relations not only with Israel, but with various Jewish groups in many foreign countries.

No wonder that Egon Bahr, spokesman for Willy Brandt, said, 'It is not that we have a Jewish problem, but that we have problems involving Jews.'

Bahr was one of a number of officials to whom I spoke. He said wryly, 'Whenever I am interviewed by a foreign journalist, I make sure that I have all my facts about the Jewish people readily available.' His hand went to the files on his desk.

Bahr is in his early forties, one of the first of the post-war generation to gain prominence in German public life. Short, heavy-set, dark complexioned, he looks more Latin than Teuton. He occupies a small, box-like office in the modern building which houses the Foreign Office. This lack of fustian is his hallmark.

Bahr chooses his words carefully, not for effectiveness, but for clarity. His mind is sharp and precise. 'The average German,' he said, 'regards the Jews as more abstraction than reality. The Jews are not physically present. Where they exist, they exist as a matter of conscience. The government, however, has a duty to deal with them, but as physical entities. History has made the Jews a governmental concern.'

He took a moment to formulate his next thought into words. Then he said, 'If there were not a single Jew in Germany, the government would still feel that it was its duty to make amends for the past. In a sense, this is what it is doing by its relations with Israel.'

Bahr is a Social Democrat and his party was the minority opposition from the founding of the Federal Republic until the formation of the Grand Coalition. Now, it is the junior partner in that coalition. Like Jews and Communists, Socialists were subject to Nazi persecutions. Some, like Willy Brandt, fled Germany. Others died in the camps.

'The question of the Jews,' Bahr said, 'is a sign of a deep split within the German people. Kurt Schumacher, leader of the SPD after the war, put the problem best. He said the German people must choose whether to regard themselves as having been liberated from Nazism or defeated in a war. His programme – the SPD programme – was predicated on the belief that Germany had been liberated.

'However, a majority of the people took the view that we had been defeated. This was because, I must admit, a large majority of the German people either were Nazis, supported them, or were willing to accept the Nazis because it was safe or profitable. Naturally they feel defeated. And a sign of their defeat is both the continued presence of Jews in Germany and the efforts of the government to make amends.

'It is this group – the defeated – who regard our efforts not as a matter of morality, but as a tribute extracted from them because they lost. It could be that this feeling will pass with time, but I do not know.

'Even though there are so few Jews, anti-Semitism does still exist. It exists both among the old Nazis and among some who were not Nazis. After all, if only the Nazis had been anti-Semites, they would not have been able to carry out their extermination policy. Much of the onus must fall on the *mitgangers* (fellow travellers).'

He shook his head thoughtfully. 'The terrible situation,' he said, 'is that the matter of the Jews has been allowed to become a political problem. All other aspects have been ignored. And yet, I suppose that the Jews are a political problem in the best sense of the word. I'll put it this way : the success of democracy in Germany can be judged by the ability to deal with all the issues raised by reason of the Jews. Whenever an anti-Semitic act takes place, it means a failure of democracy.

'If racism exists, it means our schools and teachers and institutions are not doing their jobs. What troubles me about the N P D is not that it exists, but that it attracts young people. And that these young people are vulnerable to demagogues and extremists. My God, didn't we learn any lesson from the past?'

He fingered some of his papers, glanced at some odd notes. 'We miss the Jews,' he said. 'They were always experimenters, innovators, catalysts. They are gone from Germany and it is a pity that they will not again be here in large numbers. It is a shame. A great shame.'

He was delivering a funeral eulogy.

And so did Richard Borchardt in his office a short distance away. Almost as soon as I entered, he took from his desk a cartoon that was printed in the *Suddeutscher Zeitung,* the influential Munich newspaper, some time ago. It showed two boys talking with each other. The first asked, 'Has your father had that serious talk with you yet?' and the other responded, 'Which one? The talk about the birds and the bees or the one about the Jews?'

Borchardt said, 'You see, we really are aware of this problem. Of course, the sad truth is that more young people get the facts about sex than they do about what happened to the Jews during the Hitler period.'

Borchardt is middle-aged, a cosmopolitan. He was attached to the Bonn Embassy in Washington for nine years before being recalled to Germany. 'Perspective outside Germany is different,' he said. 'The concentration and extermination camps are the symbols of Nazism to most Americans. Therefore, it does not surprise me when the first question an American asks is, "What about the Jews in Germany today?"

'It is right that they should ask it, but it throws the problems of the Federal Republic out of proportion. On the other hand, it has given the republic a chance to regain credibility with the rest of the world. Our treatment of the Jews has provided evidence of our good faith, proof that a fundamental change has taken place in Germany. Don't take my word alone for it. Ask the heads of the Jewish community.'

I said I had talked with many of them and that they agreed. But, I added, they had drawn a sharp distinction between the government and the mass of Germans.

'That is unhappily true,' Borchardt said. 'I would be dishonest if I said that everything the government has done for and because of the Jews has had the support of all – or even a majority – of our citizens. But the government accepts that it must act as surrogate for the Jews even when its actions are unpopular. An example was the extension of the statute of limitations on war-crimes trials. Surveys showed that more than two-thirds of the people were opposed.

'Just the same, the extension was voted by an overwhelming majority in the Reichstag.'

(The Reichstag vote found the S P D almost unanimous for extension, while a fairly large number of C D U members either voted against or abstained.)

'And, of course,' Borchardt said, 'our foreign relations played a part in the extension. The majority of world opinion was for the extension. We know that even after twenty years, the Federal Republic remains on trial.'

Borchardt, too, had his figures, records and statistics on hand. 'It is startling,' he said, 'to learn how many governmental problems relate to the Jews. These run from our diplomatic relations to the size of the budget.'

Then he pointed out that some of the government's efforts have never been publicized and cited the case of the women who had been used for medical experiments in Ravensbrueck. Many of these had been Polish and, after the war, Poland sought payment from East Germany for the medical care of those women who had survived. This was refused, but West Germany accepted the responsibility and paid the money asked.

'Under the law,' he said, 'we could not make any restitution to a country with which we did not have diplomatic relations. On the surface, this barred our making such payments to Poland. However, the government felt a deep responsibility and so a way was found to transfer the funds outside the usual diplomatic channels.'

(It was at Ravensbrueck that women prisoners were given gas gangrene wounds and subjected to bone grafting experiments without anaesthesia.)

Borchardt confessed that the problem of dealing with the Jews in Germany was more complex than that of dealing with Jewry. 'The farther we get from the Hitler period,' he said, 'the more difficult it is. Half of our population has little or no idea of what happened during those years. One of our most difficult tasks is imposing that knowledge on the young.

'We are handicapped because education is a local function, not a federal one. Each of the *laender* has complete control of its schools and what is taught in them. Some put a great deal more emphasis on the National Socialist era than others. By and large, however, it must be admitted that most of our teaching has been inadequate.

'One of the reasons, of course, is that there are still many teachers who served under the Nazis. Some feel reluctant, some ashamed and some guilty, when they must teach recent history. In West Berlin, a special flying-squad of teachers, all under thirty, was formed and sent from school to school just to teach this subject. But that was West Berlin. It hasn't been tried in the *laender*.'

When asked to guess about the future of the Jews in Germany, Borchardt threw up his hands. 'I can't guess about that. I can't be sure that there is any future for the Jews in Germany. That is a decision that they will have to make for themselves. It's obvious that there is not going to be any further return from other countries. The figures reveal that many young Jews leave Germany when they complete their educations. If this continues, there will be only a handful of Jews left.

'All the government can do – and it is doing it – is to make certain that the Jews are assured equal rights and equal protection of the laws. It will continue to seek to redress the wrongs of the past to the extent that that is possible. But, frankly, I think that when you look into future German-Jewish relations, it will be primarily external. It will involve governmental relations between the Federal Republic and Israel.'

He leaned back in his chair and took a long breath. 'For a

long time to come,' he said, 'I expect I will be asked these questions about the Jews. That is both right and inevitable. Many of us ask ourselves questions about the Jews. But the simple fact is that time is providing the answers, not the actions of men and governments.'

Very much the same words and concepts were expressed to me by Peter Herz in his office in the Berlin Rathaus (City Hall).

Herz, too, is one of Germany's younger politicians. He is volatile, dynamic, a spokesman both for West Berlin and for the new German democracy. He is a Christian, as is his family, but, he said, 'I had sufficient of a Jewish background for the Nazis to call me a Jew and send me to a work camp from which I was liberated by Americans in 1945. The effect of that imprisonment, of my suddenly finding myself included among Jews, has stayed with me.

'I think that it affected a great many persons with backgrounds like mine. Some even went so far as to reconvert to Judaism as a result. I would estimate that there are more than 1000 who have done so in Berlin now. And I have been told that there are 70,000 mixed families in this city.

'In the long run, I think that these mixed marriages and the children born from them, will be the only Jewishness that will remain in Germany. As time passes, the Jewish heritage will be continually diluted. Jews – as Jews – will grow fewer and fewer, I believe. This is not what we want for either Berlin or Germany, but it is what is happening.'

By reason of his position, Herz sometimes acts as an ombudsman, hearing citizens' complaints. Some of these complaints have involved anti-Semitic words and actions, but, he said, they have been relatively few and there has been no charge that a studied anti-Semitism was involved. 'These have been individual acts and words, very often the result of angry quarrels.

'On the other hand,' he went on, 'I must admit that there has been talk about the Jews in the East German government. People talk about Norden and Eisler. But you must remember that here in Berlin our life is dominated by the presence of the wall. And there are still persons left over from the Nazi period who equate Communists and Jews.'

Herz spread some of the inevitable papers about his desk. 'All these are concerned with the relationship of the West Berlin government and the Jews who are here. They disclose a sad story. They reveal that we are dealing with shadow, not with substance. We can educate. We can hold seminars and meetings. We can give lectures. We can have exhibitions of Jewish history and culture. But we do not have Jews. There is no promise that we will have them in the future.'

Then he began to discuss the N P D. He was one of the few Berliners with whom I talked who was markedly concerned about the party. 'Too many people talk about how few they are,' he said. 'What troubles me is that they exist at all. They spread their harmful propaganda. They arouse new hates and re-kindle old ones.

'There is no question but that anti-Semites have found a haven in the N P D. The party threatens not merely the Jews, but the future of Germany. After all, the few Jews who are here can, if they wish, seek security elsewhere. It would be a horrible thing if that became necessary, but they now have a place to go. I, for one, would not blame them if they did leave. I know they have suffered too much already.

'But we Germans would not have that choice. We would again be the victims of a new madness. It is up to us to meet this challenge and defeat it. You didn't have to be in a labour camp to learn what the N P D's programme promises Germany.'

A third man of good will, closer to the problems of the Jews than Borchardt and Bahr, but still apart from it. The three are fair examples of the official German attitude toward the Jews. All of them show concern, coupled with the accept-ance of the disappearance of the Jews from Germany. It was as if I had been talking to three surgeons in an autopsy room.

22. *The NPD*

THE surprising thing about the rise of the N P D is that it surprised no one. Nazi ideology was not immolated in the same bunker with Adolf Hitler. German supra-nationalism was a phoenix which did not even suffer singed feathers.

For twelve years legally, and another ten illegally, the National Socialist party had indoctrinated the German people. The effects of that indoctrination could not be erased with bombing or cannon shot. Nor could the conditioned character of the German people be reversed by either. Pavlov's dogs kept salivating after Pavlov.

Even as the war ended, two groups emerged to continue Hitler's work. One was composed of fanatical Nazis and former officers of the S S, the Gestapo, and the Bundeswehr. This group failed because it had no Ludendorff as a nucleus about whom to form. The second group was made up of Germans who had been expelled from these lands which Russia took from Germany to give to Poland. The expelles formed *landsmannschaften* (native sons' societies) and are still in existence.

When the Federal Republic came into being, the most vocal right wing party was that of the veterans. This was absorbed by the *Sozialistiche Reichspartei* which was banned in 1951 as an outright Nazi front. From the outlawed party emerged the *Deutsches Reichspartei* (D R P), which was able to elect five members to the first Federal Bundestag, one of them a handsome, personable aristocrat, still in his twenties, Adolf von Thadden. Because of his youth, he was nicknamed 'Bubi' (little boy), a name which he still bears, though his hair is greying and his face is beginning to line.

The D R P, unlike some seventy other right wing political groups, was never declared illegal. Instead, gutted by internal dissension, it must fell apart. From the time of its collapse until the emergence of the N P D, right wing Germans were politically gelded.

In 1964 the right gathered under a new banner that was strikingly similar to an old one. Where the Nazi emblem had been red, with a white circle enclosing a black swastika, the N P D flag altered it to enclose the blue letters, 'N P D', within the same circle. The similarity was, as Otto Hess, a veteran Nazi who joined that party in 1930, told me at an N P D meeting, 'not accidental'.

The Bonn government has estimated that among the party's founders there were about 3800 former S K P members and about 3500 veterans of the D R P. Another 1200 were 'old Nazis', party members before 1933.

Its ostensible leader was Fritz Thielen, a Bremen cement manufacturer. Stout, pedantic, with a wattled, grey-skinned face, he has a shadowy resemblance to Goering. He has always maintained that he was not a Nazi and relates that his father was imprisoned for removing swastika flags from the family factory.

Thielen provided the new party with a middle-class image. He gave it the appearance of bourgeois respectability. Solemn, almost dour, without charisma or flair, he gave the party a muted image. But this was his greatest weakness, for it prevented him from gaining a deep hold on the party members. Instead, it was von Thadden who emerged as the dominant public personality in the party.

In an attempt to keep control, Thielen broke with von Thadd in March, 1967, and had him expelled from the party. In a comic opera interlude that followed, von Thadden and his followers excommunicated Thielen. The second *putsch* succeeded. Von Thadden has been the leader of the party since.

What was surprising about these coups was that they should have been attempted at all. They came at a moment when the N P D was riding a wave of success. After waiting two years from the time of its founding, the N P D had finally entered the political lists and had done even better than its leaders had hoped.

Early in 1966, the N P D entered candidates in local Bavarian elections and received more than ten per cent of the vote. In such former Nazi strongholds as Nuremberg, Bayreuth and Erlangen it received almost one-fourth of the vote. This gave the party confidence enough to contest the various *laender* elections.

Under both Federal and *laender* law, members of the legislative bodies are elected on the basis of proportional representation. Any party receiving more than five per cent of the vote is entitled to have members seated.

The first two elections were in Hesse and Bavaria. The N P D went over the required minimum in both states and in Bavaria outpolled the Free Democratic Party and replaced that party in the *landtag* (state legislature).

The results were far better than those which the Nazis had attained in the same period of time. But success brought a basic difference between Thielen and von Thadden to a head. The former, whatever his concepts, was a moderate in word and action. Von Thadden was more radical. And he had the support of the party ideologues, like Hess.

If the N P D has no *Mein Kampf* as a bible, it does have its 'Twelve Principles of Policy'. Under Thielen, these were muted. Under von Thadden, they have been blared.

One of these principles has caused von Thadden some embarrassment. Defending himself against charges that his is a Nazi party, he has always reminded questioners that his half-sister was executed by Hitler for complicity in an anti-Nazi plot. On the other hand, one of the articles of faith declares that those who intrigued against Hitler were guilty of 'high treason'.

There is no certainty that von Thadden, who comes from an illustrious Pomeranian family, was ever a Nazi. However, there is no question but that he was a member of the Hitler Youth. But that I was assured by many anti-N P D Germans, was like a boy joining the Boy Scouts in the United States.

Von Thadden has developed a public personality. His voice is bland and his smile disarming. When he talks to reporters, he is the picture of innocence. 'We are not,' he says, 'anti-Semitic. We are not anti-anything. We are pro-German.'

This is the line which was taught all N P D speakers by Hess. (Late in 1967, Hess committed suicide for reasons, it is generally admitted, that were personal, not political.) Hess knew all the complexities of German law and his instructions were careful and precise when he tutored his speakers. Innuendo and indirection were the tactics he stressed and the tactics which the speakers follow.

Von Thadden, for instance, follows a Hess-manufactured line when he attacks the nuclear non-proliferation agreement. 'Such a treaty,' he says, 'will not deter other powers, such as Israel, from building such weapons.' When asked why he chose Israel as an example, he just shrugs.

The same evasion is employed by the N P D in their 'Twelve Principles'.

One declares: 'We demand an end to the lie of the sole responsibility of Germany (for World War II) whereby thousands of millions of money have been extorted from our nation.' This then is applied to restitution and reparations payments, both to individuals and to Israel.

Another of the 'Principles' calls for an end to trials of those accused of war crimes. It states:

'Twenty years after the war, we demand an end to the one-sided trials which aim at wiping out the past, while in other countries millions of war crimes against German men, women and children go unpunished.'

And No. 10 calls for 'a true picture of history. We defend ourselves against eulogies of high treason.' This is the sore point with von Thadden because of his half-sister.

But the strongest point for the millions of expellees is No. 11 which declares that 'Germany claims the territories where Germans have lived for centuries. We contest with no nation the land where it has settled, but we insist, with equal firmness, on the right to our own land.'

There is, of course, no mention of the Jews in the principles, no attack and no condemnation.

Pinning von Thadden down in an interview is like tryig to catch a fish with your bare hands. Even when you get a grip on him, he is likely to wriggle out. He is adept at evasion and obfuscation in both German and English, yet, at the same time, he gives the appearance of frankness and youthful ingenuousness. (He has cultivated that ingenuousness ever since his entrance into politics.)

He speaks in generalities. 'Our party,' he said, 'is trying again to build up the national spirit, in order that it may one day again be able to handle national problems alone.' And, 'If you don't belong to one of the major parties, you're called a Communist or a Fascist, so we're not called nationalist, but fascist. I think that all the noise about us is mainly a reaction to the hysteria of the German parties. They're not prepared to have a third German party on the scene, so they say we're fascist and anti-Semitic.'

As to the latter charge, he was quick to remark that the small number of Jews in Germany made that impossible.

About trying to reactivate Nazism, his answer was, 'Hitlerism was buried when Hitler committed suicide.'

The N P D, however, has found some of the old Nazi tactics adaptable to the present. Where once the Nazis used the slogan, *Kinder, Kuche, Kirche* (children, kitchen, church), the N P D employs *Heimat, Volk, Vaterland* (homeland, nation, fatherland).

Heinrich Fassbender, chairman of the N P D in Hesse, grew irate when an interviewer denigrated the slogan. 'Laugh if you will,' he said. 'The day will come which will wipe the laugh off your face.'

I attended an N P D meeting in Munich shortly after the break between Thielen and von Thadden. It took place in a beer hall in the Schwabing district and I was taken there by Maon Gid. "They know who I am,' he said, 'but they don't care. They say they are a legal party and that publicity is good for them. As for being anti-Semitic, they point out that they even have a Jewish nationalist who writes for their paper, the *Deutsche Nachrichten.*'

(The *Nachrichten* is the official N P D paper, but is far smaller in circulation and influence than the *National Zeitung* which speaks for all right-wing groups.)

No one barred our way into the meeting hall. There were about forty men gathered there, some of them old enough to have been Nazi party members, but the majority appeared to be under forty. In many ways it was reminiscent of the beer-hall days of the Nazis. Steins of beer were before everyone. A pleasing statement was greeted with table-thumping.

It was quickly evident that there was no dissidence among this group. They were Thaddenists and showed their approval every time his name was mentioned.

A speaker declaimed that the way was opening for Germany to reclaim its lost territories. All that was needed was a strong and determined Germany, one with its own army and its own weapons. And that day would not be long in coming.

'These,' Gid said, 'are set speeches. They always make them.'

It appeared to me that time had been set back more than thirty years. In a place like this, if not in this place, similar groups had gathered in the twenties and the thirties to listen to Hitler and his bravos. They had thumped the tables with their steins, roared their agreement with the sentiment that Germany must rise again.

And this was reinforced when a young man got to his feet and invoked the name of General Harster who had just been sentenced for his part in the Dutch murders. 'Who,' he demanded, 'has been jailed for the bombing of Dresden? They make criminals of our generals, but they make heroes of their criminals.'

The sound of steins on tables was like that of marching feet.

The meeting ended with loud pledges of support for von Thadden.

As we left, the young man who had evoked the cheers and another young man, also in his twenties, joined us. They knew Gid, but they wanted to know who I was. I told them and also told them what I was doing in Germany. 'Are you a Jew?' I said that I was.

They introduced themselves. The young orator was named Kurt Geyer. He was a student working for a doctorate in political science. The other said his name was Hans Eckart. He was also a student and he informed me that he was a relative of Dietrich Eckart, 'the great playwright'.

(Later I got a further identification of Dietrich Eckart. He had been a minor writer and a drug addict who early joined the Nazis and of whom Hitler wrote in *Mein Kampf*, that he 'was one of the best'.)

Both young men spoke English well and when they asked me if I would join them in a glass of beer, I agreed. Gid, who had other work to do, left us.

Seated in a restaurant, I inquired into their backgrounds. Geyer said his father owned a small factory and belonged to the Free Democratic Party. He had served in the army as an officer under Rommel, but had never been a Nazi.

Eckart, who had a chip on his shoulder all during the time we were together, said his family had been Nazis, 'which means patriotic Germans,' he said. 'We are still patriots.'

As we drank beer, Geyer said, 'The first thing you should know is that N P D is not anti-Semitic. It doesn't have to be for there are no Jews in Germany. We are pro-German. What's wrong with loving your country?'

Eckart said, 'You know the truth. Not a single Jew was gassed on German soil. You Americans built those gas chambers after the war to blacken Germany.'

I asked him if he really believed that.

'Of course,' he said. 'Some day it will come out like the truth came out about the nuns in Belgium in the first war.'

Then I asked Geyer if he felt the same way. 'What does it matter?' he asked. 'It's all over. I say all this talk about Jews is nonsense. I have no feeling about Jews. They don't exist for me. They don't exist for my generation. I have no guilt feelings about what happened to them. I don't care if it was right or wrong because it all happened either before I was born or when I was an infant. No one has a right to blame us for what happened.'

'And I say,' Eckart said, 'that it didn't happen. That it's all a pack of lies.'

I looked at these two young men. Both were products of the era after the war. They were well-dressed, obviously had no financial problems. This was a good world in which they lived. I said, 'There are facts, evidence. Millions of people – not just Jews – were killed by the Nazis. Women and children were among them. Doesn't this have any meaning to you?'

'Women and children were killed in Dresden,' Eckart said. 'What does that mean to you?'

Geyer said, 'Of course I don't believe in murder and killing. I tell you I'm not a Nazi. I say only that what happened had nothing to do with me. It has nothing to do with the N P D.'

Eckart would not let it go at that. 'After the war,' he said, 'the whole world was united against Germany and blamed it for everything that happened. In war, there are always atrocities. You Americans committed them. The Russians were a thousand times worse than the Germans.' His voice was so loud that people about us had stopped talking and were looking at us and listening. 'The difference is that you won and we lost. It's always the losers who are called guilty.'

Geyer tried to quiet him, but Eckart would not be quieted.

'We have paid out billions of marks,' he said, 'and still they ask for more. Why should we pay Israel anything? No Israelis suffered because of National Socialism. There was no Israel in existence.'

Geyer said, 'Keep quiet, Hans. We're not talking about Israel.'

'Why not?' His voice lifted another notch. 'I say that Germany has been blackmailed long enough. If the government has money to give away, let it give it to Germans. We have millions of refugees from the East who lost their homes and their land and their money. They should get the money.' He lifted his glass and finished off his beer in one long gulp. Then he rose from the table and said, 'I have talked enough to a Jew.' He lurched away.

Geyer said, 'You have to understand. After the war, his family suffered greatly. They went to prison. A relative was executed.'

'But they at least received a trial,' I said.

'Those trials!' He did not hide his bitterness. 'Do you call them justice? Do you call the Eichmann trial justice? Don't talk to me about trials.' Unlike Eckart, however, he had control of himself. 'I understand why a Jew should feel the way you do, but you can't expect me to feel that way. The trials were unjust.'

I said I had talked with many Germans who did not feel that way.

He shrugged that off. 'I speak only for myself.'

I asked him what appeal the N P D had for him.

'The N P D is the only way for Germany to become a great nation again. If that does not happen, then the whole country will be taken over by the Communists. You Americans must realize that we are the only people who can prevent that.'

'Do you really believe that?'

'Of course.'

There was the ring of truth in his voice, but it was a frightening ring. After I left him, I wondered how many Kurt Geyers and Hans Eckarts there were in Germany.

Dr. Jurgen Gebhardt, assistant professor of political science at the University of Munich, assured me that there were not many. 'Certainly not at this time,' he said.

Gebhardt, in his thirties, spent three years in the United States, one at Havard on a research grant, and two teaching at Western Reserve University in Cleveland.

H

To him, the NPD poses only a potential threat. 'It has not become attractive to the urban population. If it should ever get ten per cent of the city vote, then it will be an actual danger. The other thing to watch is who provides the money for the party. Until now, it has been supported by small, individual contributions. But, if it ever starts getting money from large groups, either social or financial, then there will be an actual neo-Nazi resurgence.'

Like Geyer, he does not feel that anti-Semitism, *per se,* is important to the NPD. 'They're not enough of a target. They're too few and too unimportant. That dosen't mean there is no anti-Semitism. It shows in many ways, like some of my students saying, "The only reason the Jews are here is to get our money."

'You have to realize one thing. The German people, in the main, did not care about the Jews, did not want to care about them, and did not – and do not – want to believe the evidence of what happened to them.

'That is where the NPD has been most effective and destructive. It has succeeded in casting doubts on history. It has been able to prove that a small number of the charges and claims have been falsified. It ignores all the rest and keeps talking about the false charges.

'At this moment, the German people are not actively anti-Semitic. They could become so if there were a large immigration of Eastern European Jews. Then there would be someone real against whom to direct anger and frustration if, for example, Germany should have a worsening economic recession. In such a case, the NPD could make telling points.'

Analysing the NPD further, Gerbhardt said, 'It must be realized that the party is on the majority side in a number of issues. Most Germans feel that there should be an end to the war-crimes trials. Many liberals have come to the conclusion that they no longer have any meaning and that the basic purpose they serve is political rather than judicial.

'Trials should not be used for the purpose of education, yet there are some left-leaning jurists who have behavioural concepts of the law and so conduct these trials.'

Gerhardt is uncertain as to the future of the NPD. All the other right wing parties since the war either fell apart or were declared illegal because they turned to extremism when they started to lose supporters, he said. Further, the N P D is a party without a programme. 'It is merely against certain things. It is a party of grumblers, of the discontented, of negativists.

'If some ideologist could come up with a positive programme, and if the N P D can find a leader to inspire it, then the chances for the N P D would improve greatly. As it is, they already are a major threat to the Free Democratic Party and may well replace the F P D as the third party in the country.'

(The F P D is an amalgam of the burgher classes, the small manufacturers and some large businesses. It is in favour of a *laissez-faire* economic policy, is both nationalist and neutralist. It is suffering from severe internal schisms.)

As Gebhardt sees it, any further weakening of the F P D structure will finish it. 'If that happens,' he said, 'its right wing will have no place to go but to the N P D. And that could mean a surge of solid, middle-class money into the N P D.'

In Bonn, I found a high government official who felt that Gebhardt was wrong in feeling that the N P D was not a present danger. For personal and political reasons he asked not to be named.

'The N P D,' he said, 'already exerts much influence on the government. It does this by merely existing. It is the only real threat to the Grand Coalition. The extreme left, the Communists, are outlawed in this country, so any such opposition has to be undercover and, besides, the number of Communists in West Germany is really very small. To my mind, the best way to show how small would be to legalize the party and dare it to put up candidates.

'So the opposition, as I said, comes from the right. There were two ways to meet it. One was to fight the right on the issues. The other is to try to capture that opposition by moving the government to the right. Well, that is what is happening. Because the S P D is a member of the Grand Coalition, it has accepted policies which it would have fought had it remained in the opposition.

'I'll give you an example. The government was technically neutral during the recent Arab-Israeli war, though many politicians made it plain their sympathies were with Israel. However, the S P D officially followed the announced neutrality. If the

S P D had been in opposition, I am certain it would have come out on the Israeli side.

'The same thing is true on such matters as extending the statute of limitations and liberalizing certain sections of the restitution laws. Here the coalition position was to the right of the S P D position, but the S P D has to go along.

'This is why I say the N P D is a present danger. If it goes on getting more than five per cent of the votes in different elections, it will build a solid base in the eleven *laender* and here in Bonn. If the Grand Coalition continues after the next election, the N P D will be in a most enviable position. It might well be the only rallying point for opposition remaining.

'That is why I want to see our voting laws changed so that they are like those in the United States. I would like to see elections by constituency with the man getting the highest total elected. If we do change our laws, then I do not believe that the N P D could elect a single member to any legislature. It would be the equivalent of the Ku Klux Klan running candidates in the United States.

'Otherwise, I am afraid we are going to see a bigger, stronger N P D in Germany. And if the present policy of appeasement is not stopped, it may well be sooner than later.'

In the past year, von Thadden has gained full control of the party. There is no public dissent among its members. It now has representatives in a majority of the *laender* governments. It confidently awaits the 1969 national elections and it is certain that it will then replace the Free Democratic party as the third major party in West Germany.

Numerous groups, both Jewish and non-Jewish, have called on the government to ban the party. Thus far, the answer has been that the N P D has stayed within the letter of the law. Its leaders and speakers have been well taught. An official of the Justice Ministry said, 'They have studied the law carefully. I would say they are the real experts in that field.'

There have also been calls for banning the *National Zeitung* and in the summer of 1967 both the Justice and Interior departments announced they were investigating to determine if the newspaper had violated Article 18 of the basic law. This article gives the government power to act against any newspaper which 'misuses the freedom of expression of opinion, especially press freedom, for a struggle against the free, democratic, basic order.' (No newspaper has ever been prosecuted under this law.)

But, as the official quoted earlier, said, 'We are in a dilemma. You Americans face the same one. Where does dissent end? We guarantee free speech and a free press. We don't want a nation of *Beobachters*.' (Hitler's personal newspaper organ.)

The paper did get into trouble when its July 21, 1967, edition was removed from the news-stands because it carried a front-page picture of Adolf Hitler. The picture was removed from a re-plated edition, but none of the contents of the newspaper was otherwise changed. And no government action was taken.

Garry Stindt, a Gentile, news editor in Berlin for an American television chain, said of the N P D, 'It gets away with things no other German political party has been able to do. It preaches a Nazi doctrine and sells a Nazi line. And it keeps getting stronger. The fact is that it has an appeal for a great many Germans.

'It is for God and motherhood. It calls on an end to immorality and crime. It urges lower taxes. Who can be against any of these? It has a "gut appeal". It doesn't try to reach the mind, but the emotions. Of course it is a threat to the Jews, but at the moment it doesn't need to be openly anti-Semitic. It can make its point by indirection.

'If the N P D is to be stopped, it will have to be because of international pressure. The present government is not taking any action.'

Surprisingly, the Jews in Germany are not as disturbed by the N P D as Jews outside that country. They see the N P D as more of a threat to the Federal Republic than it is to them.

Moritz Binder explained why he felt that way. Binder, a camp survivor, owns a jewellery store in Cologne. Middle-aged, he and a sister were all of a family of more than twenty who remained alive after the war. 'What,' he asked, 'can the N P D do to us that the Nazis did not do? The dead can only die once. The living can go to Israel. Besides, we are unimportant even to the N P D. We have no illusions. We are here on borrowed time.'

My own experience in talking to N P D officials and members was chilling. To many of those, the era of Hitler has become a golden age. It was a time of greatness, when Germany

was strong, prosperous and feared. It was when they paraded
in their brown shirts and polished boots and trampled down
any who opposed them.

The fact that many of them sit limply in beer halls, use
words because they fear to use action, makes them pitiable,
but does not keep them from being dangerous. They go each
day from their homes, where they relive the past, to their jobs
where they try to resurrect it.

When I talked to Otto Hess in Nuremberg in May, 1967, he
said, 'It is a spirit which we are keeping alive. It is like a small
fire which is only waiting for a spurt of air to flame up all
about.' Hess dismissed the question of the Jews. 'You are talking about the past. The Jewish question no longer exists in
Germany.'

And young NPD members, like Geyer and Eckart, also dis-
miss the matter of the Jews as irrelevant.

I felt, talking to Geyer, that he had chosen the NPD because
it was the one path of revolt open to him. And I believe that
unless an opening is made to the left in Germany, Geyer will
be joined by many thousands of young people who suffer from
a sense of frustration. German youth, like the youth of all
nations, has been inoculated with revolt. It is simply against
what is because what is does not satisfy.

Young men like Geyer have taken up the NPD because it
was the one outlet open to them. The great danger is that they
will start believing in it.

I think that it would be better both for the Jews and for
West Germany if the Jews put up a stronger fight against the
NPD, if they made it a major issue. There is too much of
the pre-Hitler feeling of self-delusion and self-abnegation about
the way the Jews are now acting. Van Dam's 'once a persecutee,
always a persecutee' is not a rationalization but a surrender.

If there had been no Hitler and no Nazis then this form of
self-delusion might not be too harmful either to the Jews or to
Germany and its hopes for a democratic future. But there was
a Hitler and there were Nazis and many of the latter still live
and thrive in Germany.

23. *The Once and Former Nazis*

JUST how many Germans were members of the Nazi party is a matter of conjecture. Immediately after the war it appeared that not a single one had survived.

Von Thadden, admitting that one-fourth of the members of the N P D executive committee had 'discharged an official function in the service of the National Socialist Party,' said this compared to 1 in 5 Germans – 12 of 60,000,000 – who were Nazis in 1945.

In 1930, six and a half persons cast votes for the Nazis, but that represented, not the party's strength, but the party's appeal.

From 1933 until 1945, party membership was necessary for the civil service, for a teacher's licence, for any number of posts as functionaries in cities, states and the federal government. A great many persons joined because they felt this was the way to promotion and economic advancement.

One man, Kurt George Kiesinger, joined because he saw membership in the party as a means of changing the party.

In 1967 this same Kurt George Kiesinger became Chancellor of Germany.

Except for diatribes from East Germany, no one has assailed Kiesinger harshly for his light brown past. No one has accused him of having taken any part in the Nazi persecutions and terrors. He held no position of major influence under Hitler.

When he was named to head the German government, the Jews in Germany made no outcry. None to whom I spoke feel that he has been less than fair or just to them during the period he has served. Some expressed a sense of shock, but most accepted his appointment as an evolutionary process, begun under Adenauer.

For it was Adenauer who first handed out indulgences to reformed Nazis, of whom the most notorious was Hans Joseph

Maria Globke, whom Adenauer appointed as his Secretary of State, where he served as the late Chancellor's closest adviser on domestic matters.

Globke had a record as a brilliant legal scholar and jurist. Hitler had called on him to codify and annotate the Nazi laws against the Jews. It was Globke who found a historic precedent for making Jews wear a Yellow Star of David in the records of the Fourth Lateran Council in 1215.

Such individual appointments might be defended on the ground that special knowledge and talents were needed in the first days of the Federal Republic and the past could be forgiven in the hope of future benefits. But Adenauer went far beyond that when he had Law 131 enacted in 1951. He was then at the height of his power, the absolute boss of his party and of the government. All it took to enact a piece of legislation – or kill it – was a word from the Chancellery.

And from the Chancellery came word to enact Law 131. This made it mandatory to reinstate into their old positions all officials who had served during the Nazi years. The reason given was that only these had the experience, knowledge and background to run the government!

If this had applied only to technicians, clerks and minor officials then the impact would not have been too great. However, what it did was to restore to the bench and the courts and prosecutor's office all the old Nazis. It reinstated all the teachers. With this one law, Adenauer had abruptly cut off from denazification both education and the administration of Justice.

It is probably most heinous that the judiciary remained in the hands of former Nazis. These included not only rank-and-file members and self-named *mitgangers* (fellow travellers), but judges who had been members of the SS and Gestapo, who had served not only on the established German courts, but had presided in the courts of occupied countries and on Hitler's 'lynch courts', the so-called 'People's Courts' which were intended merely to give a façade of legality to murder.

This was what made it possible for Dr. Edwin Schuele to serve as a war crimes investigator in Ludwigsburg before it was discovered that he was a former Storm Trooper and evidence uncovered that caused him to be charged with being a war criminal. As a result, he resigned (he was not fired) and allowed to become a public prosecutor in Stuttgart.

Other such former Nazis have been uncovered in the courts over the years. Leo Drach was serving as Chief Prosecutor of Frankenthal when it was revealed that he had been convicted in Luxembourg of causing the deaths of numerous Luxembourgers. He was sentenced there to thirty-five years' imprisonment but was released after serving only a short time. When he returned to Germany he had no problem about reclaiming his civil service post.

There were numerous others.

Rudolf Husslein, president of the Deggendorf state court, had handed down the sentences that sent four Danes to their death.

Karl Arndt, president of the highest court in Bremen, had been a member of the S S from 1933 to 1945.

Hans Eberhard Rotberg, a member of the highest court in Karlsruhe, had been a member of Hitler's Security Service during the war. (Charges against him were dismissed, his activities, according to the Federal Ministry of Justice, were 'immaterial'.)

Only revelation of his activities as in the Nazi Ministry of Justice prevented the appointment of Senatsrat (Senator) Carl Creifels to the Federal Court.

Joseph Weinicke, State Attorney of Coblenz, was charged with having sentenced a group of Luxembourgers to death.

Ernst Ehelers, a former Gestapo official, is a judge in the Schleswig Administrative Court.

Albert Leiterer, a former S S colonel who headed the Gestapo office in Magdeburg, serves in the same Schleswig court.

Heinz Rausch, who sat on one of Hitler's notorious 'Special Courts' in Magdeburg (this court dealt with 'political offences') is senior judge in Celle.

No one has a complete tally of former Nazis still sitting in the courts of West Germany. A group called 'The Association of Nazi Persecutees' has made up a list of more than thirty who were important under the Third Reich.

Egon Bahr, Willy Brandt's assistant, said, 'There is no question but that many who were Nazis are still undiscovered. It would be good, of course, if all who were Nazi functionaries could be removed from office, but that is unlikely. What is important is that the actions of all judges and public officials is under constant observation. If we cannot undo what the Nazis

did, we can at least make certain that those actions are not
repeated.'

Jews in Germany are concerned by the presence of former
Nazis in the judiciary. Ernest Landau said, 'It would be good
if they had been barred from holding office anywhere. There
is a certain contradiction that Hitler was able to run the government completely with Nazis and now we find that we cannot
run it without them. But there have been no anti-Semitic acts
by these former Nazis.

'What is shocking is not that there are former Nazis, but that
there are former war criminals and persons who have been
charged with war crimes in important positions. Some of the
responsibility for this must rest with the American and other
occupation forces. It would have been possible to exclude former
Nazis from places in the Federal government if the occupation
forces had insisted. But they did not.'

The presence of former Nazis in the educational system is
equally disturbing to the Jews. One of the most publicized cases
involved Goetz Freiherr von Poelnitz, who was the founding
rector of the University of Regensburg. Some years after he took
office, a cursory search of the files of the University of Munich
revealed that he had been one of Hitler's most virulent anti-
Semitic polemicists.

A number of teachers have been involved in anti-Semitic
actions. The first person to be convicted and sent to jail for
spreading anti-Semitic propaganda was a school teacher. Others
have had their assignments changed so that they are no longer
allowed to teach either history or civics.

Except in the rare instances where criminal charges are filed,
little publicity is given such cases. But the question of Nazi war-
crimes is another matter.

This is the most emotional domestic problem in Germany.
A 1966 public opinion poll on the subject showed that 63 per
cent of all German males and 76 per cent of all German females
wanted an end to the trials.

Under German law, only murder, or complicity in murder,
remains a punishable offence. Rape, torture and assault trials
have all been outlawed by the statute of limitations. Actual
murder is subject to the maximum penalty – life imprisonment.
Complicity calls for lesser punishment.

About 80,000 Germans have been sentenced by Allied and German courts. More than 60,000 other investigations were made by state attorneys-general and about 6100 convictions obtained. In 1967, more than 14,000 such cases were still pending.

'It may seem unusual,' Richard Borchardt said, 'that all these cases should not long ago have been cleared up, but you must remember that much evidence in these cases was deliberately destroyed, hidden or accidentally lost. Fresh facts keep continually turning up. The government feels that it must act on any evidence, no matter how dilatory.'

(A case in point was that of Herbert Wyegandt, arrested in late 1965. He had been deputy director of the Gestapo in Dusseldorf and had gone undetected for more than twenty years until some long-lost papers came to light. On the basis of these papers, Weygandt was charged with the murder of 50,000 Polish Jews at the Kulmhof death camp.)

'We want no revenge,' Rabbi Levinson said, 'but we do want justice. There is no statute of limitations for murder of other types. Are we to concede that Jewish lives are worth less than other lives?'

But many young Germans feel that the time has come to end the trials. Reinhard Haarman is a newspaperman and television writer, a member of a family that was anti-Nazi and suffered for it.

'This is not a Jewish question,' he said, 'but a German question. Each arrest, each trial, seems to many to add a further load to German guilt. Sometimes we have to ask if there is no limit. And I, for one, have to insist that I do not feel guilt. I had nothing to do with a past of which I was not a part.

'No one can truthfully call me anti-Semitic. Yet there are times when I feel the Jews of the world are asking too much of Germany, when I feel that they make normal relations impossible. All I ask is that we be given the chance to start fresh, not have mud thrown at us continually. It is not that I want to see the guilty go unpunished as I do not want the innocent to be punished.'

Unlike many Germans of his age, Haarman has no doubt about the atrocities. 'I know they happened,' he said. 'My family are examples.'

But in Hamburg, Kurt Tegge, a prosecutor in the war-crimes

trials, was met with disbelief when he talked about the atrocities. He appeared before a youth club and one of its members said, 'I don't believe any of it. I don't know anyone who'd behave like that.'

Tegge's answer was to tell of a man who had come to his office and confessed that he had been a member of SS Division 1005. 'He told me,' Tegge said, 'he had shot children. He didn't even know precisely any more how many, but he thought 114 anyway. He'd make them kneel near a pit and then he'd stand behind them and shoot them in the neck, one after the other.

'He'd volunteered for this duty and he gave me the names of eighteen other SS men, still living in Hamburg, who had volunteered.'

Another prosecutor said, 'Every one of us hopes that today will see the end of our work, but each day new evidence comes in. We learn of child-killers, of woman-killers. Of men who appeared to delight in the act of killing. They killed out of principle: the Untermenschen – the sub-humans – were there to be used or killed. They said so. It's murderers we are after. It's our duty to prosecute murderers.'

The 'Central Agency for Prosecution of Nazi Criminals' is located in the small city of Ludwigsburg, a spa twenty-five miles from Stuggart. Its director is a Bavarian, Adelbert Rueckerl, a big slow-speaking man. Middle-aged, he remembers the Nazi years. He has a staff of more than a hundred, made up of twenty-eight prosecutors, twenty-two judges, and the rest clerical and research aides.

The men and women who work in the agency have an almost monastic existence. The agency occupies a former women's prison, a cell-like building surrounded by a high wall. Every employee is a volunteer. Once each agreed to work for the agency, he had to leave his home. All live in rented rooms or small hotels. Only a very few have their families close by.

Their lives are difficult and their motives either misunderstood or misrepresented by many. Hans Bueschgens is thirty-three, a prosecutor. He said, 'People here have had the gall to accuse us of being "career-mad" because we do this work. Our every thought is concerned with horror and death. We have no personal axes to grind – at our age there is no question of personal guilt. We now lead completely abnormal lives only because we feel there is work that must be done. How can anyone believe that we would choose to live this kind of life except out of conviction?'

Director Rueckerl pointed out that there were two major misconceptions in the German mind in relation to these trials. The first was that the crimes were committed by the military in the course of a war. But the truth is that these crimes were committed by the *Schutzstaffel* – the SS – which was a civilian police group without military status.

The second is to regard all the victims as Jews. 'They killed 6,000,000 Jews,' Rueckerl said. 'We know that. But they also killed 5,000,000 Russian civilians, 2,000,000 Poles and 1,000,000 other people – Gypsies, German free-thinkers or political opponents and German insane or incurably sick. Eight million of what they called "inferior stock".

'But these dreadful numbers – 14,000,000 – are not even the point. It's the basic insanity of categorizing humanity that matters. How can we make our people understand? And, unless they understand, how can we have any hope for the future?'

But understanding comes very hard. The Mayor of Ludwigsburg appeared on a television programme and was asked his opinion of the Agency. His reply was, 'I'm not saying the Central Agency is a burden to us, but certainly it doesn't help our reputation to have them here, because surely not only in this country, but abroad as well, there is a certain smell about them, and naturally this clings to our city.'

But, day after day, new evidence arrives at the Central Agency, new crimes are discovered. In various parts of Germany ordinary men, leading middle-class lives, raising their families, are charged with having committed murders in Germany, in Austria, in Hungary, in Poland, in Russia, in the Netherlands.

Old, familiar, names appear in the newspapers and are reported on television – Dachau, Auschwitz, Treblinka, Sachsenhausen, Chelmo and Sobibor.

And Rueckerl said, 'The day will never come when we can say, "It's done now, it's finished." There is no end in sight except a biological one, when at last they will all be dead. And then it will only be done if, in the meantime, we have succeeded in teaching those who come after us. The only guarantee of it never again happening lies in knowledge.'

But much of the diffusion of knowledge remains in the hands of the former Nazis. And a generation has grown up which finds itself seeking questions for which no satisfactory answers are being supplied. Theodore Luckner is a philosophy student at the University of Frankfurt. He is twenty-four, earnest, intospective. One of his professors suggested I talk to him because 'he is at the crossroads. The way he feels now, he can go all the way, either to the left or the right. He's full of doubts and frustrations.'

Seated in a coffee house, Luckner poured out his confusions. 'My parents,' he said, 'were passive anti-Nazis. My father got into trouble once because he helped some Jewish friends. My mother had a Jewish grandmother, but nothing ever happened to her because of that. I don't have any Jewish feelings. I don't identify that way.

'When I was growing up, I was told the Nazis were bad. Not devils, but bad. In my mind, I separated Germans into two groups, good Germans and Nazis. Then we started getting the truth about the terrors and the tortures and it made me sick. When I first heard the story of Anne Frank, I cried. And later I read all the evidence in the Eichmann case.'

He buried his head in his hands and stared down at the table. He took a fork and started tracing figures on the cloth, then dropped the fork with a clang. 'I was a German. The men who killed Anne Frank were Germans. Eichmann was a German. But I couldn't believe I was like the others. I couldn't. I told myself the Nazis were a special type of German and that they were now all gone. That they had been eradicated.

'But I knew it wasn't really so. Every day there were stories in the newspapers about the men being tried for war crimes. They were all such respectable people, ordinary people. And suddenly Kiesinger became Chancellor. And do you know something –' his face twisted into an unhappy smile – 'there weren't as many people upset about that as were about Willy Brandt being named Foreign Minister.

'It was all right for Kiesinger to have been a Nazi, but it was wrong for Brandt to fight the Nazis. They'll never forgive him for that. Not just the N P D, but others. Look at the stink that was made when his son was in that movie.'

(Brandt's son appeared in a picture called 'Cat and Mouse',

and, in one scene he used an Iron Cross in what the N P D called a degrading manner.)

Luckner has no interest in party politics. Like many other young people, he expressed his opposition to the Grand Coalition by saying. 'Black plus Red makes Brown.'

'You don't know what to believe,' he said. 'You're lost. All this talk about democracy doesn't mean anything. Even the N P D says it's democratic. Now that they're together, you don't know what either the C D U or the S P D stands for. One of them is as bad as the other.

'This is supposed to be a new Germany. Maybe it is. But I don't know what kind of a country it is. You have the feeling that there's nothing worth fighting for. It's all a sham. There's no anti-Semitism now not because people have changed, or been taught that anti-Semitism is wrong, but because there are no Jews.

'And you can't even say that the Nazis were bad because if they were, then what are so many of them doing running the country now?

'We haven't been left anything that we can have any faith in. Nothing at all.'

In his anguish, young Luckner had crashed hard on the truth. There is an absence of faith in West Germany. In its government, in its leaders, in its future, and even in faith itself.

24. The Church

In 1937, Dr. Hans Kerrl, Nazi Minister for Church Affairs, addressed a group of what William L. Shirer called 'submissive churchmen'. This group, composed of both Protestants and Catholics, heard Kerrl declare the new Apostle's Creed, the new Nicene Creed, the new Athanasian Creed, the new Augsburg Creed.

It was based on two principles:

'Positive Christianity is National Socialism.

'The Fuehrer is the herald of a new revelation.'

With this statement, the Christian religion was temporarily replaced in Nazi Germany, not to return until after Hitler's defeat. It is one of the great shames of the German people that the vast majority accepted it. This included both religious and lay leaders.

And, yet, it is not historically out of context with German history. Church and State have been intertwined as long as there has been a Germany. Charlemagne established the Holy Roman Empire and was legitimatized by Pope Leo III, who crowned him. (And whom he restored to the Papacy.) A millenium later, the Kaiser was the head of the Protestant church in Germany and the noblemen of his court served as his bishops.

Whether Germany was Catholic or Protestant, the Jews were always the object of persecution. The *servi camerae* were never allowed to forget their place. Adolf Stoecker, who served Wilhelm I as the last royal court chaplain, ordered the Jews to be 'publicly condemned, beaten and abused'.

Both churches were always authoritarian. Luther had laid the foundation for his followers by taking the side of the nobles in the Peasants' War, and had set a precedent for future centuries. During the few years of the Weimar Republic, the Lutheran church played a strong part in undermining it. The Catholic church gave it little support.

While Hitler and the Nazis were moving toward power in Germany, there was no opposition from any major religious leader and support from many.

The 'German Christians' Faith Movement', made up of a large segment of German Protestants, was organized in 1932 and promised full support to the Nazi race doctrines and to the leadership principle and sought to bring into being a single Reich Church which would make the Protestant Church a part of the Nazi totalitarian structure.

The leaders of Catholic Action, a major force in German Catholicism, were early Hitler supporters.

In the hours before Hitler was granted dictatorial powers by the Reichstag, he told its members that the Nazi 'ambition is a peaceful accord between Church and State.' And, as bait for votes from the Catholic Centre Party (which he later received) that his government hoped 'to improve our relations with the Holy See.'

One of Hitler's most fervent supporters in the days when he came to power was the Rev. Martin Niemoller, the World War I submarine commander who entered the Ministry. In his auto-biography, published in 1933, Niemoller wrote that the destruction of the Weimar Republic meant an end to 'years of darkness', and promised the 'national revival' for which he had so long fought, for a time as a member of the *Freikrops* from which so many leading Nazis emerged.

A large majority of Christian religious leaders accepted on face value the Nazi promise that there would be 'liberty for all religious denominations of the state (except the Jews, of course) so far as they are not a danger to... the moral feelings of the German race. The party stands for positive Christianity.'

When Hitler did gain power, he gave public praise to the Christian faiths as 'essential elements for safeguarding the soul of the people.'

Only a few months afterward, he signed a concordat with the Vatican which guaranteed the freedom of the Catholic religion (he was nominally a Catholic) and promised the church the right to 'regulate her own affairs'.

I

All during this period few voices, and none loudly, were raised by pastors or priests against the Nazis.

It was only when Hitler began his drive to mortice all forms of Christianity into his totalitarian state that opposition developed. Hitler's cynicism did not allow sanctuary behind the Cross.

There is a parallel between the reactions of the Church and that of the Jews in the first years of Nazi domination. In neither case, apparently, could these victims of Nazism bring themselves to believe that Hitler meant what he said and what he did.

It took four years for the Catholic church finally to rise against Hitler. Meanwhile he had violated the Concordat, dissolved such Catholic groups as the Catholic Youth League, executed Erich Klausener, head of Catholic Action, arrested and imprisoned thousands of priests, nuns and lay leaders, many of them on charges of 'immorality' that seemed to have been drawn straight from Boccaccio's *Decameron*.

Finally, in 1937, Pope Pius XI attacked the Nazis in an encyclical titled *Mit Brennender Sorge* (With Burning Sorrow) which charged Hitler with violating the 1933 Concordat and accused him of sowing 'the tares of suspicion, discord, hatred, calumny, of secret and open hostility to Christ and His Church.' There was no mention in the encyclical of Hitler's treatment of the Jews or of his racial doctrine.

The Protestant Church, more closely interwoven with the German state since the time of Luther, never completely broke with the Nazis. It was a national, rather than an international, church and its ties to the state were strong. In July, 1933, representatives drew up a constitution for a new 'Reich Church', and it was given legality by the Reichstag.

Naïvely, most Protestant leaders had believed that this new church would be autonomous. They quickly learned that this was not the case. A Reich Bishop was to head the Reich church and religious leaders chose as their candidate Pastor Friedrich von Bodelschwingh. Hitler, however, had his own candidate, Ludwig Mueller, who had been an army chaplain in World War I.

Mueller had been an early Nazi, was a slavish follower of Hitler, and an active proponent of Hitler's racial theories.

The full force of the Nazi machine was put to work to effect Mueller's election. The government dissolved a number of Protestant organizations, blockaded some churches and turned both the S A and the Gestapo loose to terrorize potential voters. The night before the election, Hitler made a campaign speech on radio to urge Mueller's election.

Mueller was elected and this resulted in a breakaway from the newly established church by a group composed of members of the 'Confessional Church' and the Pastors' Emergency League, whose spokesman and leader was Niemoller. More quickly than most he had learned the meaning of Nazism. But it would not be until three years later that Niemoller and his followers would break completely with the Nazis and challenge Nazi doctrine. From 1933 to 1936 the quarrel with the Nazis was over control of the church. In May, 1936, the leaders of the Confessional Church for the first time publicly attacked anti-Semitism.

A year later, all efforts at conciliation having failed, Nazi authorities arrested Niemoller and sent him to prison. There he became a symbol of the Protestant revolt against Hitler, but he did not represent the majority of Protestant clergymen and, far less, the majority of Protestant laymen.

In the spring of 1938 the great majority of Protestant pastors took an oath of personal allegiance to Hitler.

The facts show that the opposition to Hitler in the organized churches of Germany was part of the old struggle for power between church and state. Hitler's racist theories and his campaign of persecution against the Jews were not basic to that opposition. There were, of course, hundreds of priests and pastors who fought Hitler and condemned his racism. Many were tortured and killed for their courage. But all these were personal acts.

In the beginning, both organized churches were Hitler's supporters. They turned against him primarily in defence of themselves.

Jewish leaders in Germany today look back on the actions of Christian religious leaders as part of the history of relations between Christians and Jews in Germany. Rabbi Schereschewsky said, 'We have been persecuted by other faiths, but that was never the whole side of the story, though it was the greater one. The other part is made up of the actions of those who risked lives, fortunes and family in behalf of Jews.

'I think there is a spirit of tolerance and understanding in Germany now such as never before existed, despite harmful incidents which might arise.'

One such 'harmful incident' had arisen only weeks before I talked with the rabbi in Cologne.

A Frankfurt newspaper printed an interview with Rabbi Max Nussbaum, a German born refugee from Hitler, who had come to Germany to visit from Los Angeles. Rabbi Nussbaum quoted Josef Cardinal Frings, Germany's most eminent Roman Catholic prelate, as saying that the Jews had provoked the wrath of the Nazis by parading their wealth, that there was no proof that 6,000,000 Jews had died as the result of the Nazi terror, and that Nazism would not again revive in Germany because there were no Jews.

The story shook Germany. Many found it hard to believe because Cardinal Frings had a reputation as a liberal, earned by his actions in both Vatican Councils, where he had been one of the leaders in the fight to clear the Jews of guilt for the crucifixion of Christ.

Others quickly pointed to the Cardinal's age (he is over eighty) and suggested that this might be a reason for his statements.

The Jewish community divided. Some felt that Rabbi Nussbaum should not have quoted the Cardinal because it would only revive old hatreds. Others said Rabbi Nussbaum had no right to make public a private conversation.

Hendrik van Dam was unhappy because 'now real anti-Semites can say they are only quoting the Cardinal.'

Certainly the *National Zeitung und Soldaten Zeitung* seized the opportunity. The newspaper ran a front-page picture of the Cardinal and captioned it, 'He's Our Man'.

Within days, some facts emerged. The most important of these was that the Cardinal had said the things attributed to him by Rabbi Nussbaum. However, the Cardinal said, they had been taken out of context and had been offered argumentatively, not as beliefs.

In Cologne, Wilhelm Unger, chairman of the Brotherhood Week ceremonies, offered his resignation. 'I could not continue with Cardinal Frings as the principal speaker scheduled,' he said.

Unger was prevailed upon to meet with the Cardinal. At the

meeting, the Cardinal assured Unger that he certainly did not hold the sentiments that had been printed and was prepared to make a public statement of his true views.

(When I interviewed Rabbi Nussbaum in Los Angeles some time later, the rabbi said that he had quoted the Cardinal exactly because he felt it was imperative that those views be made known. 'I was shocked,' he said, 'to hear them. All I could do was wonder how many others felt the same way. One means of learning this was to talk to the newspapers and get the whole matter into the open.')

Not long after meeting with Unger, the Cardinal sent a statement to the Society for Christian-Jewish Co-operation in which he said:

'Vigilance is in fact necessary if the barbarism of National Socialism is not to return one day. Under it, our Jewish citizens suffered most terribly.'

Shortly afterward, addressing the crowded audience at Brotherhood Week ceremonies, the Cardinal again called for vigilance. This was not enough for Unger who followed him on the platform and told the huge crowd that the Cardinal had made a retraction of the views reported by Nussbaum.

'I believed,' Unger said, 'it was absolutely necessary to make this plain. It had to be on the public record.'

The *National Zeitung* charged that the retraction had been extorted by 'Jewish blackmail'. It stated, as it had before, that there was no 'proof' that 6,000,000 Jews had died because of the Nazis. And it called again for an end to reparations to Israel.

Every element of the establishment – Jewish and Gentile, foreign and domestic – rushed to stamp out this brushfire before it spread. The issue quickly became not whether the Cardinal had been correctly quoted, but whether it was politically correct to publish his remarks.

The Jewish issue, which Adenauer and others who followed him to power believed had been settled with restitution and reparations, with constitutional provisions, was suddenly unsettled. No, unsettled is the wrong word. The issue, which so many had called dead because they wanted it dead, had proved that it still had life.

And the culture in which it revived, was the culture of religion.

The Cardinal had done what the NPD and the *National Zeitung* had found beyond their powers.

Christian leaders, desperately seeking to return Christianity to Germany, where Hitler had prostituted it, hastened to repeat that no church today accepts anti-Semitism as an instrument of policy. Jewish leaders, reverting to the period when Hitler first rose to power, sought to deny a reality once more.

I talked with Monsignor Erich Klausener in Berlin about the position of the Catholic Church today. He is the son of the leader of Catholic Action who was killed by Hitler at the time of the Roehm purge.

(His death was due to his relations with the anti-Hitlerite group of which von Papen and other notables were members, not because of a revolt against Nazism *per se*.)

Monsignor Klausener is handsome, erudite, articulate, cosmopolitan. He is a former Fulbright scholar who spent time in the United States. In many ways, his is a position analogous to that so long held by Bishop Fulton Sheen in the United States, an accomplished spokesman and public relations man for his deep faith. He is both sincere and diplomatic. And when I talked with him, there was a young man present to make certain that we had no semantic difficulties because of Monsignor's Klausener's excellent English and my limited German.

'There is,' he said, 'no anti-Semitism in the Church and none in Germany of which I am aware. There is a danger, however, that an excess of philo-Semitism can cause a reaction. We must return to a normal situation. The young people are more than twenty years away from the persecutions. They feel no direct responsibility and have no personal knowledge of the past. It is they who might revolt against philo-Semitism.'

He sees the present small Jewish community as a safety valve against anti-Semitism. 'However,' he said, 'if there were to be a mass emigration of Eastern Jews, then it could be different. These immigrants would not be regarded as Jews, but as East Europeans, and this, I fear, would be resented. Our young people today are really not aware of what Jewishness is. They have had almost no opportunity to learn.'

Mgr. Klausener does not believe there is any religious backing for the growth of nationalism in Germany. 'I see no relationship,' he said. 'The NPD has had no greater success in Catholic regions than it has had in other regions and, in some instances, even less. I know of one vice-president of the N P D who resigned because he felt the party's platform and actions violated his convictions as a Catholic.'

He is troubled by attacks on public figures for their actions during the Nazi era. 'This,' he said, 'is a type of German McCarthyism. It takes the form of searching for some kind of Nazi past. I say it is wrong to say now that nothing is important but what a man did thirty years ago. This denies that a man can change and grow and improve.

'What too many people forget is that it was impossible to survive without some form of collaboration. This was the case of the Church as well as that of some individuals. The Church supported Hitler only when he became head of the government and even the Bishops' Conference made it plain that it did not endorse the ideological position of the Nazis. Besides, it was expected that when Hitler took office, he would tone down some of his radical positions and become more responsible.

'It was always the primary duty of the Church to protect itself. In the Netherlands, where the Church fought the Nazis, the result was that Catholics of Jewish descent were imprisoned and executed.'

Mgr. Klausener believes that the play, 'The Deputy', gave a false picture of the attitude and actions of the Vatican. 'The Pope,' he said, 'had to be restrained from speaking out. When he sent a pastoral letter to be read in all the churches of Poland, it was Cardinal Sapiela who suppressed it because, as he told the Papal emissary, "the next day we will all be in concentration camps and there will be no priests for the people".'

Klausener offered further evidence that the Catholic church in Germany had done what it could to aid the Jews. 'Brazil,' he said, 'would take only converted Jews, so papers were forged, baptismal certificates provided and other papers procured. This satisfied Vargas. (Getulio Vargas, dictator of Brazil from 1930 to 1945.) What could be done, was done, and at great risk.

'Many individual priests attacked Hitler. Father Bernard Lichtenberg, Dean of the Berlin Cathedral, began to offer a special prayer on behalf of the persecuted after the Crystal Night. He did this night after night until he was denounced by two visitors from outside Berlin. Then the Nazis imprisoned him.'

At present, the Church, he said, is involved in a reconciliation with the Jews. Many prominent Catholic clergy are taking part in inter-faith groups. The age-old attempts at converting the Jews in Germany have been halted.

'The problem Germany faces,' he said, 'is not that of the Jews, but of increasing democracy. It is an element of the German character that it deals in absolutes. This applies even to government. If government is not perfect, many are ready to discard it. They forget that government is a human institution and, for that reason, has human weaknesses and human failings.

'The German people, especially the young, must recognize that the only way to keep liberty is to restrict abuses of it. The Church is doing all it can to teach that. It includes the Jewish problem, but it is not limited to it.'

Monsignor Klausener sees all German problems from the perspective of the Church. It must do its 'primary duty'. That is why, for example, it fights against sectarian control of the schools. Why it insists that the Concordat signed with Hitler must be honoured. To a great extent, he sees the Jewish problem as having been solved because there are so few Jews in Germany.

But Professor Helmut Gollwitzer, teacher of Protestant Theology in the Free University of Berlin, has no such confidence.

Gollwitzer is an outspoken liberal. A small man, with twinkling eyes and a slight figure, he regards theology as a field that includes man's relationship with man as well as man's relationship with God. His teaching methods are Socratic, but the lecture hall and the meeting place, the public platform and the outdoor rally have replaced the *agora* as the site for his teaching.

'Nazism,' he said, 'revealed the Germans as the least Christianized people in Europe. There were many churches, but few Christians. Anti-Semitism was an inevitable by-product.

'The German churches were always political. Under Hitler, they realized that their intervention into politics was a fault. It made them vulnerable to politics. For a time, they became more religious and introspective.'

Gollwitzer contends that there was a reversion after the founding of the Federal Republic. Pre-Hitler Germany had had a majority of Protestants, but the new country had a majority of Catholics and it was headed by a devout Catholic who was a product of the old, political Church.

'The metamorphoses under Hitler were not permanent,' he said. 'The Church returned to its old mistake of political Catholicism. This is evidenced by the Catholic line of the C D U and is an obstacle to creating democracy in Germany.

'The Protestant Church, on the other hand, has taken a new position since the end of the war. Formerly it had been nationalistic and monarchical. It had been oriented to the right. Today there is a significant, non-conformist, liberal trend within it.

'History has shown that wherever a form of government contains a theocratic element, non-conformity has been attacked. In Germany, where the church was part of the government until the founding of the Weimar Republic, the Jews were non-conformists and active anti-Semitism was the result.

'My father was a Lutheran minister and his politics were very conservative. He was an anti-Semite. As a boy, I was enthusiastic about Hitler and his anti-Semitism seemed natural to me. It was only later, when I came to the University to study that I met any Jews that I began to question my attitudes and those of my father.

'As time passed, of course, I matured. My politics became liberal. Anti-Semitism became abhorrent to me.'

The big change which has been effected since the end of World War II, Gollwitzer feels, is that the 'naturalness of anti-Semitism' has been eliminated. 'Students today,' he said, 'do not have to overcome personal anti-Semitic sentiments. They are not brought up with them.'

Gollwitzer stressed the word 'students'. He said, 'Anti-Semitism decreases as education increases. The very young and the non-academic youth are more anti-Semitic than other groups.'

Gollwitzer maintains that the Protestant church has transcended old prejudices and attitudes. 'The Protestant Church,' he said, 'now supports complete separation of Church and State, voluntary payment of Church taxes, and national community schools where religion is taught on a non-sectarian basis, unlike the present confessional schools.'

Further, Gollwitzer said, the Protestant Church is now liberal politically. 'On the matter of recognizing the Oder-Neisse line,' he said, 'the Protestants have shown a far greater willingness to accept the political realities than the Catholics.'

As Gollwitzer sees it, there are Jews, but there is no Judaism, in Germany. 'The Jewish influence in art, culture and business has been destroyed. Only in education do we see it today. This last is especially true in the Free University of Berlin. The proportion of Jewish professors is greater than it was before 1933. Under the Weimar Republic, no German University had a Jewish *Rektor* (dean). We have already had three at the Free University.

'On the other hand, a brilliant young Jewish professor was recently offered a post there and refused it. He said, "You already have enough Jewish Professors." Here you find a hangover from the past. There is still intellectual fear, even though there might not be physical fear.

'All German life shows the lack of Jewish influence. We miss their criticism, their involvement, in our politics and our society. We have no Tucholskis, no Maximilian Hardens. We have no one to stir up the animals. And even when the Jews inter-married and were assimilated into non-Jewish Germany, they brought with them their scepticism and their sensitivity.'

But not all Protestants agree with Gollwitzer that so much has changed. One who does not is Gunther Gensch, an *oberstudienrat* (high school teacher) in Cologne. Until recently, he was a teacher of religion (Protestant), but now has been restricted to teaching physical education. He is white-haired, with drawn features and eyes which have a deep light glowing at their back.

'I grew up,' he said, 'during the Nazi years. I was inculcated with the Nazi ideology. I was an anti-Semite. During the war, I was a pilot in the Luftwaffe. Afterward, I went back to the university and took my degree in Protestant theology. I entered the university with the prejudices that I had been taught. Nothing that I learned there altered those prejudices. Only, instead of being an active-anti-Semite, I became a passive one.

'I readily accepted that the Jews were to be despised because they had first rejected Jesus Christ and then destroyed him. It almost seemed as if it were necessary to be an anti-Semite in order to be a good Christian.'

Gensch became a teacher in 1953. In 1955 he began teaching in Cologne.

'I think it was about 1962,' he said, 'that I began to be deeply troubled. It seemed to me that I didn't know anything about the Jews, their history, their relationship to God. I set out to learn what I could about the Jews. The more I studied, the more I came to feel that teachers like me were continuing Hitler's work.

'We were really teaching anti-Semitism. I checked into the books that we were using for religious instruction and compared them with the books that had been used during the Third Reich. I was shocked when I found that many were the same, that we were still using Nazi texts, containing Nazi language, and preaching Nazi ideology.

'And I saw, too, that many of the same teachers, who had sworn fealty to Hitler, were still teaching in the schools.

'I brought this to the attention of the head of the school. He said that he would examine the books and he did so. As a result, one of them was banned but the rest were continued in use.'

(A continuing study of all books being used in German schools is being made in many *laender*. Changes are continually being effected.)

Gensch also discussed books and teachings with other instructors. 'Some of them,' he said, 'agreed with me, but said that I was making a mistake by pressing my point. They said that I hadn't discovered anything new; that everyone was aware of the facts but few were interested in making changes. A few said, "If you feel that way, you're not a Protestant. You're a Jew." I told them that, in some ways, I might be.'

Shortly afterward, two special investigators came to the school and questioned Gensch, his pupils and his fellow teachers. These were not civilian investigators, but religious investigators. In a matter of weeks they handed in their report. Gensch was removed as a teacher of theology, forbidden to serve as a lay preacher, and told he could no longer refer to himself as a 'Protestant'.

'All this,' Gensch said, 'happened to me within the confines of the school. It was treated as an administrative matter, but by the religious, not the civil authorities. I was not made the target of abuse. I found no personal antagonism. But I could not find any understanding either. No one really cared if the charges that I had made were true. All that counted was that I had challenged authority.'

Gensch acknowledges that his is an individual case. 'No one thinks in terms of teaching anti-Semitism. But no one believes that it is necessary to change the books and the teachers, to review our theology, so that the church will cease being the last bastion of Nazism. The students trust us and have faith in us. If we teach

Jewish guilt, if we do not refute known untruths, then we are laying a foundation for a new anti-Semitism.

'Sometimes I think that the God who was born on the Cross was killed in the furnaces of Auschwitz.'

All the evidence I found reveals that the old, church-inspired and church-condoned, anti-Semitism no longer exists in Germany. But, at the same time, it reveals that the country was virtually de-Christianized by Hitler.

If it was, as Gollwitzer called it, the 'least Christianized' country in Europe before Hitler, its post-Hitler state was one of not being Christian at all.

After 1937, the Catholic church existed only as a paper organization in Germany. It was suffered to continue as a showpiece, but it played no important part in German life. The hierarchy of the Church was aware of this and accepted it because it was powerless to do anything to change it.

The 'Postive Christianity' of the Nazis, with its folk-god, Hitler, was absolute denial of Catholicism.

The Protestant dilemma was, unhappily, not so great. Many Protestants, both clerics and laymen, were able to synthesize their religion with Nazi teachings. Those who did not, like Niemoller, and spoke out found themselves in the same camps, ovens and gas chambers as Jews.

What Protestant church organization there remained in Germany after Hitler was tarnished. It had been part of the Nazi regime.

The Catholic Church did not have this to overcome. Its hierarchic organization enabled it to begin functioning at once. With the founding of the Federal Republic, it became part of the power structure. Though Gollwitzer's opinion is coloured by his political philosophy, it is nonetheless the truth he spoke when he said there was a strong Catholic influence in the C D U. And the C D U governed the country.

In 1948, the majority of West Germans were Catholic. The great majority of Catholics voted for the C D U. Many factors have weakened that Catholic influence in recent years. Today, the majority of West Germans are non-Catholic. The C D U is now not the sole ruler, but a partner in the Grand Coalition.

But, in the first days of the Republic, the Catholic church returned to the *status quo ante* Hitler. It saw its first task as re-establishing itself. Its thoughts and its actions were turned inward. This was no time for innovation or reacasting of church doctrine. Jews, their fate and their future, were not matters of first import.

Since then the spirit, the words and the works of Pope John XIII had had their effect on the Church in Germany. But it has not completely replaced the spirit of Torquemada among all its communicants. The Pope sat in the Vatican for only five years; anti-Semitism has had a history in Germany more than a hundredfold those five years.

Even the most liberal Catholic churchmen unhappily admit that there still remains a residue of anti-Semitism. Old prejudices and old hates still remain. It took governmental action to get a church to remove murals depicting the Jews as ritual killers. A Cardinal Frings can make a slip of the Freudian tongue.

But, as Gensch's experiences demonstrate, there are also anti-Semitic vestiges among the Protestants. Who can erase the writings of Luther? True, such theologians as Reinhold Niebuhr, Paul Tillich and Gollwitzer advance new concepts. The bitter experience that was Hitler has caused a rethinking among some, if not all, Protestants in Germany.

But there remain some who adhered to Hitler's Chaplain Mueller, who accepted *Mein Kampf* as a new Bible.

No Jew to whom I spoke in Germany believes that there is in that country today any anti-Semitism that stems from church teachings or church action. Not even those most disturbed by the statements of Cardinal Frings felt they had anything to do with church policy.

But what disturbed me was something implicit and explicit in what both Klausener and Gollwitzer had said : That anti-Semitism was decreasing in Germany because it had so few Jews upon which to feed.

It disturbed me because it is so often the strongest influence in German thinking about Jews.

25. The Vacuum

THERE are institutes for the study of the Jews and their history in many cities of Germany. In Cologne and Hamburg and Mainz and Tübingen and Giessen and Muenster and Frankfurt.

Almost every University has departments on Jewish religion, history and culture.

Exhibits of Jewish history and art have been shown throughout Germany.

'The Jews,' said Werner Krauss, 'are of great historical interest to the Germans. They have little present reality.'

Krauss is a student at the University of Frankfurt. He is taking his doctorate in Jewish history. He was born in 1943 in Solingen. His father was employed in a steel factory there during the war until 1944 when he was drafted into the army. He was killed on the Russian front.

'My father,' Krauss said, 'was a good Nazi. He hated the Jews. Maybe that is why they haunt me. I don't know any Jews. I have no business with Jews. Still, they dominate my life.'

We had met only minutes earlier in a coffee house frequented by University students. He had sought me out, having heard from someone at the University what I was doing. Almost from the instant we had shaken hands and taken our seats, he had been talking at me. It was as if he were afraid that I would not hear him out if he delayed. His voice was intense, emotional.

Now, as we were being served our coffee, his troubled eyes roved the room. He waved a hand at the others in the room. 'Ask them about the extermination camps. About Belsen or Treblinka or Sachsenhausen. They'll tell you they don't know anything about them. It's the truth because they don't want to know. If they knew they would have to condemn their own country and that means condemning themselves. So they tell you it all happened before they were born and they don't know anything about it.

'You know –' his lips twisted into a smile that hurt – 'you know, it's true. They don't. Not even the ones studying with me. We know all about the distant past, about the Maccabees. We can give you the whole story, from Mattathias to John Hyrcanus II. But those are Jews in history. They're not people.'

He gulped down some of his coffee. 'You're writing a book about ghosts,' he said. 'And they exist. They haunt all of us. Because we don't know the real reason for what happened to them here. If it had been only a few who were responsible, if only a few had been murderers, then we could adjust to what those few did. But the more we learn, the more we hear, it seems there were only a few who were innocent. All the rest killed and let others kill.'

His knuckles tightened about his cup, as if he were going to pulverize it. 'Don't they trust us? Don't they think they can tell us the truth? Don't they know that every time we hear the word "Jew" the pretty picture of Germany fades away?'

I told him about Professor Gebhardt, in Munich, who had said that the Germans had not cared about the Jews in the past and that they did not care now.

'I care,' he said. 'Not because of the Jews, but because of myself. I have to know what kind of man I am. I have to know what kind of men we all are. You will be talking with important people. Tell them it's time to tell us the truth. If they don't, we won't be responsible for what happens.'

A short time later he left me.

If Krauss thought he was speaking for the great majority of Germans, then he was wrong.

In Cologne, Frau Jutta Bohnke-Kollwitz is in charge of the German-Jewish library. It was founded ten years ago because of the demand by students at the University for books telling about the Jews. A bookseller, Karl Keller, was so inundated with requests for such books that he could not fill the orders. Further, there was a paucity of books dealing with the period between 1933 and 1945.

The Federal government, the North Rhine-Westphalia *Land* and private sponsors joined to finance the library. Now it contains more than 10,000 books dealing with the history of the Jews and especially oriented to the history of Jews in Germany.

Frau Bohnke-Killwitz, a Gentile, daughter of a famous German artist, was asked to become director.

'Like so many Germans,' she said, 'I had a deep interest in the Jewish question. I realized my knowledge was limited. I didn't know the historical background, the reasons why for two millenia the Jews had been persecuted and hounded. I could not only help others to learn, I could help myself.'

When the library began to operate, she said, there was a great demand for books. Both young and old were interested in the history of anti-Semitism, in the German experience, in Israel.

'We had,' she said, 'many older people who came here from all over the place. It was as if they had been cast away on a desert island for years and now wanted to learn what had happened during that period. Today it is different. Few non-students visit the library and the number keeps growing less all the time.

'The subject does not agitate people the way it did earlier. Some people say they've heard and read enough about the Jews and that it is time for Germany and the Germans to start thinking of other things. It seems that a great many people have grown tired of the past.

'In addition, there is the vacuum of Jews in Germany. It's much easier to be interested in Israel as a nation than in Jews as Jews. Israel exists. But time has destroyed even the memory of the Jews in many persons. To the young, they are almost fictional characters. And to many of the old, they are reminders of a past they would like to forget.'

Klaus Jacobi, a senior editor of the magazine, *Der Spiegel*, agreed with Frau Bohnke-Kollwitz. Seated in his handsome office in Hamburg, Jacobi said, 'The Jewish problem, as such, is no longer newsworthy. However, German newspapers are still extremely sensitive about matters affecting the Jews and so they give extra space and prominence to stories out of Israel or statements by important Israeli officials. This also applies to stories that emanate from major Jewish organizations in the United States.'

A handsome, impeccably dressed man in his early forties, Jacobi is a representative of the new Germany, just as is the magazine he edits. He is technician, rather than scholar. He could be a magazine editor in the United States, more interested in circulation than content, in the balance sheet than in influence. He is a product of what so many call the 'Americanization' of Germany.

To him, the Jews are editorial matter. He accepts the absence of Jews from German society as a *fait accompli*. 'It has had,' he said, 'a negative result on German culture and science, which is regrettable. A great loss is felt in research. But I believe this has been an irreversible process.'

Then he gave another viewpoint on the absence of Jews that, he prefaced, would be 'cynical sounding'.

'The simple truth,' he said, 'is that the absence of Jews has made possible the campaign against anti-Semitism. If there had been more Jews in Germany these last twenty years they would have served as a constant reminder of their persecution by the Germans. They would have caused the Germans, out of a feeling of guilt, to be more aggressive against the Jews.

'This way, the Germans were able to deal with an abstraction not a reality.'

I asked him if he wasn't saying that the way to end anti-Semitism was to do away with the Jews.

'In a sense – I told you I would sound cynical – that is true. It's not a course that I advocate. I would be far happier if the Germans – if all people – could be cured of racism by reason and understanding, but that doesn't seem to be working anywhere in the world.'

Then I asked if he wasn't saying that the situation in Germany was little different in 1967 from what it had been in 1933.

'It's far different in actuality,' he answered, 'but not psychologically. And certainly that was more true right after the war. I believe the young are far less anti-Semitic than their parents. But I've told you what I believe the reason to be. Among the older generation you will continue to find the old habits and beliefs.'

As I left him, he said, 'You know, if the Jews were as important in Germany today as they used to be, the chances are that I would not be occupying this office.'

To Jacobi, this present Germany is a country to which he has easily accommodated. Intellectually he is aware of losses suffered by reason of the destruction in the past, and the absence now, of Jews. But there is another side to the coin, his own 'cynical' side. And since it is this other side of the coin that shows, he accepts it.

After all, life, psychologically, emotionally and even financially, is better for many Germans under these present circumstances. They can reject all unhappy memories, perhaps even believe that those did not occur.

In Frankfurt, Ernst Goldschmitt discussed this further. Goldschmitt is a motion picture distributor with his main offices in Frankfurt. He is of German background, but was born in Switzerland where his father settled in 1919.

'The Germans,' he said, 'don't want to be faced with Hitler or Nazism. They don't want to be reminded of that period. An example was the picture "Judgement in Nuremberg", which told the story of those trials. The Germans simply would not attend this picture. Nor would they go to see "Is Paris Burning?" Both these pictures asked questions of Germans which they do not want to answer.'

('The Sound of Music', the most successful picture ever made, was a failure in only one country where it was shown – West Germany. Its anti-Nazi message was unwelcome there.)

'There has been a change as time passes,' Goldschmitt said. 'For instance, the Anne Frank picture was a sensation when it was shown here a number of years ago. There is a question in my mind as to whether it would be even moderately successful now. It isn't a question of their being more anti-Semitism. I don't believe there is. It is a matter of their wanting to cover up the past, to bury it.

'On the other hand, they are interested in pictures about Israel. The Germans liked "Cast a Giant Shadow", which was the story of the founding of Israel and the first Arab-Israel war. Pictures made in Israel do good business.'

Goldschmitt said the situation was much the same in East Germany as in the Federal Republic, but for different reasons. In East Germany, the authorities wanted no pictures which did not follow the party line. The anti-Israel attitude of the government, for example, would make it a waste of time and effort to try to sell 'Cast a Giant Shadow'.

'In addition, there is no stress on the persecution of the Jews in East Germany. An anti-Nazi picture, of course, is salable, but only if it is not based on what happened to the Jews. Over there, they are not so interested in wiping out the past as they are in re-writing it. The only basis they use to judge a picture is its propaganda value.'

Nor is it solely the Germans who think it helpful to black out the past. There are some Jews in Germany who believe that the constant reminders are no longer necessary.

Dr. Hans Lamm is very active in Jewish affairs, not only in Munich where he lives, but throughout Germany. He has served as secretary of the General Federation of German Jews and almost from the time that he was liberated from a concentration camp has been involved with all the problems of the Jews in post-war Germany.

He is an assistant principal of a Munich high school and a prolific writer, both for German and English language newspapers and periodicals.

'We must,' he said, 'look at the picture as it is today and not always hark back to the past. The Jews today are equals. We have every right that others have. I would say that there is less anti-Semitism in Germany than in the United States or France. True, there were many well-educated Germans who were pro-Hitler and practised anti-Semitism, but I believe all these have had their eyes opened.

'This doesn't mean that we will forget, but it does mean that we can forgive. I lost all my family. I had my time in the camps. I don't think anyone expects me to forget those things, but I cannot let them blind me to the fact that this is a changed Germany.

'All you have to do is look at the attitude towards Israel. That country has been substituted for the Jews who once were in Germany.'

And, in many respects, it has been. Nothing proved this more than the attitude of West Germany in June, 1967, when the Arab-Israel war erupted.

26. The Nations

DIPLOMATIC relations between the Federal Republic and the nation of Israel were formalized in August, 1965. The two nations had had various forms of contract for more than twelve years before, but both domestic and international politics had forbade an exchange of Ambassadors.

In the period when both nations had begun to function, the wounds, the hate and the bitterness that had resulted from the Nazi persecutions were still fresh. In the late 1940's and early 1950's, there were few Jews who believed that any Jews should remain in Germany. Most advocated *Chissul*, the termination of Jewish life in Germany.

Various Zionist organizations forbade every type of Zionist activity in Germany and the Zionist World Organization maintained this ban for many years. The fraternal order, B'Nai Brith, for a long time withheld permission to reorganize the lodges which had thrived in Germany before Hitler.

No Israeli government, in that period, could have survived if it had established formal relations with any German government.

The West Germans also had problems. They had to perform a delicate balancing act of their own. One of the cardinal tenets of their foreign policy was the 'Hallstein Doctrine', a declaration that West Germany would not maintain diplomatic relations with any country, except Russia, which recognized the East German government.

But, if they felt that way about East Germany, the Arab nations, with whom West Germany had established diplomatic and trade relations, felt as strongly about any nations which recognized Israel. So West Germany had to keep this in mind.

On the other hand, the nations which guaranteed the existence of West Germany – the United States, England and France – confidently awaited some action by Adenauer's Germany to show to the world that it accepted responsibility for the destruction of Jewish lives and property during the Nazi era.

The simplest solution, one which would cause least political turmoil in Tel Aviv and Bonn, and, at the same time satisfy the West without alienating the Arabs, was to develop an unofficial relationship.

Both Ben Gurion, in Israel, and Adenauer set to work to create such an instrument. As early as 1952 the first German-Israeli Reparations Agreement was signed. Over the course of a dozen years these 'unofficial' diplomats arranged for payments of hundreds of millions of dollars to Israel, for trade agreements, for cultural exchanges, for all the minutiae that accompanies relations between two nations.

In the middle fifties, more and more efforts were made on the part of the Germans to better relations with the people of Israel, as opposed to the government of Israel. A large number of private groups were formed in Germany to that end. The Israeli government welcomed such actions, but the Israeli people did not.

Germany remained anathema in Israel. Orchestras refused to play the music of Wagner and Strauss. German films were banned. Israeli doctors pledged to boycott an international medical meeting if German was one of the languages spoken.

The simple fact was that three-fourths of the population of Israel was made up of Hitler's victims, men and women who had fled their native countries to escape the certain death that awaited them if they fell into Nazi hands. The death that had come to six million of their relatives, friends and neighbours.

Yet, in Germany, Israel had become the one symbol of Judaism that had a real meaning. Germans could seek to strengthen ties with that country even while seeing the number of Jews in Germany steadily decrease.

And, as was to be shown as late as 1967, the Germans could express admiration for a small country, with limited men and manpower, which could administer a resounding defeat to a group of giant neighbours.

Many young Germans joined groups seeking better relations with Israel. Other young Germans made visits to Israel. And nearly all of them found themselves rejected. Still others were told bluntly not to bother to make the trip.

Between 1957 and 1967 the person-to-person relationship between the two countries worsened. The Eichmann trial, of course, was a factor. To the Jews, it recalled the horrors of the past. To the Germans, it was as if all Germans had been placed on trial when Eichmann went into the box.

Still, in 1965 the two countries had reached a point where they could give each other mutual recognition. A great many individuals in both countries remained opposed, but the two countries agreed the time had come to legitimatize completely their relations.

In Israel, survivors of the Hitler years demonstrated when the first German Ambassador, Dr. Rolf Pauls, handed his credentials to the President of Israel. When Asher Ben Natan followed the same protocol in Bonn, the N P D and other right wing groups fumed.

For almost two years a period of correctness, but without warmth, followed.

Die-hards in Israel made contracts between the two countries difficult. The nationalistic surge in Germany was accompanied by continued attacks on Israel, on financial settlements, on economic ties.

In May, 1967, all this changed.

Nasser blockaded the straits of Aqaba and announced that 'We shall not accept any possibility of co-existence with Israel.' Ahmed Shukeiry, head of the Palestine Liberation Organization, said, 'I can't imagine that even a single Israeli is going to be left alive once the battle begins.'

It seemed as if almost all of Germany seized on this as a mass catharsis that would enable it to eliminate, once and for all, its guilt about Hitler and the Nazis.

As the crisis grew, West Germans made it more and more evident that they supported Israel. The government officially was neutral, but politicians of both the C D U and the S P D made public proclamations of where they stood.

But it was the people, rather than the politicians, who gave the best picture of what was happening. A monster rally was held in Berlin in support of Israel at which Helmut Gollwitzer and Gunter Grass, Germany's most noted writer, were the principal

speakers. Organized by the Societies for Christian-Jewish Coopera-
tion, it was intended to give moral support. It turned into financial support as well.

Rabbi Nathan Peter Levinson had helped organize the rally.
'We hoped,' he said, 'to elicit German sympathy. We found that
it was already present. The audience was not satisfied with
speeches but began to collect money spontaneously. Paper bags,
old hats, any container that could be found, was used to hold the
collection.'

There was another form of support that broke all German tradition. For the first time in German history an ecumenical service
was held in Germany, this in the Kaiser Wilhelm Memorial
church. A Protestant choir, a Jewish cantor, and clergymen of the
Protestant, Catholic and Jewish faiths prayed together in German and in Hebrew.

Again, the Protestant Bishop of Berlin took part in a special
service for Israel and broke another precedent when he preached
in the Berlin synagogue.

All over West Germany pro-Israel demonstrations took place.
In Munich, more than 10,000 persons gathered on June 5 in the
Koenigplatz, where Hitler had once shrilled his hatred of the Jews,
to show their support of those same Jews. The sponsors of the
rally were the major political parties, both branches of the Christian church, trade unions and the youth organizations of Munich.

What was in their minds was made evident when there was a
sudden stillness in the group when the main speaker reminded
the crowd that he was speaking only a hundred yards from what
had once been 'a great murder centre', the headquarters of the
Nazi party.

And another stillness when a speaker said of the crisis, 'if this
act of madness were to succeed, then this would be the consistent
continuation of the campaign of extermination against the Jewish
people begun by Hitler.'

Other meetings and rallies took place in Nuremberg, Frank-
furt, Essen, Hanover and Offenbach. The German Federation of
Trade Unions announced that it was purchasing $750,000 worth of
Israeli state bonds.

Hundreds of young Germans rushed to the Israeli Embassy in
Bonn and to Jewish or Israeli offices in the rest of West Germany
to offer their services to Israel. If they could not fight, they hoped

to replace those who were leaving the *kibbutzim* and the factories to fight.

Throughout West Germany placards and signs appeared reading 'Now We Have an Opportunity for Reparation', and 'Are Six Million Victims Not Enough?'

Support for Israel was widespread, but not unanimous. The far left and the far right once again united as they had during the period of the Hitler-Stalin pact and, again, Jews were the victims.

East Germany, of course, supported the Moscow line. As the crisis deepened and turned into war, *Neues Deutschland*, the official newspaper, radio and television all joined in calling what was taking place 'Israeli aggression', 'American Imperialism', and 'the new Hitlerism'. Such former Jewish refugees from Hitler as Norden and Eisler ordered a propaganda barrage that likened Moshe Dayan to Hitler and the actions of the Israelis 'a new Auschwitz'.

And, in the Federal Republic, the *National Zeitung* used almost the same words in describing both crisis and conflict. It accused Israel of 'unleashing its third war of aggression against the Arabs' and of 'committing war crimes'. It charged the Bonn government of submitting to 'Zionist blackmail' and sacrificing German interests for the sake of Israel.

But almost every other West German newspaper supported the Israeli cause in its editorials and equated the Arab threats to extinguish the living Jews in Israel with Hitler's to extinguish them in Central Europe.

Looking back at that period, Rabbi Levinson said, 'I do not know the reason for the reaction of the German people to the Israeli crisis. Years of teaching, inter-faith movements, efforts by political and religious leaders were not able to accomplish what a few days of war and a military victory did – a rapprochement between the Jews and Germany.

'I don't know if it was a sense of wonder that Jews could do such a thing at all, an identification with the story of David and Goliath, or a German admiration for military accomplishment. One thing, however, is true beyond doubt; the majority of Germans felt a sincere joy.'

In my talks with Germans, it appeared to me that all of these figured, but that there was a deeper psychological reaction.

Dieter Bidnowski, a West Berlin student who went to an Israeli *kibbutz*, said, 'The older generation is too old and they cannot free themselves of guilt. But we young people can do so. We all know that the Nazis did great harm. This was our opportunity to show that we are different.'

But an older German, Kurt Peters, offered another reason that included his generation. Peters had fought in the war, first in the *Afrika Korps* and later in Italy. 'Most of us,' he said, 'knew that we could never make our peace with the Jews in Germany. Maybe it was too much to ask because many of us could not forgive ourselves. I, for instance, was never a Nazi, but I was never against them. I never did anything to help the Jews and then I fought for Hitler with all my heart. I told myself that I was fighting for Germany.

'But when this happened in Israel, it was different. In a way, we were able to transfer the identity of Hitler to Nasser, of the Nazis to the Arabs. Years later we were able to act and think in a way that we now knew was right. And, at the same time, we did not have to condemn ourselves and our country.'

Gunter Grass offered another explanation and one which involved Germany's most controversial writer in still another controversy. Grass said, after the Israeli victory, 'There is now a sincere and spontaneous upsurge of sympathy for the bravery of the Jews in their struggle to protect their homeland and have a dignified life.'

He went on to say that a tour of Germany had revealed to him a 'healthy, new attitude' on the part of Germans towards Jews. He said, further, that this presaged a 'more normal relationship between the two'.

Then he added, 'Up to now much of the dialogue about the fate of the Jews in Germany was haunted by conscious or unconscious guilt or impeded by recriminations. I am convinced that a new situation has emerged which gave us a possibility to express our solidarity for Israel and the fate of the Jews without our feelings being hindered by the past.'

Few Germans have been as outspoken about that past as Grass. He bitterly assailed the naming of Kiesinger as Chancellor because of Kiesinger's Nazi past and called on Willy Brandt not to join in any Grand Coalition with Kiesinger. And, in the critical days of May and June, he was one of the leaders in the battle to align West Germany fully with Israel.

Yet his statement aroused a bitter answer from author Hans Habe who had been a refugee from Hitler. He called Grass's statement 'impudent' and added, 'It is typical that the Jews have to prove themselves valiant warriors – which they have been for five thousand years – to impress Herr Grass and his fellow Germans.'

My own experience has been, however, that just this was important to many Germans. Many of them were proud of 'their Jews' in Israel, forgetting the circumstances which had resulted in their being in Israel.

But, whatever the reason, the period of the crisis and war was a major turning point in the relations of Jews and Germans in Germany. For the first time the Nazi years and the terrors were transcended. The relationship between Jews and Germans had taken a permanent change.

In the months since there has been a shaking down. The emotion has died. Today there is, again, a placidity to relations between the two groups.

And it is a good time to render the answers to the questions that brought me to Germany, to give a verdict – my own, of course – on the situation of the Jews in Germany today.

27. *The Answers*

I WENT to Germany to find what it is like to be a Jew in Germany today.

I was there from January to September, my stay overlapping that last, great crisis in German-Jewish relations, the war between Israel and the Arab nations. All that time I questioned and assayed.

I sought answers to the questions I raised in my preface. I had to learn if it was true, as Gudrun Tempel had written (in 1962), that 'the sin of the Germans was not that they were Nazis during the Hitler years, but that they were not anti-Nazis then and they are not anti-Nazis now'.

And if Karl Jaspers, probably the outstanding German philosopher of this era, was correct when he wrote in his book, *The Future of Germany*, that:

'Today (1967) we face no Hitler and no Auschwitz, nor any similar threat, but the Germans as a whole seem unregenerated from *the way of thinking* that allowed Hitler to rule.' (Italics mine.)

I found my answers. They were in the words of Max Jacoby and Klaus Jacobi, of Hendrik van Dam and Itzhak, of Werner Krauss and Hans Eckart, of Inge Deutschcrone and Hans Rosenthal, of Egon Bahr and Otto Hess.

Yes, I found my answers.

The gap between Jews and Germans has been designated the *unbewseltigte vergangenheit* (the awful past). Reparations, slogans, laws – not even time – have closed it. The Jews stand on one side and the Germans on the other.

It haunts both Gustav Herzog, who still lives in it, and Adolph Von Thadden, who denies that it ever existed.

The feeling of guilt is universal and miasmal. Gentiles and

Jews are trapped in it. Mendel Karger-Karin, a German Jew, wrote in the foreword of his book, *Israel and Us*, that his book 'did not constitute an evaluation of the Jewish community in Germany, even if it takes on that function for certain penpushers who have taken it upon themselves to designate the Jews of Germany as second-class Jews.'

Pride is mixed with the guilt among the Jews, pride and a unique awareness of their being Jewish. Memory and experience have joined to effect this.

They lived and suffered through the Hitler era, not as men and women, as Germans or Poles or Russians or Roumanians, but as Jews. It was because they were Jews that they were persecuted, tortured, incinerated, gassed, and shot. And, as Jews, they survived.

Now they prove to the world that fire could not immolate them. Bullets could not destroy them. Nor gas. Not even the grave could hold them.

It is a feeling that is beyond religion. They could deny Jehovah and still boast of being Jews. None regards his survival as personal. It was a victory for all Jews. Nor does it have the arrogance of thinking of themselves as the 'chosen people'. The six million who perished were also chosen.

No, it is a conviction that their spirit could not be killed.

George Steiner, scholar and critic, has written that no one who did not suffer their experience can truly comprehend it. This is true, but it is also true that their experience infects others. I know that when I was among these Jews in Germany, I felt for the first time that there was more to being a Jew than just being Jewish.

I do not intend to portray the Jews in Germany as other than ordinary men. Their distinction is that they had an extraordinary experience. Certainly Lazarus was changed after he was raised from the grave.

Yes, I found my answers. I have reported them.

But I learned something else, something which cancels all the answers, makes them irrelevant. It was a fact that emerged more clearly day by day, interview by interview.

It was that history will list one final victory for Adolf Hitler.

In a short time – and no one, not Jews nor Germans – can halt it, Germany will be *Judenrein*.